Transforming
Teacher Education

Transforming Teacher Education

Lessons in Professional Development

Edited by
Hugh T. Sockett, Elizabeth K. DeMulder,
Pamela C. LePage, and Diane R. Wood

Foreword by David T. Hansen

Bergin & Garvey
Westport, Connecticut ● London

Library of Congress Cataloging-in-Publication Data

Transforming teacher education : lessons in professional development / edited by Hugh
Sockett . . . [et al.] ; foreword by David T. Hansen.
    p. cm.
  Includes bibliographical references (p.) and index.
  ISBN 0–89789–790–0 (alk. paper)
  1. Teachers—Training of—United States. 2. Teachers—In-service training—United
States. I. Sockett, Hugh.
  LB1715.T673 2001
  370'.71'173—dc21   2001018477

British Library Cataloguing in Publication Data is available.

Library of Congress Catalog Card Number: 2001018477
ISBN: 0–89789–790–0

First published in 2001

Bergin & Garvey, 88 Post Road West, Westport, CT 06881
An imprint of Greenwood Publishing Group, Inc.
www.greenwood.com

Printed in the United States of America

The paper used in this book complies with the
Permanent Paper Standard issued by the National
Information Standards Organization (Z39.48–1984).

10 9 8 7 6 5 4 3 2 1

Contents

Illustrations

Foreword

David T. Hansen

This wide-ranging, spirited book will be of interest to anyone who wants to learn more about the inner workings of educational reform. With teacher development as their prime focus, the authors attend to every aspect of reform. They describe the vision that guided their effort, their attempts to build a supportive institutional structure, their curricular and pedagogical undertakings, and their attempts to communicate and collaborate with the many persons who cross the stage of the drama they describe. Readers who follow their account to the end will no longer be able to think about educational reform, especially in teacher education, in quite the same way.

The book pivots around an innovative master's degree program for teachers. That program was embedded in the Institute for Educational Transformation, housed at George Mason University. (The name has since changed to Initiatives in Educational Transformation, a change discussed in the book). The chapter authors include the former director of the innovation, the faculty who were involved in teaching and administering the program, and teachers who studied with them and who were invited back to lead discussions with subsequent groups of master's degree students.

The authors' vision centers around the idea that both teaching and teacher education are moral rather than technical or instrumental endeavors. The authors acknowledge that teachers must have curricular knowledge and pedagogical skill. The book is replete with their accounts of how they teach, whether in the teacher education classroom or in school classrooms where we hear from graduates of the program on how their experience has transformed their practice. However, although skills are indispensable, the authors argue that these must be embedded in a dynamic vision of education. They criticize the ways in which technique all too often takes on a life of its own, typically as a result of unrelenting pressure on teachers to raise students' test scores, adhere to myriad standards, and otherwise toe the instrumental line. According to the authors, a moral vision of practice can and should replace what they call the dogmas of control and the quick-fix. Their purpose is to illustrate how a moral vision can be enacted in practice.

As just mentioned, the authors report on virtually every aspect of their innovation—and then some. Their attention both to broad purposes and to minute details demonstrates how any serious attempt to change practice will be unwieldy, contentious, and subject to sudden shocks, reversals, and (happily) successes. Hugh Sockett, the director of the innovation, once described teachers as "guides through difficulty," helping students to meet and embrace the very real difficulties in genuine learning. In likeness, this book discloses that for an educational reform to succeed, all participants must become, in one way or another, each other's guides through difficulty—a level and quality of collaboration and communication that is challenging to build and to sustain.

In an unsparing, frank way, the authors recount their joy in accomplishment and their despair in failure, often on the very same page, even in the very same paragraph. They describe why change can be so difficult, and why institutions so often appear intractable. They capture tensions in classrooms in which, as teacher educators, they walked a fine line between dictating to teachers how they should regard their work, and respecting teachers' dignity as persons who dwell on the proverbial frontline day after day. They describe the delights and the deepened learning that took place in school classrooms when participating teachers, renewed and inspired intellectually, learned to work with the young in innovative, challenging, enjoyable ways. In between such passages, they pen one painful word after another in recounting how misunderstanding and mistrust between reform partners mushroomed virtually out of control, even as the parties overlooked the shared values and ideas that often, in fact, seemed to outweigh their differences. Then, in the very the midst of these heartfelt conflicts, the authors portray the intellectual and moral transformations many participants underwent, as they learned to work in teams, to alter their conceptions of diversity and culture, to change the way they perceived immigrant parents and children, and much more.

In this moral drama of reform gone both awry and well, the authors illuminate what it means to cultivate personal agency. They describe educators and parents who are seeking to participate in policy issues that affect them and, above all, that affect children. These men and women want to move beyond merely reacting to policy, or merely adopting a passive stance. Once more, the authors straddle a fine line here, between the Rodney Dangerfield stance that too often characterizes some teachers' talk—"I don't get no respect!"—and the more mature stance that says teachers, like all educators, must learn to win and re-win their voice, especially in a pluralist culture such as that in the United States.

Every generation of teachers, and every individual teacher at whatever level of education, has to articulate, enact, and then re-enact time and again, personal agency. Nobody, and no institution, can ever "give" agency to them. At the same time, however, administrators and policymakers can be a whole lot more supportive than they often are, another truth that this intense account of educational reform reveals.

One more truth stood out as I read these chapters: If educators attempt seriously to place the moral at the center of their work, they are guaranteed to multiply the challenges they face (even with all the institutional support in the world). Almost by definition, the moral life is complex, contested, often ambiguous, and, above all, a matter of lifelong learning, lifelong hope, and lifelong persistence. There is never closure, because both self and others grow (hopefully) and alter their perceptions, aspirations, conduct, and more. To become a good parent, a good teacher, a good citizen—a "good" anything in the moral sense of that term—is a permanent adventure. As one of the participating teachers says about collegial teamwork, "I am beginning to suspect that you don't ever really get this perfectly right." But if perfection is for immortals rather than for mortal educators, the authors of this book show that it is possible to move closer to, rather than farther from, what is right for teachers and students. They show that although the adventure of becoming good is permanent, it can also be wondrous and the source of some of the deepest satisfactions human beings can feel. Their achievement is to help us see, concretely, how ready and willing so many educators are to strive for these satisfactions.

Preface

Putnam (2000) described the ways in which Americans are withdrawing from community, becoming less participatory in public and private organizations and thereby degrading what he called "social capital." Workplaces are, however, taking on new forms, where community becomes more important than function. The dot.com corporation, for example, looks strongly to the character of its community, rather than simply to paper qualifications of individuals. Individuals in their turn are choosing much more selectively the character of the workplace, rather than merely going for the stock options, the perks, or the salaries.

Universities and schools are deeply conservative institutions, mostly resistant to organizational change or innovation, and sometimes with only a rhetorical sense of community. This book describes an attempt at program innovation, rooted in a conception of moral professionalism (Sockett, 1993), which challenged most of the conventional parameters defining professional education in teaching. It took place at George Mason University (hereafter GMU) in Fairfax, Virginia, under a president, George W. Johnson, who believed that traditional practices had to be transformed in his aspirations for GMU as "the new American university." He offered constant support and encouragement for which we are profoundly grateful.

The authors are existing and former members of the faculty at what was the GMU Institute for Educational Transformation (IET), together with teachers who studied with them in the school-based master's program that IET invented. To all the school teachers, to their students, and to other faculty not contributing to this book, the authors are also truly grateful: They gave IET both ideas and inspiration. The authors also wish to acknowledge the support of many former and existing superintendents in Virginia school divisions, especially Lowell Lemons (Waynesborough), David Martin (Henry County), Jake Burks and Dennis Kellison (Orange County), and Edward L. Kelly (Prince William County), but not forgetting James Moyers (Manassas Park) and Jim Brumfield (Fauquier County) who are, alas, no longer with us.

The authors also acknowledge the following organizations: *Education Week* for permission to reprint most of Hugh T. Sockett's article, originally published as "School-Based Master's Degrees" on October 19, 1994 (vol. 14, no. 7); and George Mason University for permission to print IET material and for the use and citation of student comment, which is anonymous except where cited. We would also like to thank the Columbia Heights West Teen Photo Project, especially the director, Paula Endo and also Albert Hernandez and Lyn Min for permission to publish their poems and self-portraits. These poems and accompanying self-portraits were part of an exhibition entitled Beneath the Surface: Photographic Self-portraits. Finally, we would like to thank David Lees, Theresa Rigsby, and Lissa Soergel, who helped to prepare the manuscript for publication. We would especially like to thank Jane Yates who has not only helped us with preparation of the manuscript, but who has been dedicated to the IET program since its inception. Jane worked diligently behind the scenes for 10 years to make sure the program ran smoothly, constantly struggling to reconcile our nontraditional structure with the requirements of the university bureaucracy.

Many of these chapters began life as presentations at international and national conferences, including the American Educational Research Association, the American Association for Colleges of Teacher Education, the International Teacher Research Conference, and the Ethnography Conference at the University of Pennsylvania.

All royalties are to be donated to the Children's Defense Fund.

Hugh T. Sockett, Elizabeth K. DeMulder,
Pamela C. LePage, and Diane R. Wood
Fairfax, Virginia 2000

Transforming Teacher Education
Hugh T. Sockett

In the twentieth century, faith in the power of science emerged alongside growth in the power and influence of the state. Science was not merely the deliverer of brilliant technologies but it contained a view of scientific method (Nagel, 1950), which spread into the human and social sciences. Psychologists at the beginning of that century, for instance, began to believe that they could in principle describe, explain, and predict (and thereby control) everything, provided the human being was seen as a machine, not a conscious organism (Skinner, 1975). Such principles carried over into social practice, where technical bureaucracy became the paradigm of social organization. As the Protestant ethic withered, this bureaucracy created its own norms of practice, often in direct contrast to the personal moral beliefs of the individual (Jackall, 1988). With such ideas of control, human beings could become mechanical producers (witness Charlie Chaplin's *Modern Times*), or they could be controlled at all levels of organizations (witness *The Organization Man*), or, horrifically, they could be processed into gold, hair, and ashes in the moral nihilism of the Holocaust.

Yet science brought with it another important social expectation: the general belief that there exists a neat solution to every human problem, even though that thought runs completely counter to intuition and to most people's everyday experience. This quasi-scientific view of solvability became embodied in the American love of the "quick-fix." Solving problems demanded constant scientific "experiment" and subsequent changes in practice. The pervasiveness of this view may even contribute, tragically, to the adolescent contemplating suicide because his or her problems seem unfixable. Two ideas, therefore, were combined: first, that everything in human affairs could in principle be controlled

and, second, that everything could be quickly fixed. These are immensely se-
ductive ideas for politicians and bureaucrats. Their combination has proved
deadly for public education.

Science and the mechanistic application to human affairs became powerfully
interlocked. From this dysfunctional marriage emerged a system of public education in which, at the end of the twentieth century, few appeared to have
much faith (Finn, 1991); in which children had little confidence (Hersch, 1998);
in which there was demonstrable lack of democratic community, lack of responsive partnership with parents, and, inevitably, alienation and demoralization
of teachers. Politicians and bureaucrats seek to impose ever stricter hierarchical
controls on schools, and their agents, misled by the dogmas of scientific rationality, provide them with the tools. Citizens, lured by the quick-fix, demand
results *now*, so public education has become a system particularly prone to
hucksters, as William James suggested it would. Agents and hucksters, it has to
be said, are often found in universities.

The tragedy is that, in the whole saga of public education, the university is
a prime suspect, perhaps even a culprit. First, it has allowed and encouraged
the development of education as a quasi-science, not as a human study. It has
developed criteria of progress that depend on external funding. It has turned
professors into experts, not learners and (God forbid!) professional partners with
schoolteachers. It has made its colleges of education almost universally disliked.
Like the duenna in Murillo's famous *Girl with Her Duenna*, the rest of the
academy sniggers behind its handkerchief at substandard educational research it
regards as neither empirically competent nor philosophically germane. The
schools and teachers often see little or no value or relevance in schools of
education for the hucksters and the agents are their enemies.

Within universities and colleges, schools of education have chosen two paths
on their own. First, many of them are more like schools than they dare admit.
Too many have adapted the ecology of school organization to the academic unit
of the university, especially in top–down bureaucratic management, the creation
of dependency between students and faculty, and the appointment of managers
who are no more serious scholars than many school principals are instructional
leaders. Given that many teacher educators were socialized into the institutional
norms of schools before joining universities, it is also not surprising that there
are even elements of anti-intellectualism in schools of education just as there
are in schools. Given such characteristics, teacher education institutions often
lack the strength that comes from constant self-critique and reflection.

But, second they have been willing bedfellows with the university and its
dominant scientific epistemology. For all the critical theory, enlightened cognitive psychology or modern commitments to reflective practice, most of these
institutions have chosen Thorndike over Dewey (Lagemann, 2000) deferring to
positivism in a field of human action manifestly unsuitable for this doctrinaire
view of science. They have marginalized work that was not "re-search." They
have fashioned institutions, which contain positivist principles in their deep

structure. They have bowed low before an epistemology that separates values from facts and ends from means, finally establishing values as necessarily relative. Morality (values and ends included) thus become irrelevant to education, in general, and to teacher education, in particular, because pedagogy is reduced to a set of techniques as defined by scientific facts. As an intellectually uncertain and later disreputable field, education has lacked the intellectual caliber to work itself out of the vortex of decline, primarily because it has failed to make any case that it is an epistemologically coherent as a discipline (Sockett, 1988c).

The history of teacher education in the 20th century pressed forward by establishing a lamentable and growing distance from moral thought. At the beginning of 2000, two interesting reports revealed clearly the deep-seated confusion in university teacher education, if it were not already perspicuous. In May, the National Council for Teacher Accreditation (NCATE, 2000) announced that the accreditation of colleges and universities would in the future be based on teachers' ability to have children learn. (You mean, no one thought of doing that before?!) In June, the Public Agenda Foundation (Farkas, Johnson, & Foleno 2000) published its report *A Sense of Calling*. Young teachers, we are told, are hungry for technique, yet their motivation is strong and idealistic. Teacher education as presently constructed can answer neither of these interests. It cannot equip young teachers with classroom skills because the complexities of the classroom change readily and highly skilled practitioners alone, not academics, are competent to do that work. Nor can it nurture the idealism at the beginning or during a career. It cannot give young students a moral education, for it has neglected the moral framework within which "a sense of calling" (and much else) can be examined. It has gratuitously, even systematically, ignored the phalanx of 20th-century moral philosophers with a great deal to say about education as a moral endeavor—Dewey (1938), Oakeshott (1967), Peters (1966), Greene (1988), Scheffler (1985), Martin (1992), Polanyi (1958), MacIntyre (1984) and others—most of whose names and work are completely unknown to teachers. Moral thought has been largely absent from teacher education so that the dogmas of control and the quick-fix have been left unchallenged.

Given this, how then does a committed critic conduct him or herself within such institutions, whose pseudo-scientific tentacles reach into every corner of the operation from curriculum planning to student evaluation and, of course, to human relationships? How does one grapple with deeply rooted institutional conventions that one sees as simply wrong? How does one respond to statements like "our job is to produce knowledge," or "you can't construct a curriculum without objectives," or "teachers can't do research," each of which seems empty, confused, or simply false?

This book describes one such attempt. Its authors believe that it has wider relevance for modern professional education. Teaching, it can be argued, has developed as a technical production process, backed by a naïve belief in the power of science and a commitment to hierarchical structure in educational organizations. With such a process come technical experts, children viewed as stereotypes, managers who need only be managers not educators, and a drastic and unbridgeable gulf among practitioner, researcher, and administrator. Above all, there arises justified public discontent.

How can this system be turned on its head, at least in teacher education? By treating colleagues and students as partners, by focusing on the predicament of unique cases, by developing a sense of research as systematic inquiry made public that challenges the normative practices of science, and by putting at the center the moral thought and responsibility of the teacher. With the opening of moral perspectives, it is thought, teachers will grasp or find the significance of their commitments, start to understand their practice as moral not technical and help transform themselves as well as their students.

THE CONCEPT OF THE INSTITUTE FOR EDUCATIONAL TRANSFORMATION (IET)

The attempt to grapple with this complexity took institutional form through the foundation at George Mason University in 1992 of the Institute for Educational Transformation. At that time, there had been much public political talk about the need for *reform* in public education. As its title indicates, IET was interested in transformation. Rhetorically, we aimed to develop new systems, new products, new experiences, new approaches, and new roles, preferably all at once. Although we appreciated that reform was important and that new concepts and ideas could emerge out of that, we set ourselves more ambitious targets, attempting, if you will, to change the paradigm of change.

Traditionally, teacher education in universities works only with schoolteachers and administrators. Yet of course, families, communities, and local businesses have major interests in public education, and the university could in principle be connected to them. The struggle was to articulate this frame of broadening responsibility for IET, mindful of the ambitious structural innovation it would imply, the political obstacles it would encounter, and the barriers that would have to be surmounted or removed.

Fundamental to the emerging institutional concept was the idea of the professional as a *reflective practitioner*, a term first used by Schon (1983). For us, reflective practitioners would be technologically skilled professionals, working in teams, with a commitment to continuous improvement through sophisticated intellectual and moral study of their workplaces. This concept was not merely for teachers. Rather, the impact of technological and other changes was producing people in the modern workplace who needed a sense of themselves as agents, as people with a battery of skills, dispositions, and competencies that could be applied in different contexts.

Second, making moral thought the basis of all activity and organization was paramount (Sockett 1993, especially chap. 8). This would affect and influence not just curriculum practice, but the character of research and the character of continuous improvement in the new institution. Such a drastic change would call into question many established political habits in the university bureaucracy.

A third fundamental important principle (Goodlad, 1990) was that a university was an institution of great relative wealth and influence with an obligation to, and a self-interest in, public education. We reasoned that universities could and should be active instruments of social justice, especially for teacher educators. With academic freedom, it seemed to us, must come social responsibility in practice, not in the abstract. Public education as a practice and a democratic ideal came to be seen as resting on a tripod of support from teachers and their schools, local and regional communities, and universities and higher education. The task of transformation evolved as one in which each of these three was a target for mutual initiatives, with overlapping interrelationships as critical.

Teachers and Schools

As IET faculty, we looked at teachers and their schools. We saw institutions as well as individuals as an important focus for our work. For example, we developed a "one-division strategy" whereby we worked with a specific school division, providing a variety of services, teaching, and assistance to the school board, principals, schools, central office, and teachers within a common and agreed framework. We devised a school-based master's program, the major topic of this book, which brought in substantial numbers of teachers in teams from schools. We planned to build on work with individual schools once a critical mass of their teachers had graduated through the program. We sought to link schools to their local communities in specific areas, and we connected some of the school teams to business advisers.

The Local Community

There are two ways in which we approached the local community—through the business world and the local neighborhood. The business world was represented by a nonprofit corporation we founded (IET Inc.) Its directors raised money from individuals and corporations to provide support for IET graduates to continue research built on technology, teaming, and continuous improvement. Visiting schools with members of the Board to judge proposals for grants began to open up links of new kinds between business and schools. Educators are wary of business, given the baleful influence of Taylorism. Yet, sophisticated modern business takes seriously ideas derived from the quality movement, of which Deming was the main proponent. Although many of his principles are rooted in measurement, he stressed the moral health of an organization, as, for example, in his injunction "Drive out fear!"

On the neighborhood community side, IET sought to build community projects, which could interact with public education. The U.S. Department of Housing and Urban Development provided initial funding to a community development project known as the Urban Alternative. Out of it grew computer learning centers, an early childhood program, a teen photography project, work with families, and more recently, a political effort to involve the low-income, largely immigrant community in a massive redevelopment project that directly affects their lives. Members of faculty were and are deeply involved in this project, seeking to link the work of the community to the schools and to teacher education.

University and Higher Education

The final leg of the tripod is the university and higher education in general. Strategically, IET had created alliances across the university. It was strongly interested, given its mission, in transformative ideas in this sector. The foundation of a new undergraduate college with a strong base in experiential learning and new curriculum design was a natural ally in the university. IET was a major contributor to the master's in New Professional Studies, described in the following section. There were advanced plans to develop this program on Andros Island in the Bahamas with the College of the Bahamas where the GMU Center for Field Studies had a marine ecology base and a central need to find ways to support the poor local community. We provided technical assistance to a Brazilian university and to Levinsky College in Tel Aviv in the development of new teacher education programs, which became the foundation for their work and the basis for a worldwide network of institutions with similar interests as ours.

Table 1.1 illustrates the concept that emerged (with the three main "legs" of the tripod across the center) and an indication of the institutional steps IET took.

ABOUT THIS BOOK

The development of this institutional concept was not completed before a university reorganization in 1998 led to IET (renamed Initiatives in Educational Transformation) returning to the Graduate School of Education from which it had been separated in 1992 (see chap. 14). The diagram reveals that a start was made on each sector. However, it was in the development of a school-based master's degree program reflecting the "new paradigm for research and development partnerships" that the model became fully developed. That model is the topic for this book.

The book is divided into four parts, each dealing with major aspects of the program, its development and implementation. The first part contains three chapters on curriculum and pedagogy. Because there was no proven blueprint for an effective master's program, especially one that connected to children's learning, IET sought to provide faculty teams with as much space as possible to work and rework the central ideas of the program as creatively as they could and into different formats. This autonomy meant, say, that the class of '94 based at one

Table 1.1
The Development of the Institutional Concept

Transformation = New Systems, Products, Experiences, Approaches, Roles
*
The New Professional as Reflective Practitioner
*

An educational transformation network (ETN) linking professionals to the university	The business community: Enabling business talent and expertise to support public education	Worldwide transformation network in education through a consortium of higher education institutions
*	*	*
An ETN was created as a social, political, and intellectual organization of alumni, students, and faculty	IET Inc as the nonprofit organization proving business support through consultancy and grants	Experiences in Israel and Brazil with plans for the Pacific Region and the Bahamas. IET ideas also used in U.S. universities
*	*	*
Teachers, children, and their schools	Families and communities	University transformation
A new paradigm for research and development partnerships academics, practitioners, and communities	Local communities institutional and neighborhood capacity building	The university in the community: Faculty and students in partnership with business and local communities
*	*	*
Development of joint publications, school-based projects, and books	The urban alternative: A model for community and school partnership in South Arlington	Faculty and students contributing to research, teaching and experiential learning in local communities

campus would have a different emphasis from the class of '95 based at another. Yet there was another important radical assumption. Faculty believed that both the curriculum and the pedagogy, and thereby the teachers' learning experiences, were also experiences teachers could use with children in their classrooms. That belief is borne out by the constant description of classroom innovations by teachers. These three chapters, therefore, celebrate that possibility, but they describe a particular curriculum emphasis (chap. 3) and a particular pedagogical approach (chap. 4), neither of which was universal as was the practice of teachers working in teams (chap. 5).

Improving Children's Learning, the title of Part II, is a task common both to teachers and to teacher educators. Indeed, its achievement perhaps should be the central criterion whereby all programs of professional development are evaluated, especially innovations such as this. Once one moves away from the simplistic notions of the dominant paradigm, this ideal presents difficult, complex, and unexplored issues within a moral paradigm with which no one, including IET has yet struggled effectively. For the moment, therefore, it is a matter of gathering together differing perspectives necessary to identifying the ways forward to this ideal, in this case those of faculty and classroom teachers. The perspective of teacher educators in the first part describes the sheer complexity of morally grounded practice and the challenges it presents. Two chapters by teacher alumni describe different projects that wrestle with new ways to understand children's learning experience and how its improvement can be described.

No program in contemporary America can ignore the fact of race and the many cultures in American society. The real work of education, however, dwells in the particular and the specific. Contexts, personalities, identities, and lifeworlds matter to teaching and learning. Children and teachers enter classrooms with past knowledge and experiences, with aspirations and dreams, with fears and anxieties, and with attitudes and beliefs. The parents who send their children to public schools hold a wide spectrum of hopes and expectations regarding classroom learning. The nested communities—business, neighborhood, religious, civic, ethnic—that look to the schools for social and economic amelioration frequently demand contradictory agendas. The chapters in Part III, Diversity and Dialogue, explore the moral issues that schools face in a society whose ideals demand democratic pluralism, specifically the intersections of individual identities with social institutions. The too often sublimated issues of race, class, and ethnicity in public schools affecting so many lives in public education invite the question implied in each chapter: How can public schools as institutions be both responsive to the needs of individuals and also encouraging of a common good? Specifically, issues of identity and oppression, creating honest dialogue among teachers, and the character of conflict of ideals and cultures between teachers and families of recent immigrants are the topics addressed in these three chapters.

The final part of the book is called Framing Professional Critique. For those who espouse the moral paradigm, an honest dedication to self-critique and a willingness to take risks when advocating for positive change are paramount. They will be prepared to reveal tensions in their professional lives, which are not often found in print as they confront norms in bureaucratic institutions. However, a dedication to continuous improvement in the context of critical cultures calls for risk and disclosure—a type of truth that can be found only in the passionate stories of people who care. The risks lie in naming problems, which many would prefer to have left quiescent. The final three chapters describe different individual perspectives focused on the challenge of the innovation to IET faculty, the effect of the Virginia Standards of Learning on professional integrity, and how the course of an ambitious innovation can attract professional hostility that, it is argued, undermines academic freedom.

These perspectives on the program are prefaced in the following chapter with a description of the educational rhetoric of IET and an account of its institutional shape and program reality. First, the degree, although originally conceived as a master's in education, formed the basis for a universitywide master's in new professional studies, which has different professional tracks. In the second part, the path from rhetoric is explained by the first national public statement of the program's direction, from which the primary ideological document in IET emerged. *Beliefs and Principles in IET Practice*, also contained in chapter 2, sets out the shared program beliefs, the curriculum and pedagogical principles being followed, and the kinds of experiences teachers studying the program would undergo. In a brief final section, the atypical organization of the program as it appears to the teacher student is described, which completes the orientation to the ideas then explored in the main body of the book.

From Educational Research to Program and Skills

2

From Educational Rhetoric to Program Reality

Hugh T. Sockett and Pamela C. LePage

From the foregoing philosophy, the master's in new professional studies, a new degree for GMU, was developed for various professions and was explicitly dedicated to a basis in moral, rather than empirical thought. This development coincided with the IET's foundation. It emphasized philosophy rather than traditional educational psychology, learning communities and partnerships over individual expertise, and morality as the crucible for thinking about professionalism, in this case teaching. Professionals other than teachers would also work from a common structure including four compulsory courses in ethics, epistemology, qualitative research methods, and a workplace-based project.

The design of this degree makes a substantial contribution not only to teacher education but also to professional education writ large. With the exception of law and medicine, there is immense fluidity in the work of many professional schools and in emerging new professions (e.g., technological management). There are also existing professions seeking to revitalize their work. At GMU, for example, nursing studies used the framework of this degree in the development of team structures at a nearby hospital, fostering cross-professional partnerships of doctors, nurses, technicians, and administrators. In technological management, the School of Business created a (very expensive) learning experience in this degree with a strong emphasis on ethical and epistemological issues. The Program in Social and Organizational Learning was a front-runner in creating teams among students studying their own workplaces, whether from corporations, or local and federal government. The significance of the program design was twofold. First, it enabled traditional programs to experiment and face the contemporary workplace challenges of their students. Second, it promised the possibility of interprofessional programs across the university that, for teachers, could have become a significant experience had the innovative style of President Johnson been continued by his successor.

How this conception played into the degree design was articulated in an article for *Education Week* (Sockett, 1994) published about the program. It appeared when IET was still within the university's Graduate School of Education, hence the references within the article. However, some outdated information has been deleted. Yet this extract encapsulates clearly the program's founding rationale and is therefore worth reproducing here.

How do you improve education? There are two obvious answers to that question: Control teachers more effectively, or find ways to enhance teachers' professionalism, creativity, and autonomy. Control implies tighter accountability (through merit pay, state or local mandates), and treats teachers as technicians implementing the political will. Autonomy implies trusting teachers and having systems (for example, in site-based management) that give them opportunity and incentive. It assumes teachers are morally committed professionals. The dominance of the "control" ideology is mirrored, however, in many professional-development programs, typically in the short, in-service programs that instruct teachers in the latest fad. So we have few examples of what professional development based on the importance of teacher autonomy would look like.

Master's degree programs for teachers exemplify the control ideology, and are a primary link between teachers and academics. In 1990–91, in the most recent federal accounting, there were 88,904 master's degrees awarded in education. Many university faculty members see them as a sorting mechanism for education doctorates. Implicit in the degree structure, in fact, is the view that theoretical knowledge is developed in the university and passed on to technician-teachers to implement in their classrooms. Treated as isolates in their workplace, teachers take courses which may, or may not, have an impact on what they do in classrooms or how they view their work. Programs usually demand evening attendance after a heavy day's work. They seem to pay little attention to teacher wisdom, and may retain their popularity more because of their cash benefits than because of the benefits flowing from any serious study of individual classrooms and work situations. The structures themselves may have longevity also because they match an overall university degree system.

We must completely reconstruct the university's relationship with the teaching profession, beginning, I think, with the master's degree. To do this, we need to be committed to the importance of teachers' autonomy and moral agency. We must recognize at the outset that we don't know what professional development can be because we have no idea what a 25-year career in the classroom ought to look like. Without some overarching conception of an "ideal" career and its professional-development needs, how can we determine what an academic program should look like?

Over the last two years, my university in Fairfax, VA, has been trying to develop ideas within a radically different master's degree—and we are just beginning. We aim to end the disconnect between degree programs and the teacher's work, and we believe we have found a way to do that, consonant with quality. There are seven major features of what has come to be called, at George Mason University, the "School-based" Master's

Degree. The following seven features reveal the radical and ambitious character of what we seek to do and may be a model for others:

- We don't recruit any individual teachers; we select teams from schools. We may be the first program in the country to do this, but whether or not that is true, we have been amazed by the impact of this relatively simple innovation. Teachers tell us of the importance of our inviting them to discuss individual draft assignments with members of the team before submitting them to us. They develop extensive and profound professional and personal relationships driving their work that replace the isolation they felt as "a colleague" who vaguely knew what others were doing. They work intensively at teaching and studying their teaching together. While mutual support is always important, making an impact on a school culture with a team that reaches out to other faculty members is seen by these degree candidates as an essential duty. This team intimacy has also had marked influence on how they view their students and the way knowledge is generated and transmitted within a school culture. We have now come to believe that the premier way to end the isolation of teachers and to promote changes in school culture is to invite teachers to study their practice intensively in teams.

- We commit half the formal structure of the degree to school-based work. This recognizes the teachers' expertise as professionals because we at the university level define ourselves as "coaches" assisting them in working with the research techniques they have learned. This means we often have to be in schools, too, and we have developed, in addition, extensive e-mail links to keep the interaction constant. The fact of our students' doing research on their teaching also seems to recast the relationship with students in the classroom. Teachers report that the adoption of the role of teacher-researcher changes their approach to pedagogy. It becomes questing, rather than authoritative, and this finds its place in getting students to be reflective learners.

- We have abandoned entirely the semester–credit-hour structure in terms of the character of master's-degree candidates' learning experience. We still have the formal "catalogue description" of the degree with its 10 courses and 30 credits, but this gives no guide to the scheduling. We work with what we dub "short-fat" and "long-thin" courses, weaving a coherent pattern of learning across the two years (plus a summer workshop) of the program. This means we have also junked the evening work; we have three summer workshops and release days and Saturdays to bring us to equivalence with other master's programs. Yet that equivalence is illusory. Most teams spend at least three additional hours a week on their work. Everyone starts and finishes at the same date. Thankfully (as we haven't worked out what would happen), no one has tried to transfer to another program. The retention rate through the program (completed in July 1994) was 97 per cent; only four out of 143 teachers dropped out.

- We are creating a teaching partnership of depth between academics and practitioners. We have used our faculty slots to hire outstanding practitioners with years of teacher-researcher activity behind them. The teaching teams are interdisciplinary, consisting of practitioners from schools and college faculty from education, social science and the humanities. Where possible, faculty also develop roles as coaches in one or more of schools with which we are partners.

- Casting aside evening teaching and working with daylong intensity has forced us to design a new pedagogy which focuses more rigorously on our own teaching and engages the members of the program in that adventure. We began by thinking of the day in four blocks and felt the need to have the third block devoted to some kind of non-sitting activity. After much discussion, we came up with what we call the "pasca" pedagogy: presentation, analysis, strolling critique, and collaborative argument (see chap. 4, herein).

- The whole group of 140 teachers attends the presentation, breaking then into five cohorts (with six or seven teams, integrated by school division and grade-level work) for analysis and the establishment of questions and problems. The "strolling critique" segment (in school teams) is usually done after lunch and enables the students to walk around and talk together, specifically defining their agenda for the final session. That session, "collaborative argument," is where we are trying to use Richard McKeon's (1944) ideas about "the architectonics of learning" in a pluralist framework.

- We are searching for a new assessment system, which overcomes one huge obstacle to profound change: the grading system. We have not yet succeeded in breaking the stranglehold conventional grading has on the psyches of everyone who has ever been to school, especially teachers. But we are struggling with what we call "targets of quality," described in a matrix of five areas and three levels of understanding, against which we invite teachers to assess their own work. We take the assessment process very seriously, writing copiously and carefully about each candidate's work, and using the "targets" to make a judgment. The basic drive, of course, is for continuous improvement, and we have found many of the ideas from the Total Quality Management movement useful, especially in our own self-evaluation.

For us, rethinking professional development has been a process of accelerating fast-tracking. We design as we build. In business terms, our goal is a better product at lower cost. In moral terms, we seek to enhance teacher professionalism and emancipate teachers from the dogma in which they are ensnared. In practical terms, we are creating a framework schools can palpably touch, as they witness the effect it has on their teachers.

Our sense is that if we want to transform the university's relationship with the teaching profession, all of us, teachers and taught, have to treat the degree as if it were an extensive partnership research-and-development project. The intensity and the excitement of the venture is richly rewarding.

BELIEFS AND PRINCIPLES IN IET PRACTICE

In 1995, not long after the *Education Week* article appeared, IET faculty members wrote a Teaching Team Document that described their approach to teaching and learning in the new program (Atwell-Vasey, Gerow, Sevcik, Sockett, & Wood, 1995). Its title *Beliefs and Principles in IET Practice* indicates that the program was a curriculum not designed by objectives (as rational science would demand) but by principles (which morality cannot abjure). It was intended to provide information for new faculty and students, but also to act as a basis for continuous improvement of IET practice. It described the ideological core of IET as a *learning community*, suggesting that because matters of governance are not separable from practice, the document would become an explicit and comprehensive statement of beliefs and principles, a *modus operandi*, and a set of standards against which improvement could be measured, and individual and team conduct judged. Its authors also saw it as constantly subject to revision as IET sought continuous improvement by inviting examination and critique by both faculty and students. Its content thus provides a clear statement describing the ambitions of the program.

The standards established here are very stringent, even as they are open to constant interpretation. Inevitably, there are anachronisms: in 1994, the program began a policy of leasing laptop computers for teachers in order to be able to insist that technology was a part of every teacher's life. That has now been completely superseded. The significance of the document is to be seen not in terms of successes or failures so much as the way in which establishing the ideology and the procedures as guidelines provided a clear sense of direction for people drawn from very different backgrounds.

A New Approach to Professional Development for Teachers: A Team Document

Since 1990, members of IET have been developing a new conception of a master's degree for serving teachers. Specifically, we sought to end the disconnection between degree programs and the teacher's work and to find a way to improve dramatically the intellectual quality of professional education, while improving the standards of commitment toward the profession. As we worked, our discussions focused on these aims, eventually evolving into a position paper by the beginning of 1995:

The degree is dedicated to the examination of four central questions:

- How do we understand ourselves as people and as teachers?
- How do we create knowledge of our world through the forms and genres of language?
- How do we seek knowledge and understanding of our world, of students, classrooms, and schools?
- How do we build learning communities and reflective practice?

The degree program is grounded by seven seminal features:

- Curriculum and pedagogy as primary intellectual and practical interests
- Work in teams
- Reflective practice
- School-based inquiry
- Intensive scheduling
- Integrated technology
- Continuous improvement

We articulated each of these features of professional development, not just in terms of what is received as curriculum by the teachers who study with us, but as matters in our own development, direction, and inquiry. For example, because we require teachers to work in teams, we ourselves work in interdisciplinary teams in an effort to understand the complexities of collaboration and develop new approaches to it. For each of these seven features, we articulated beliefs and principles of procedure to which we are committed as a faculty team, and then laid out specific learning experiences that we deemed essential to accomplish our educational aims.

As our document took shape, we saw it not as a blueprint but as a provisional statement of a present position. In that spirit, we invite critique by those who study with us, those who might wish to come and work with us, and any other professionals interested in the task of innovation and finding new directions in professional development.

Hence, our *beliefs* taken together form a strong ideology of professional development, but they are essentially contestable. Our *principles of procedure* are not goals. They describe, rather like guidelines, the ways in which we intend to work, both in teaching and management of the whole program, as well as in our own thinking and planning. The *experiences* we describe are not intended to be exclusive, but illustrative of what a teacher will enjoy as he or she approaches the program as a learning commitment.

Although recognizing the contingency of the document that follows, we view it nonetheless as a kind of manifesto calling for changes in the programs of professional development of teachers. We would not be disappointed by those who see it as such or cavil at such a perspective.

THE SEVEN SEMINAL FEATURES: BELIEFS, PRINCIPLES OF PROCEDURES, AND VARIETIES OF EXPERIENCE

On Pedagogy and Curriculum: Beliefs

- Development and innovation in teaching and curriculum are at the core of continuous improvement.
- All teachers should model approaches to teaching and curriculum and provide models of reflection on teaching.
- Different models of pedagogy and curriculum are essential to a stimulating learning environment if it is to foster a shift from an instrumental to an intrinsic view of the worth of what is being learned.
- Team members are both experts and apprentices in the continuous improvement of pedagogy and curriculum.

On Pedagogy and Curriculum: Principles of Procedure

- Deploy models and approaches to teaching, curriculum, and reflection that emphasize a search for insight, not a quest for truth.
- Continuously develop new forms and styles of teaching as part of a need for more interesting pedagogies, and articulate their rationale.
- Integrate curriculum through the 2 years of study, promoting both lateral and recursive examination of the material across courses.
- Plan curriculum and pedagogy so that in concert they are complementary rather than contradictory.
- Build the assumption that reflection and study are of noninstrumental, intrinsic worth.
- Enable team members to become both experts and apprentices in teaching and learning.

On Pedagogy and Curriculum: Varieties of Experience

- Conduct conversations, discussions, analyses, and debates with teachers studying with us.
- Experience extensive thought and reading, writing, and disseminating of new understandings and perspectives.
- Participate in learning in seminars with colleagues, through electronic connections, and through new work and discussion with children.
- Experience ambiguity, uncertainty, challenge, and difficulty as a necessary mode of learning, within contrasting pedagogical and curricular forms.

On Work in Teams: Beliefs

- Individuals benefit from working together and learning how to do so.
- Working together is complex and difficult and requires considerable energy and dedication.
- Collaborative communities have mutual perspectives as well as multiple individual perspectives with separate, sometimes competing or conflicting interests. But individual perspectives also frequently have overlapping interests, areas of expertise and unique strengths and weaknesses.

On Work in Teams: Principles of Procedures

- Negotiate shared issues, a common agenda, and a vision for the future of the team's work.
- Celebrate and appreciate those issues, agendas, and visions that are an individual prerogative.
- Create and employ a significant regular schedule to foster a meaningful team experience and the development of collaboration.
- Develop the exercise of a complex set of skills to enhance collaboration (e.g., listening, clarifying, building on, asserting; avoid blocking and dismissing).

On Work in Teams: Varieties of Experience

- Regular (weekly, bi-weekly, monthly) meetings with agreed time and agenda.
- Mutual acceptance of changing roles (e.g., facilitator, note keeper).
- Diplomatic persuasion; controlled anger; mystification; stress; intense dialogue; contrasting emotion; self-discovery; discovery of deep dissent; learning through criticism; flashes of insight linking dissimilar issues; anxiety and concern over responsibilities to team, all arising from a team functioning collaboratively as well as independently on matters of teaching.
- Rigor in team research; relating and critiquing a single collaborative project or individual projects related to the program; working as a response or problem-solving group in support of writing and publishing an individual's or the team's research.

- For faculty: teaming with current faculty; working as an adviser; establishing a team and individual identity.

On Reflective Practice: Beliefs

- Effective and moral teaching requires deliberate, ongoing reflection and the careful articulation of the moral and epistemological assumptions made by individuals.
- Reflective practitioners strive to uncover and critique their own values, assumptions, and biases, examining constantly their day-to-day strategies, intentions, and decisions.
- Reflective practice demands individual contemplation and collegial dialogue.

On Reflective Practice: Principles of Procedure

- Articulate and critique practical knowledge, emergent theories, deeply held beliefs, and values.
- Inquire into the interactions among practice, theory, belief, and cultural influences.
- Move beyond consideration of what works to imagine, invent, and enact what is possible.
- Create an agenda moving constantly beyond cultural constraints to reclaim personal and professional perspectives.
- Build the capacity to view schooling from multiple perspectives.

On Reflective Practice: Varieties of Experience

- Write journals and autobiographical narratives about experiences in learning and teaching.
- Articulate, analyze, and debate practical knowledge, emergent theories, deeply held beliefs and values in conversational, seminar, and forum settings.
- Experience uncertainty and indeterminacy as valuable concomitants in reflection along with discovery.
- Think and act as a member of a learning community with questions: What has this society made of me that I no longer want to be? What has this society made of teaching and learning that I no longer want them to be?

On School-Based Inquiry: Beliefs

- The needs of students and the potential and limits for school change become more visible when teachers study education in the context in which they work.
- When school is a naturalistic base for teacher inquiry and research, problems in teaching or curriculum are not idealized, but grounded in the complexity and difficulty in which teachers present themselves in schools.
- Teachers appear more enterprising and autonomous in the conduct of school-based inquiry, providing a model for students in which teachers are seen, and students may see themselves, as people who construct knowledge and critique knowledge.

- When teachers' inquiry and research projects are based in their own practices, they are more likely to lead to action.

On School-Based Inquiry: Principles of Procedure

- Contextualize work with teachers, legitimating and fostering thick description of cases, individuals, and circumstances.
- Develop relationships in and promote evidence-based knowledge about school communities.
- Build ethical criteria for the conduct of inquiry across institutions and among individuals.
- Provide models of university-based inquiry to demonstrate complexity.

On School-Based Inquiry: Varieties of Experience

- Discover how far we can see institutional and individual weaknesses and strengths.
- Appreciate the contributions children make to understanding the context of school.
- Confront interpersonal and professional tensions arising from new perspectives on one's work.

On Intensive, Teacher-Friendly Scheduling: Beliefs

- It is necessary to have time for study and reflection that fits the rhythm of the teachers' work and family life.
- A professional community can arise only from intensive and profound experiences together.
- New complex material cannot be easily mastered without continuous study over a long period of time.

On Intensive, Teacher-Friendly Scheduling: Principles of Procedure

- Create forms of scheduling that maximize opportunities for prolonged study and community building.
- Make an individual's family commitments an essential component in constructing learning experiences, within the context of the individual's commitment to the program.
- Consonant with purpose, be open to frequently reordered schedules.
- Publicize schedules and changes responsibly and as early as possible.
- Create opportunities for examination of priorities.

On Intensive Teacher-Friendly Scheduling: Varieties of Experience

- Participate in intensive study in full-day summer workshops, school-day release and Saturday sessions in addition to regular individual study and site-based work in school teams.

- Construct a way to do scholarly, social, and political work on educational issues within the heavy demands of family and teaching (e.g., anxiety and tension arising from work–family commitments and the complexities of their resolution, discovering the extent of personal support from family members).
- Enjoy the exhaustion provided by determined intellectual rigor.

On Integrated Technology: Beliefs

- An increasingly technological world requires integration into the program of technology issues and its practice.
- Access to technology raises issues of equality and changes relationships between faculty and students and between the teachers in the program and their students.
- Only compulsion in the use of technology will bring many teachers into the technological world.

On Integrated Technology: Principles of Procedure

- Employ computer technology as an integral feature of pedagogy and curriculum and as a conspicuous and continuous medium for communication among faculty and teachers on the program.
- Seek regular and continuing instruction to improve expertise.
- Provide opportunities for all to learn from those who know (e.g., children).

On Integrated Technology: Varieties of Experience

- Hold intellectual discussion through electronic conferences.
- Communicate by e-mail.
- Conduct periodic in-service training for faculty and teachers on the program to stay abreast of the potential for learning through technology and of the most recent developments in distance learning and communication.
- Surf the Internet.
- Change relationships with children.

On Continuous Improvement: Beliefs

- Conventional systems of testing and grading are enemies of change.
- Continuous improvement must be viewed as an educational commitment by all educational institutions and individuals as teachers and learners.
- Multiple forms of experience and presentation are vehicles for continuous improvement.
- Public accountability is a critical element in designs of continuous improvement systems.

- Public statements of standards and targets of quality should be seen as stages in the development of quality by an individual not benchmarks defending the purity of an academic offering.
- Standards and targets of quality are essential for orienting teachers and learners and should be kept under constant review.

On Continuous Improvement: Principles of Procedure

- Negotiate, publish, and use agreed standards and targets of quality as criteria in working with teachers.
- Devise and foster innovative forms of presentation as indicators of continuous improvement.
- Install practices celebrating continuous improvement across the organization of teaching and learning.
- Publicize the rationale for the commitment to continuous improvement.
- Engage external reviewers for each program as part of a strategy of benchmarking across institutions.

On Continuous Improvement: Varieties of Experience

- Construct illustrative portfolios including, for example, writings, tapes, and descriptions of team experiences to demonstrate quality.
- Cope with anxiety and fear in assessment.
- View work done in the program as public and as having implications for the workplace.
- Examine how principles of continuous improvement can be applied to work with children and expressed to parents. (Atwell-Vasey, Gerow, Sevcik, Sockett, & Wood, 1995)

THE ORGANIZATIONAL STRUCTURE: A TEACHER'S EXPERIENCE THROUGH THE PROGRAM

So far, we have discussed the rationale, philosophy, and beliefs and principles of the program; we now turn to the structure that has remained fairly consistent since the early 1990s. In subsequent chapters, the authors describe in detail important aspects of the program. What we attempt in this section is to provide a brief overview (a bare-bones skeletal structure) describing how teachers currently (and historically) have experienced the program. We expect this will help orient a reader to the broader experience discussed in more detail later.

Because teams of teachers are recruited from individual schools, teachers are expected to work together through the application process and once admitted, they attend an orientation where they are given precourse requirements to read imaginative literature and other relevant material in preparation for the first summer session. Typically, 75 teachers are recruited for a new class (e.g., Arlington Class of '99). They are recruited from elementary, junior, and senior high schools so they are given the opportunity to engage in dialogue across grade levels and school divisions. The larger class is broken into three cohorts of 25 students, and usually each cohort has the same faculty leader for 2 years. In fact, the new group will have the same faculty team (3 faculty for 75 students) working with them for 2 years to complete their degrees. Depending on the number of students, faculty teams range from two to five members who collaboratively teach all the courses offered. The program is structured so that the teacher-students attend three summer institutes and two academic years. We present the program here as a teacher might currently experience it.

First Summer Institute

All the summer institutes are held in July. All class days run for 8 hours. The first summer session lasts 2 weeks. During this time, the teachers start their work in Moral Professionalism; Technology; Culture and Language; and Beginning Research. The focus is on having teachers get to know each other and build cohesive, moral communities in their teams, cohorts, and graduating class. But, we immediately start working on complex educational issues. Many groups use narratives, storytelling, and drama as pedagogical strategies to help groups share and build trust while also probing deep educational problems relevant to their lives. During the first summer, we also focus on team development, technology access, and basic research methods.

All of the faculty teams integrate course content to some degree. Some teams integrate so intensely it is difficult to differentiate the days according to traditional course descriptions. Other teams do not integrate quite as much, but all courses are expected to build on and reinforce the others.

First Year

During the first academic year, the teachers attend four class days during each semester (for two semesters). In the past, this has involved coming on two Saturdays and on two weekdays. In the beginning, many of the partnering school divisions gave teachers' release days to join the program. Over the years, some of these school districts have reluctantly turned away from this commitment because of the shortage of substitutes. But, there are still some districts that maintain this benefit for teachers. On Saturdays, all the teacher-students and the entire faculty team attend, and the days are structured much like those in the summer session. During the week, individual cohorts of 25 students come to class. Cohort days are slated for work that requires more intense individualized teaching (e.g., technology and research). The Saturday sessions are reserved for classes that lend themselves to large-group presentation and discussion.

During the first year, the teachers focus especially on their first-year research projects due at the end of the year. They also undertake other assignments including theoretical essays, journals, curriculum projects, and technology portfolios, as well as a large quantity of assigned readings.

The college faculty not only teach on Saturdays and during cohort days, they also visit schools (approximately once a month) where they work with teacher-students to develop their research, design curriculum projects, lead discussions on readings, and clarify assignments. They also encourage productive team relationships.

Second Summer Institute

By the second 2-week summer session, the teachers know each other better. They have built some team cohesion and are ready to struggle with complexity and to confront sensitive controversial issues. Early in the first week, they finish their first-year research course by presenting in an informal conferencelike fashion to their peers, while critiquing each other's work and presentations. They also begin course work in Epistemology, Culture and Language II, and Advanced Research, which requires the team research project.

Second Year

During the second year, the teachers develop and complete a team research project. Concurrently, they work on other assignments to complete several other courses. One particularly significant assignment is an exit portfolio, which they present at the end of the program. This project requires teachers to reflect on their professional growth over the 2-year period working with us. The second year, because of the intense demands of the research project, faculty typically spend more time visiting teams in their schools. Purposes for these increased visits are twofold: to help with the uncertainties and dilemmas of the qualitative research process and to support teachers as they work through the complexities of collaborating on such a project. Collaboration is difficult work, but it can also be deeply rewarding. Faculty work hard to help cohesive teams maintain a critical edge and to advise troubled teams as they work toward resolving conflicts and reconciling differences.

Last Summer

Finally, during the last summer, in school teams, the teachers present their research to each other in a formalized conferencelike structure. This conference lasts 1 week. Faculty create professional schedules and invite guest speakers to present. We invite principals, teacher-colleagues, district administrators, and other members of the community to take part in these celebratory presentations. During that final week, the teachers also provide feedback to the program and to the faculty. And most important, they are given the opportunity to reflect on their experiences and develop a vision for their future.

PROGRAM EVALUATION AND SCHOOL CHANGE

Whether a program has moved successfully from rhetoric to reality depends to a large extent on evidence of the program's effectiveness. The IET faculty has always been concerned with whether the program has an effect on children's learning. In the second section of this book, we focus on our struggles and our successes as we seek to work with teachers to improve children's learning. In fact, faculty members have been involved in different kinds of program evaluation over the years that seek to probe the quality and effects of a variety of program initiatives. Our evaluation strategies have evolved in three ways. First, we began evaluating the program almost exclusively through teacher self-reports. Next, we broadened our focus to evaluate intellectual and academic progress by analyzing graduate student products. Most recently, we have followed alumni out into the schools in an attempt to understand further and to document changes. In this section, we provide a brief overview of some of the projects that college faculty and teachers have been working on over the years that speak to the effectiveness of the program. Some of these efforts are described in detail in subsequent chapters, but a quick overview will help orient the reader to a variety of program evaluation efforts.

Teachers' Self-Reports

The IET faculty has always been meticulous about asking teachers for feedback about the program. Not only does the faculty ask for end-of-year evaluations, reflective essays, and verbal critiques, but they also ask teachers to write reflections on every class session. So the faculty has accumulated a large amount of evaluation data from teachers, especially about their attitudes toward the program.

Efforts to evaluate IET date back to the first year of the program, when IET was required to submit a detailed quantitative evaluation of the program to the Graduate School of Education of which it was then a part. This consisted of detailed accounts of student performance, analysis of teaching, specifically in teams, attendance, and other such measures.

In a more recent study, Rigsby and DeMulder (1998) examined end-of-program essays by 103 graduating teachers for patterns, variety of experience, and outlier responses about the influence of the program on their thinking, attitudes, and teaching practices. Teachers described important changes they had experienced in their professional and personal lives that tended to fall into eight broad categories, including: an ability to see children and classrooms through new lenses and perspectives, empowered professional voice and judgment, improved professional and personal relationships, improved teaching practices and changed educational philosophy, greater knowledge of or sense of self, increased technology proficiency, improved understanding of the writing process and improved writing style, and greater involvement in mentoring and modeling for others. This teacher's reflection highlights some of these changes:

The ways in which I've changed during . . . [the program] . . . are so intertwined that it is difficult to discuss them as separate entities. I guess an umbrella statement would be that I am willing to take risks that will benefit the students in my classes. Specifically, because my teaching strategies have changed, I hear my students' voices much more than my own. Because my relationship with my students has changed, I am not afraid of them anymore. Finally, because my confidence has increased, I can evaluate and improve my teaching practices rather than feel overwhelmed by them. In short . . . [the program] . . . provided the motivation, opportunity, and support I needed to transform myself into a happier, more effective teacher.

Teachers attributed personal and professional changes to both particular experiences in the program and to the experience of the program as a whole. For many of the middle-aged and older women, reading feminist theory, sometimes for the first time, was often transformative. For teachers mired in the bog of "tried and true" methods, it was confrontation with a variety of alternative pedagogies. For younger teachers, it was often the reinforcement of the idea that teachers are experts who need strong professional voices. Some teachers found it to be particularly confirming to develop strong, collaborative relationships with team members (although other teachers found teaming to be quite difficult and unrewarding).

Teachers described aspects of the program that were particularly challenging or that lacked the support they needed, and this information helped faculty to improve the program. For example, the feedback received about the many challenges of teaming and experience with mediating team conflicts led faculty to spend more time on team development and approaches to collaboration. Many teachers struggled with technology and expected more support and training than the program provided, reflecting the faculty's struggle to learn, teach, and incorporate state-of-the-art technology in the program. Feedback from teachers pushed the faculty to seek funding for a technology coordinator for the program, to commit to building their technology skills, and to incorporate the use of technology more fully in the program.

While Rigsby and DeMulder (1998) sought to understand the teachers' overall experience in the program, other faculty members have focused their research on certain features of the program. For example, Ann Sevcik and Sharon J. Gerow in chapters 4 and 5 report their research on pedagogical innovation and teaming. Additional research has sought to understand teachers' attitudes toward special curriculum innovations. Wood and Hicks (Hicks, Foster, Williams, & Wood, 2000; Hicks & Wood, 2000; Wood, 1996) worked together for a number of years on developing and evaluating an arts-based curriculum.

Research that has primarily depended on teachers' self-reports has drawn from many data sources. Besides written evaluations and reflective essays, teachers have been invited to work with faculty as partners to develop a new vision for teacher education. For example, LePage, Boudreau, Maier, Robinson, and Cox (2001) conducted a 2-year study that sought to reinvent the relationship between college faculty and K–12 faculty. In that study, a small group of faculty and graduate students met together for over a year and engaged in dialogic inquiry, collected surveys from students, and interviewed alumni. Ultimately this group worked to untangle the complexity of developing reciprocal and collegial relationships and maintaining partnerships, given the barriers associated with traditional school and university settings.

Analyzing Student Products

Self-report research, which has helped us to understand teachers' affective experiences in the program and their attitudes on its effectiveness, has been important, not only because it provided feedback for continuous improvement, but also because it helped the faculty to "justify" their methods. At this point, few people would argue that teachers do not like the program and that IET is not transformative: "Yes, I completely shifted my focus toward continuous improvement and embracing areas of challenge. Prior to the program 'failure' was frightening—to be avoided. After the program, 'failure' is always seen as an opportunity to learn and reflect. My way of thinking about the children has changed—they work with me. I have learned to appreciate their wonderful ideas."

But, teacher self-report research has always been under suspicion for three reasons grounded in both methodological and political concerns. First, people have criticized self-report as a method of data collection. Self-report is dependent on time and place and subject to uncontrollable variables like fear of authority. A teacher could provide very different comments about the program on a "bad day," or an exceptionally "good day." Some may be afraid to "speak the truth." Others may desire to please faculty members. But, the frequency and consistency of some of the data collected over the years makes this argument less of a concern. Second, this research method demands careful analysis. Evaluators must analyze self-reports with a critical eye. For example, if teachers told us they thoroughly enjoyed the program because it was easy and served to validate their existing beliefs and strategies, that would not constitute evidence of its effectiveness given IET's principles. A third concern, which is political and related to the second, is that given the rise in the importance of standardized test scores, many districts design mandatory inservices focusing directly on how to effectively teach toward state-mandated standards, and many will not provide money for professional development unless teachers are taking classes focused on specific subject area content. Therefore, glowing self-reports of program effectiveness could be read as a relief from the strains of test-driven accountability and not convincing evidence of the program's worth.

The reluctance to lend credibility to teachers' opinions, however, may be just one more example of how teachers are not treated as professionals. Besides being disrespectful, such an attitude is unproductive because the school districts' lack of trust invites teachers to view additional coursework as a way to earn pay increases, without seriously considering what they really need to improve their teaching. The IET program addresses teachers' needs for continuous learning in specific content areas in three ways. First, a teacher could ask to take 6 units (two classes) of "content classes" in both the first and second year. Because we have nontraditional scheduling and the rest of the university does not, scheduling this type of specialized program can be difficult, but the option is certainly available. Second, the program encourages teachers to address whatever issues in their teaching are most problematic. Through action research, essays, books, and collaborative dialogue, teachers are encouraged to follow their own path and make decisions about what types of learning will help them to improve. They can study content through the required assignments, or they can work with advisers to develop special projects that focus on content. Third, a major goal in this program is to reawaken a teacher's interest in learning. We found through program evaluations that many teachers leave the program anxious to learn more about curriculum, pedagogy, and subject area content. After they graduate, many more are willing to admit they need to learn subject area content, seek additional schooling, and experiment with new methods as indicated by some quotes from an alumni survey:

Most obviously I see differences in how I teach reading—[a] direct result of my research. I also feel more qualified and competent than I had before.

I have more courage to try new teaching methods and experiment with alternatives.

I continue to engage in informal teacher research and reflective practice to improve my teaching.

I have been writing grants, reflecting and reading about my practice.

I am forever ready to learn and educate myself in different areas of education.

I would like to receive current information and updates on people and happenings, and the latest in technology and curriculum. Now I feel isolated from the learning environment.

After working with approximately 850 practicing teachers, we found that many realize as they gain experience in the program that they did not struggle with "content" in a meaningful way until they began to change their attitudes about learning and professional responsibility. In addition, although many authority figures are convinced that teachers need more content knowledge, many of the high school teachers who have come through our program have made it very clear that is not what they needed.

While the IET faculty respects the voices of teachers, and takes their self-reports seriously, other sources of evaluation data have also contributed to our understanding of the impact the program has on teachers and their students. For example, faculty have assessed teachers' moral and intellectual development and academic progress by examining graduate student products. Sockett and LePage (2001) analyzed products that were developed over a 2-year period, including admission essays, computer conference postings, and end-of-year portfolios. Initially they were seeking to understand the teachers' use of moral language. What they discovered was a pattern of moral and intellectual development that occurred throughout the program from beginning to end. They found a significant pattern of change in the teachers' views of (1) autonomy and agency, (2) reflection, and (3) collaboration and community.

Data from computer conferencing over the years has provided a fruitful source of information for exploration into teachers' development. Robinson and LePage (submitted) conducted a study on computer conferencing itself as a pedagogical tool. Their goal was to understand both the teachers' affective experience of Web conferencing and their pattern of learning in this new environment. What they found was that although the teachers were talking about significant changes in their attitudes toward knowledge and learning, for example, in an epistemology class, their words were not translated into actions associated with the conference itself. So, in other words, teachers were talking the talk, but not walking the walk.

In a final example, Wood (2001) used a case-study approach to analyze two teacher research projects in-depth. In her study, she candidly discusses the problems embedded in a program devoted to raising teachers' voices while also enriching their lives. She illuminates her own struggle to have the teachers seriously entertain multiple perspectives on an issue without overwhelming, yet again, the authority and expertise teachers build from practice. These efforts are fraught, highly complicated by the gendered nature of teaching, the differential power arrangements in schools and districts, and the epistemological and moral development of individual teachers.

So far, teacher research reports provide the main source of data for determining whether IET has had an effect on children's learning (see Part II). We have also used self-report data because teachers frequently tell us their children's learning has improved as a result of implementing strategies they learned in the program. Using self-report and teacher research for evaluation is limited. Self-report is helpful, but it is important to seek first-hand information about children's learning. And the IET faculty views teacher research first and foremost as a way for teachers systematically to inquire into, and experiment with, new methods and ideas. Many teachers come to know and trust some of the program's basic principles as a result of their research studies, not before. These research studies can only provide information about children's learning while the teachers are in the program and conducting research. Whether the teachers maintain enthusiasm and continue to use new methods or strategies, and whether these methods and strategies continue to improve children's learning, are questions yet to be explored with alumni.

Following up with Alumni

When examining both teacher self-reports and student products, the goal has been mainly to understand the teachers' experience of the program and their intellectual development process. The IET faculty has also been interested in maintaining a connection with our alumni and ascertaining whether and how the teachers are transferring their knowledge into their daily work life.

In the beginning, the program worked to maintain a connection with alumni in part by developing a teacher researcher center and an alumni organization called the Educational Transformation Network (ETN). These efforts had some success in supporting alumni, but neither effort thrived and ultimately both were discontinued. Part of the problem was that faculty just did not feel they had time to continue devoting energy to this type of alumni and school reform initiative, given the lack of support and encouragement from the university.

To assess whether the program has made a difference for teachers in their classrooms, a few years ago the faculty sent out an alumni survey that specifically asked the teachers whether what they learned in IET was useful to them in their classrooms (LePage & Kirk, 1999). The results from the survey revealed that the teachers were overwhelmingly positive about the long-term effects of the program: "I'd just like to say, while I remain a critic of some of the program —hardly a week goes by when I don't use some idea, strategy, or concept from IET in classroom teaching."

Beyond a simple survey, however, faculty members have been designing research projects that go beyond self-report to understand whether teachers are actually making use of some of the skills and habits they learned in the program. For example, Givens-Generett and Hicks (2001) are now conducting research by interviewing alumni and observing classrooms to determine whether alumni have been able to maintain the enthusiasm, the dedication, and the initiative that many exhibited when they graduated.

In addition, LePage, Decker, and Maier (2001) designed a project in partnership with the faculty at the George C. Round Elementary School (Manassas, Virginia), where a large percentage of teachers were IET graduates. At Round, they met with teachers (both alumni and other colleagues) once per month, set up and maintained a conference space, and worked with teachers to complete a collaborative research project aimed at enhancing instruction and workplace environment. Part of IET's initial vision was to bring together a large number of teachers from different schools in teams so that ultimately they might develop a common language and work toward a common vision. The goal was school transformation. The deputy superintendent, the principal, and the teachers considered the project a success, and similar projects in IET, perhaps on a larger scale, have been considered. But the longer-term effects are still being assessed, both for this project and for the program as a whole.

CONCLUSION

This chapter has explained how rhetoric was translated into program reality. It forms a skeleton in which all the chapters in the four following parts can be understood. In subsequent chapters, the authors elaborate on the details. For those interested, it is also possible to read a more detailed description of the structure and content by visiting the IET Web site at http://www.gmu.edu/department/iet/.

PART I

CURRICULUM AND PEDAGOGY

Because there was no proven blueprint for an effective master's program, especially one that connected to children's learning, IET sought to provide faculty teams with as much space as possible to work and rework the central ideas of the program as creatively as they could and into different formats. This autonomy meant, say, that the class of '94 based at one campus would have a different emphasis from the class of '95 based at another. Yet there was another important radical assumption. Faculty believed that both the curriculum and the pedagogy, and thereby the teachers' learning experiences, were also experiences teachers could use with children in their classrooms. That belief is borne out by the constant description of classroom innovations by teachers. These three chapters therefore celebrate that possibility as they describe a particular curriculum emphasis (chap. 3) and a particular pedagogical approach (chap. 4), neither of which was universal as was the practice of teachers working in teams (chap. 5).

In chapter 3, Diane R. Wood describes her conception of connecting the IET curriculum ideal to the theme of the American Dream. After describing its origins, she examines its main components and the difficulties her team encountered in implementation, specifically in terms of opening access to knowledge; democratizing practices of teaching and learning; promoting professional habits of inquiry, collaboration, and reflection; fostering professional autonomy; and promoting teachers' public accountability.

In chapter 4, Ann Sevcik describes how, from the outset, substantive dialogue was demanded as a central part of the pedagogy. From that commitment was developed a scheme for the work of a full day, known as PASCA, an acronynm for presentation, analysis, strolling critique, and collaborative argument. After describing the PASCA rationale, design, and development, she describes the experience of working with one cohort within the new class of '98 (i.e., in summer 1996). Working with Sarah Kaesar, her co-facilitator, she developed a research project, which, for various reasons, was not completed, but was formed in this 2-week set of experiences. Building on Richard McKeon's four-part analysis of methods of argument (agonistic, logistic, dialectical, and problematic), she describes and analyzes the shifts in the work of the cohort as they grapple with fundamental ideas in moral professionalism, concluding that such work could be developed in graduate classrooms in universities.

In chapter 5, Sharon J. Gerow describes her own commitment to the development of teachers working in teams in IET, using data gathered over several years for her doctoral dissertation. First, she discusses the formation and organization of teams, the development of early conflicts, and the significance of environment and time in the creation of a working team. She then analyzes the moral issues, which arise from team relationships, the development of team identities and examples of destructive patterns of behavior. She concludes with an example of a procedure for a team, which is a dramatic test of individual accountability to other members.

3

Teacher as Citizen: Professional Development and Democratic Responsibility

Diane R. Wood

Twenty years as a practitioner in schools, I remember with occasional bitterness the succession of dreary in-service classes, and particularly vivid is the memory of an autumn ordeal during the direct instruction craze. I watched, alternately amazed and amused, as our well-manicured workshop leader demonstrated hand signals for us to introduce to our students (thumbs up for *understand*, thumbs down for *don't understand*, thumbs sideways for *not sure*), a guaranteed strategy, she argued, for efficient, on-the-spot assessment. Perfectly turned out in her corporate suit and knotted silk scarf, she energetically stalked the auditorium stage, occasionally dazzling us with her smile. High student achievement, she assured us, was only as far away as the bulleted techniques listed on her flip chart.

Listening to her, I resisted an overwhelming compulsion to raise my hands in the air—both in a decidedly thumbs-down position! My mind wandered in protest to faces of troubled teenagers in my inner-city school. I wondered what all this had to do with the poverty, drop-out rates, unwanted pregnancies, and substance abuse that permeated their worlds. Most infuriating was the way this woman proceeded as if there were nothing to contest, as if we, the teachers in the room, had somehow reached a consensus about what our students should learn and why. When a few brave souls did raise questions, she smiled condescendingly and delivered a pep talk about combining high expectations with the "latest research." Realizing our speaker, like so many before her, simply preferred not to clutter her mind with our untidy realities, we settled into polite inattention.

Experiences like this one fuel my disdain for teacher-development approaches that substitute technical solutions for conscientious dialogue and critical reflection. They make me impatient with teacher education programs that masquerade technical rationality (Schon, 1983) as common sense and ignore the profound moral responsibilities inherent to educating children (Sockett, 1993). But, most especially, having seen educational fads come and go, I am tired of hierarchical school cultures that reward teachers for obediently following the latest "experts" instead of building knowledge from lived experiences and collegial dialogue. Ironically, teachers, charged with educating children for a democratic society, have precious few opportunities to exercise their voices or control their profession. Although teachers ostensibly educate *for* democracy, their professional experiences *with* democracy are scarce.

In the first part of this chapter, I outline the rationale for a curriculum for teachers built around the idea of the American Dream as an evocative manifestation of the democratic ideal. In the five following parts, I examine central components of the curriculum and the difficulties we have encountered in their implementation. These are as follows:

1. Opening access to knowledge.
2. Democratizing practices of teaching and learning.
3. Promoting professional habits of inquiry, collaboration, and reflection.
4. Fostering professional autonomy.
5. Promoting teachers' public accountability.

I conclude by adumbrating briefly why such a teacher education curriculum has the potential to contribute significantly to democratic aims for education.

THE AMERICAN DREAM: THE CURRICULUM ORIGINS

Having now become a teacher of teachers, I work with colleagues to create forums where democratic dialogue can flourish and teachers can struggle openly and collaboratively with educational issues, not from the standpoint of technique, but with social justice and democratic citizenship in mind. Such experiences seem to renew appreciation for democratic practices, such as dialogue, argument, persuasion, deliberation, negotiation, and dissent—all crucial for a free society. They provide inspiration teachers need to transform how they think about their profession and how they go about their work.

The familiar *moral* arguments justifying a democratic society carry direct implications for the public schools serving that society. First, the ideal democracy, which demands for all its citizens dignity, freedom of expression, autonomy, and access to opportunity are the very practices required to create and sustain moral communities. Second, teachers in public schools, therefore, have a *moral* responsibility to develop a capacity for citizenship in the nation's children. Children need experiences in establishing and negotiating shared interests.

They need opportunities to articulate their opinions and to entertain arguments against them. They need to develop criteria for evaluating opposing viewpoints. They need the chance to make choices and to live with their social consequences. Third, teachers need to develop their own citizenship in professional contexts that allow similar social practices. They need work cultures that honor their voices, open spaces for professional choices, encourage collegial dialogue, and build on their expertise and knowledge. School cultures that foster democratic practices are more likely to develop in *both* teachers and students an appreciation for and a commitment to democratic life.

In the summer of 1996, I became the designated team leader of the IET program at the Arlington campus of GMU. This draws teachers from three jurisdictions, all with widely diverse populations, a full range of socioeconomic levels, and a recent influx of new immigrants from all over the world. Flying home from New York City one evening and pondering on the curriculum, I imagined the Statue of Liberty, somewhere in the darkness below. How ironic it is, I thought, that a country with such a symbol of opportunity constrains so many, including the minority and the poor children consistently denied access to an equitable education, many of whose newly arrived immigrant parents risk so much in the hopes of better lives. I thought of the many teachers I have known who work hard to meet children's needs, but whose voices seldom influence educational policies (see chap. 13, for instance). From that journey arose a commitment to design a curriculum around democratic education as a moral commitment.

My colleagues and I began to build a curriculum around the theme of the American Dream, hoping that by emphasizing an idealized version of the United States as a "land of opportunity," we might set a provocative interpretive frame for reflection, analysis, and critique of public education (Wood, 1996). How did the schools facilitate or hamper the dreams of children and their parents? For whom were opportunities opened and for whom foreclosed? What could teachers do to better serve the interests of a democratic society? How free were they to do so? We reminded ourselves that the etymological root for *profession* is the verb *to profess*. Thus, to belong to a profession is to affirm or proclaim something of value. How might teachers, we asked, affirm and proclaim a commitment to democratic life through their work with students?

We, then, turned these questions on ourselves. We saw five ways in which the curriculum could be structured as an affirmation of democratic values:

• Opening access to knowledge.
• Democratizing practices of teaching and learning.
• Promoting professional habits of inquiry, collaboration, and reflection.
• Fostering professional autonomy.
• Promoting teachers' public accountability.

OPENING ACCESS TO KNOWLEDGE

We want teachers to question the notion, widespread in contemporary society, that knowledge belongs to experts. If both teachers and their students are to see themselves as partakers and builders of knowledge, and if teachers are to share what they know in public forums, they need to come to grips with epistemological complexity. People in a democracy, after all, need to be sufficiently knowledgeable to make good personal and civic choices and control the direction of their lives.

We invite teachers to think of knowledge as an evolving rather than a fixed concept. By introducing constructivist epistemology (Belenky, Clinchy, Goldberger, & Tarule, 1986; Kegan,1982; Minnich, 1990; Vygotsky, 1978), we ask teachers to recognize knowledge forms as the social constructions they are, always open to refinement, correction, rebuttal, and expansion. We present knowledge, therefore, as perspectival, relational, contingent, partial, and situated. We invite teachers to consider whose knowledge becomes codified and authoritative and why, so that they will investigate intersections of power and privilege with curriculum (Harding, 1991; Renyi, 1993).

These efforts require both historical perspective and epistemological investigation, including a search into lived experiences. Thus, teachers in our program learn about the changing notions of the curricular canon. They learn about Taylorism and technical rationality and confront the devaluing of practitioner knowledge (Cochran-Smith & Lytle, 1992, 1999; Grumet, 1988; Schon, 1983) in favor of outside expertise. During their first days with us, they write autobiographical narratives of teaching and learning experiences and search these texts both for assumptions about knowledge and for embedded forms of practical wisdom. As they begin to articulate their "tacit knowledge" (Elbaz, 1983; Polanyi, 1958), they share it with colleagues, have it critiqued, and begin to see the power of grassroots, collective knowledge, lying outside the boundaries of traditional authority.

This range of individual experiences seems either to help teachers begin to see the value of building on the knowledge of learners, or, to affirm that conception in those who already hold it. "Now that I see what confidence it gives you to know that you *do* know something and expand from there, I want to do the same thing for the kids in my classroom" (Cathy Hix, class of '98). Many teachers in the program make more concerted efforts to surface and use the knowledge that children bring with them to classrooms. IQ and standardized test scores become debatable constructions rather than descriptions of fixed realities (Gould, 1996; Oakes & Lipton, 1999; Smith, 1995). As they work through a curriculum project that requires them to monitor closely the progress of two students through a series of assignments, they consider and discuss the relative influence of both context and heritable endowment on children's academic achievement. For most, assessment becomes a matter of constantly adjusting teaching practices to the needs and interests of students and not an exercise in measuring relative mastery over a prescribed curriculum.

Needless to say, we run into serious barriers. State mandates requiring high-stakes testing perpetuate old ideas about the static quality of knowledge and privilege some forms of knowledge over others. No matter how well we do at giving teachers a sense of their own intellectual potential and at giving them the space and time to mount arguments against these forms of assessment, they must live with the realities of the tests.

Moreover, most of the teachers in our program are themselves products of public schooling. Typically, they have been socialized to respect the authority of the text, to privilege abstract over practical knowledge, and to defer to outside experts, all of which are reinforced in their workplaces. Although in the beginning, many welcome the idea that knowledge built from practice has value, over time, as they note differences in opinions among colleagues, they become disturbed by the prospect that a variety of conclusions can be drawn from similar experiences. Moreover, as they develop habits of reflection, most identify inconsistencies in their own thinking. Some teachers express dismay that we make an already complicated job more complicated by raising problems and offering few solutions, a view that could be attributed to the epistemological development of individual students (Belenky et al., 1986; Perry, 1970). However, we suspect that, in many cases, these attitudes result from the socialization of teachers into school cultures, where authoritative certainty tends to prevail. Thus, experiences with the IET program can be unsettling, especially given the "endemic uncertainties" (Lortie, 1975) that already characterize the professional lives of teachers. As professors, we struggle to find the right balance, knowing that university life supports the luxury of ambiguity more easily than the daily press of meeting children's needs.

Thus, we try to emphasize standards for trustworthiness and credibility, such as use of evidence and logical argumentation. It is not as if all opinions are as good as the next, we argue. It is difficult, of course, for anyone to hold "commonsense" knowledge up to scrutiny, and there is a certain freedom in relying on outside expertise and top–down directives. Professors, after all, cite authorities in making arguments. Both teachers and professors sometimes flinch at the prospect of sorting through complex, sophisticated arguments in order to construct opinions. It is easy for teachers, especially, to feel an overwhelming sense of futility if they suspect hard won opinions will not be taken seriously by those in authority. It is not unusual to hear in the first few months exasperated comments like, "I can't be bothered with all these side issues; I just want to be left alone to do my job." Of course, given the crushing job descriptions demanded of teachers, we hardly blame them. Nevertheless, we persist, knowing that, without sufficient teacher input, educational policies will continually miss the mark.

Most teachers, managing to work through these issues, begin to assay knowledge from a Deweyean (1916, 1938, cited in Gouinlock, 1994) and constructivist perspective. This empowers them to see their own professional knowledge as socially valuable. They begin, in fact, to take conscious responsibility for it by subjecting it to reflection, critique, dialogue, and multiple perspectives. We nudge them further by challenging them to consider how academic knowledge and human intelligence can better serve democratic life. How, we ask, might they use their knowledge in service to civic society? There is much to be done, as Dewey (1954) reminded us, "The prime condition of a democratically organized public is a kind of knowledge and insight which does not yet exist" (p. 166). The "right course," he insisted, "is to bring the best intelligence we can command to bear upon social problems" (cited in Gouinlock, 1994, p. 189). Teachers' knowledge, traditionally dismissed, has the capacity to contribute immeasurably to understandings about public education.

DEMOCRATIZING TEACHING AND LEARNING

Not only do teachers need to democratize notions of knowledge for themselves and for their students, they need to democratize processes of teaching and learning. For years, public schools have afforded certain predictable groups of students less access to curricula than others (Belenky et al., 1986; Darling-Hammond, 1997b; Delpit, 1995; Goodlad and Keating, 1991; Ogbu, 1990; Solomon, 1992). For the sake of democratic life, teachers working together need to find the means to open access to all children. Similarly, university professors need to open access for learners in their classrooms.

As IET faculty, we attempt to open the curriculum to our own students—the teachers—in a number of ways. We employ participatory pedagogies, encouraging teachers to read and critique one another's work and to grapple together with ideas that emerge from their course work and lived experiences. We encourage the use of professional dilemmas as touchstones for critiquing theory and as departure points for dialogue and scholarly inquiry. We offer repeated opportunities to fulfill criteria for any given assignment. We choose a wide range of readings to include a variety of perspectives in an attempt to make the curriculum inclusive. In addition, we have integrated the arts into the program both because teachers find them inspirational and because they offer an alternative language for conveying significant ideas.

For a curriculum project that we assign during the second year, we ask teachers to explore their own inclusive pedagogical strategies. In preparation, they read and discuss Delpit's (1995) and Solomon's (1992) critiques of schooling as a white middle-class endeavor. They turn to Noddings (1992) and Smith (1995) for ideas about building a caring relational environment, safe enough for learning. They consider Dewey's (1938) and Freire's (1970) calls for a problem-posing, dialogic curriculum that builds around the needs and interests of students. They read Belenky's and her colleagues' (1986) take on classrooms built around the notion of "connected knowing." As faculty, we frequently learn from the pedagogical creativity of the teachers.

Once again, standardized testing raises a serious challenge to our work, constraining both our efforts and those of the teachers. Because teachers feel pressed to drill children in the facts and concepts required to pass high-stakes, multiple-choice examinations, creative curriculum projects can seem hopelessly idealistic and irrelevant. We have seen teachers begin such projects only to abandon them in frustration. Recognizing these difficulties, we try to bolster their efforts at innovation by providing readings in assessment (Calkins, Montgomery, Santman, & Falk, 1998; Wiggins, 1993). We hope to strengthen their critique of standardized tests (and most are critical of them), as well as their resolve to avoid narrowing the curriculum, while they still prepare children for the tests. As professors, we struggle with how much to acquaint ourselves with the particulars of these tests without being co-opted by their agenda. We want to devise with teachers ways to marshal the support of administrators and parents against high-stakes testing, but we know the political risks are mostly theirs. Given present political conditions, the heavy, debilitating restraints on creative, responsive teaching are pervasive in both school and university classrooms.

A second challenge opens as we consider Gutmann's (1999) claim that public schools need to provide children with the knowledge, skills, and experiences necessary for deliberative democracy. That is, children need to understand and exercise basic freedoms, while respecting those of others. Some teachers resist, claiming freedom for children requires abrogation of adult authority. We counter that, although children need guidance and direction, they also need increasing opportunities as they mature for making choices, exercising their voices, and experiencing the social consequences of both. They need to witness and participate in social situations where the exercise of individual rights need not preclude the promotion of common interests.

Thus, during the first summer working with teachers, we assign the *Declaration of Independence*, the *Preamble to the Constitution*, and the *Bill of Rights* and then ask teachers to consider the implications for public education. We establish forums to discuss these issues both in class sessions and via electronic conferencing. As they confront conflict and disagreement among themselves, they struggle to define criteria for a credible argument, to appreciate both the value and the difficulties of an open exchange of ideas, and to assess contradictory claims on the same issue. These firsthand experiences deepen their understanding of challenges endemic to democratic dialogue.

Again, these processes can go awry. Some teachers use open forums to proclaim inadequately supported opinions, even personal prejudices. We have had experiences of unreflective, racist, sexist, or homophobic remarks accompanied by injured feelings, both in class and online. On the one hand, teachers have requested that we play a more authoritarian role and set rules for their discussions. On the other, others have accused us of trying to interfere or control too much. Throughout, we insist on civility but try to avoid squashing robust, although sometimes heated, professional exchanges. We struggle with what our role should be as we hear some teachers express reductionist notions of democracy, such as "the majority rules" or democracy means "I can say and do as I please." When we raise the issue of minority rights, some accuse us of "political correctness." When we declare that democracy demands common ground as well as individual freedom, some teachers complain they are being coerced to conform. We watch with anxiety as a few teachers retreat in silence while others dominate; then we work gingerly with the community to correct the situation.

Yet this is both the price and the value of having serious discussions with teachers as opposed to the formal question-and-answer structure typical of most instruction. As we struggle to work these issues through, we try to be open with teachers about the process. A few of them, unfortunately, decide that creating more democratic classrooms is too much work or ultimately unrealistic. Some of our fiercest critics, however, have come back after graduation explaining that, once out of the program, they could not get these ideas out of their heads. As Josh Strong, (class of '98) put it, "I resisted the whole notion for 2 years but couldn't stop thinking about it. Now, I'm convinced I've got to give kids a chance to practice living in a democracy."

PROMOTING PROFESSIONAL HABITS OF INQUIRY, COLLABORATION, AND REFLECTION

Just as democracy is always in the making, democratic education should be as well. For this reason, we actively promote habits of inquiry, collaboration, and reflection in our program, encouraging teachers to think of teaching and learning as continuously in need of change and renewal. We believe that if teachers experience the power of these habits of mind, they might be more likely to incorporate them in their work and to view them as essential for the profession. It is our hope, of course, that they will also see these habits of mind as crucial for their students' development as well.

Our program recruits teachers in school teams (see chap. 5), and these become communities in miniature, a ready context for democratic practices. For Dewey (1916/1985) democracy is the idea of community itself. It embodies the conditions, the processes, and the ends—all inseparable—for uniting people in common purposes. As a result, democratic life carries inescapable moral implications (Dewey, cited in Gouinlock, 1994; Gutmann, 1999; Spring, 1999), particularly regarding justice and inclusion. Habermas' (1991) ideas resonate with Dewey's as he grounded "moral norms in communication" (p. 195), something he called discourse ethics. Fundamental to these ideas is public access to "communicative action." For him, citizens have the *moral* obligation to set the conditions for inclusive participation. They must recognize the sanctity of every human life, see the benefits of diverse perspectives, honor open dialogue, and act in accordance with these values. So with teacher teams.

In order to accomplish the various tasks, assignments, projects required, however, and to do so democratically, teachers need concrete support. We invite them to play the role of "critical friends," teaching them ideas from composition theory about how to give feedback to colleagues. We expose them to Dewey's

(1916, cited in Gouinlock, 1994) conception of "method," which he defined in democratic terms. This entails the naming of a social problem (in the case of teachers, a problem in teaching and learning). It requires reflection on both potential and actual social consequences of the problem and then systematic investigation into it. As understandings emerge and solutions take shape, the process demands continuous self-reflexivity and eventual communication with outside audiences for input and critique. The aim of social inquiry is to guide purposive action in service to a better society, a fundamentally democratic goal. In that spirit, we teach qualitative research methods and encourage teachers to situate their research efforts in authentic social situations, considering them part of a larger dialogue supporting democratic life (Booth, Colomb, & Williams, 1995).

Throughout, we urge reflection, both collective and individual. We warn teachers to "beware of common sense" and to question their own assumptions and beliefs. Primary to our purposes here is attention to multiple perspectives, again a democratic value. We try to emphasize both the risk to and the value of identity in a pluralistic, democratic society. We introduce concepts such as *resistance theory* (Solomon, 1992) and *White privilege* (McIntosh, 1988). Teachers encounter "outsider" perspectives through imaginative literature and the arts. They get in touch with their own experiences of oppression and marginalization through autobiographical narratives. As they entertain a range of others' perspectives, through research interviews, assigned readings, and collegial dialogue, many grow in appreciation of dialogue across disciplines and differences.

Refusing to suppress individual identities in the name of group conformity is, of course, an essential democratic principle. Dewey (cited in Gouinlock, 1994) wrote, "the conception of common good, of general well-being, is a criterion which demands the full development of individuals in their distinctive individuality, not a sacrifice of them to some alleged vague larger good under the plea that it is *social*" (p. 192). When individuals speak from the fullness of their own experiences and from their own vantage point, authentic common ground is more likely to emerge, making understandings about the world more complete (Minnich, 1990).

As teachers struggle to promote classrooms where social order and individual differences co-exist, however, they run into problems and so do we. Simply proclaiming that "everyone has a right to speak and be heard" does not ensure that it will be so—either in teachers' classrooms or in ours, or in their teams. Social patterns of exclusion, repression, and discrimination are often unconscious. Power often works invisibly. As professors, we worry about our voices drowning out the voices and dissent of the teachers, and we examine our own unconscious assumptions. We know that they, too, struggle to uncover deeply rooted assumptions that may affect their responses to students. Both they and we must consider how power plays out in classrooms and attend to the complexities and potential cruelties of student peer cultures.

In order to address these issues, we take a hard look with teachers at patterns of success and failure in classrooms. We ask them to evaluate who thrives in their classrooms, which parents exercise influence over school policy, and which rarely darken the school door. We ask the teachers to evaluate us as professors. For whom are our pedagogical strategies working and not working? How do issues of power and control invade the university classroom? Opening these issues up can be incredibly uncomfortable. It is easy to view discussions about classroom practice, particularly those centered on diversity and difference, as accusations rather than explorations. But the stakes are too high to avoid the subject. The invisible walls of privilege, power, and prejudice too often constrain individuals from learning and democratic participation.

FOSTERING PROFESSIONAL AUTONOMY

Again, Gutmann (1999) argued that the basic professional responsibility of teachers is to "cultivate the capacity for deliberative democracy" (p. 76). Such a capacity requires people to think for themselves, to be critically reflective, and to act on their own consciences. Necessary for full participation in a democracy, these habits of mind are also essential for developing a sense of autonomy. Those teachers who have developed as autonomous professionals are more likely to help children develop a sense of autonomy.

Professional autonomy, according to Gutmann (1999), must strike the right balance between "insolence," which results from "too much autonomy," and "ossification," which results from "too little" (p. 77). Teachers typically suffer from the latter, having insulated themselves from storms of criticism and contradictory advice. At first anxious to make a social contribution (Cohn & Kottkamp, 1993; Goodlad, 1984; Gutmann, 1999; Jackson, 1968; Lieberman & Miller, 1992; Lortie, 1975; Sarason, 1982, 1996), many lose a sense of purpose when faced with bureaucratic controls and practice ossifies.

Democratic dialogue offers the necessary antidote to either professional insolence or ossification. A professional should be responsible, judicious, and deliberative by holding expertise in dialogue with the opinions and desires of the public. Professional autonomy, in other words, needs sanctioning through democratic exchange.

Paradoxically, whether or not officially or democratically sanctioned, teachers inevitably exercise autonomy. The press of daily life in classrooms demands scores of teacher decisions, tailored to particular situations and students. If teachers are to avoid becoming either arrogant or rigid in their decision making, they need opportunities to reconsider decisions in institutional contexts that support and encourage open dialogue, the sharing of experiences, and continuous learning. Teachers need to develop and exercise responsible professional judgment.

Of course, even relieved of authoritarian controls, teachers are perfectly capable, like the rest of us, of relying on unconscious routines, habits, and assumptions. Although most people value the idea of freedom, it requires concerted efforts to develop the "wide-awakeness" (Greene, 1988, 1995) to envision the alternatives that freedom requires: "When people cannot name alternatives, imagine a better state of things, share with others a project of change, they are likely to remain anchored or submerged, even as they proudly assert their autonomy" (p. 9).

In our curriculum, we work hard to open learning spaces where teachers can name alternative possibilities for their work. Through Boal's (1995) Theater of the Oppressed, we work with teachers to stage past experiences with oppression in order to imagine alternative responses and better outcomes. We teach Rose's (1995) *Possible Lives* to offer portraits of teachers who succeed despite the odds. We study together the implications of a democratic approach to education (Apple & Beane, 1995; Dewey, 1938; Greene, 1988, 1995; Meier, 1995). In their own buildings, teachers conduct seminars on democratic possibilities for their classrooms. They read novels, such as Fitzgerald's (1925) *The Great Gatsby* and Morrison's (1973) *Sula*, to explore the characters' hopes and dreams for a good life and the social barriers that contort or strangle them. As they discuss these novels, they imagine together how democratic schooling might open possibilities for more constructive, fulfilling lives.

Just as teachers need more autonomy, children also need to learn to exercise autonomy, or ownership, over their learning (Dewey, 1916/1985; Meier, 1995; Oakes & Lipton, 1999; Smith, 1995). We find many teachers in our program expressing increasing interest in helping children to accomplish precisely that. Particularly in their curriculum projects, teachers explore how to develop their students' voices and provide more room for students' choices. Some adopt these themes for their research projects. As Julie Harrington (class of '00) explains: "We need to teach questioning and openness. . . . If we could challenge ourselves as teachers to foster and accept hard questions from our students, then we'd be serving democracy and not the status quo. In a democracy, we should be encouraged to see beyond partial knowledge and to get in conversation with others." Having a degree of freedom to choose, to speak, and to act builds that sense of agency so necessary for democratic citizenship.

Gutmann's (1999) warning that autonomy without dialogue can result in "insolence" has relevance here. Not only professional teachers but children need to develop moral responsibility along with personal agency. In our program, we ask teachers to generate moral norms for their relationships with one another over the 2 years and to encourage the same processes in their classrooms among students. Sometimes this process—both in our classroom and theirs—bogs down in difficult, tedious conversations. Time for course content seems sacrificed, and yet, in classrooms with democratic aims, this process should become essential content.

This is especially true given the way children struggle with relationships in classrooms. They, too, deserve opportunities to develop norms for community. Of course, some at early developmental stages will have difficulty recognizing the impact of their actions on others, and some will be drawn more to individual liberties than to social responsibilities. Nevertheless, they need practice in developing capacities for both. They need opportunities to move beyond behavior sanctioned by "praise and blame" (Gouinlock, 1994; Kohn, 1998) to self-disciplined decisions about how to conduct themselves not only in their own interests but in the interest of democratic living (Dalton & Watson, 1997). Autonomy without social responsibility is no virtue.

PROMOTING PUBLIC ACCOUNTABILITY

Popular notions of teacher accountability hinge too much on standardized test scores. Professional accountability should be based on whether or not teachers respond effectively to the needs of students, assess their teaching practice against the academic achievement of their students, avail themselves of continuous professional learning, collaborate with colleagues, view themselves as "stewards" (Goodlad, 1984) of their schools, and contribute to the growth of their profession. Accountability also demands regular dialogue with parents and a commitment to the welfare of the larger society. Teachers who see themselves as democratic citizens, I argue, are more likely to be truly accountable.

Commitment to citizenship, among teachers and others, however, cannot be taken for granted. Dewey (1954) warned years ago of "an eclipse of a public" intimidated by technical expertise and bewildered by the complexities of social problems. Citizens, who feel remote from or inadequate for public decision making, eventually disengage. The public's disengagement threatens participatory democracy; and teachers' disengagement from a public threatens good teaching. Sociologies of teaching (Cohn & Kottkamp, 1993; Jackson, 1968; Lortie, 1975; Sarason, 1982, 1996; Waller, 1932/1967) have long described teachers' work as sequestered behind classroom doors, rarely visible for public critique or appreciation.

People, Dewey (1954) argued, come together to form a public when they recognize vital interests and see the need to work together to preserve, negotiate, or expand those interests. The challenge for teachers, we believe, is first to recognize the important role and responsibility public educators have toward a democratic society and, second, that public education represents a common interest of all democratic citizens. Having acknowledged a common interest with and a responsibility to the public, teachers who are citizens need to muster the wherewithal to summon it.

When we ask teachers in the program to consider who they believe has a vested interest in what they know and do, invariably, they name parents. For teachers, parents are the obvious and primary public (Jacobs, 1997). Unfortunately, relationships between teachers and parents are too often adversarial (see chap. 11). Parents tend to focus on the needs of their own children. Teachers necessarily have to be concerned with groups. Parents frequently expect special consideration and exceptions to be made for their children. Teachers rely on fair and consistent treatment for all children. Some parents, intimidated by school authority, do not know how to advocate successfully for their children. Others, more privileged, intervene too much. Some teachers, understandably smarting from a lack of respect from the larger society, control parents' access to and influence on information and decision making.

In our program, we try to encourage dialogue between teachers and their students' parents. We ask teachers to conduct open-ended interviews regarding parents' hopes and dreams for their children. We urge them to share their own hopes and dreams for students with parents. We encourage them to read Tillie Olsen's (1961) *I Stand Here Ironing* and Edward Jones' (1994) *The First Day*, both short stories about school officials ignorant of or insensitive to parents' struggles. We draw on the experiences of teachers who are both parents and teachers, asking them to share with their colleagues how each role informs the other. In providing these experiences, we hope teachers will discover the common ground they invariably share with parents—the welfare of children.

We urge teachers, therefore, to create public forums for parents and teachers to meet together and discuss educational aims. We try to convince teachers in the program to communicate their purposes and practices to parents, keeping them informed throughout the school year. Parents, we believe, need to be educated by teachers about the realities of classroom teaching and learning; and teachers need to be educated by the perspectives of parents with intimate knowledge of their children. If all involved can manage candid and open exchanges, including challenges and mistakes as well as successes, then perhaps teachers and parents might learn together how better to respond to children's needs and promote their welfare.

Even beyond communication with parents, we encourage teachers to develop a public voice. We take seriously Giroux's (1988) suggestion that teachers become public intellectuals, working in public spheres for the good of children and their learning. As teachers finish their research projects, we encourage them to make their findings public by presenting them to colleagues, parents, administrators and other school officials. We advocate presentations at conferences and are developing a Web site for posting their studies. Besides sharing their research, we urge them to take an informed stand on public educational issues and try to develop forums for their opinions to be heard.

Increasingly, we are displacing routine academic papers with assignments for teachers to write letters, articles, and position papers for public consumption. Again, this is not always easy, particularly because we have found some teachers fear public presentations of any kind other than in front of children. This is understandable since most teachers work in cultures where exchanges with adults are rare and where following directives is rewarded over voicing opinions. Over the years, however, we have seen a majority of the teachers who work with us develop both the capacity and the taste for making what they know and learn public.

It is our hope that when teachers come to terms with their public responsibilities as citizens, they will recognize the need to develop similar capacities in their students. "Public schools are not merely schools *for* the public, but schools of publicness: institutions where we learn what it means to *be* a public because they establish us as a public" (Barber, 1997, p. 29). Less than half of the U.S. population voted in the 1996 national elections. Teacher educators like ourselves must accept responsibility for the following difficult agenda and share its complexities with teachers:

• What kind of public are we creating of future generations in public schools?
• Does the tight control of teachers' and children's minds and behavior in most schools contribute to complacency and passivity regarding citizenship?
• If children spend inordinate amounts of times with teachers who become primary models for adult behavior, what do they witness with regard to their teachers' participation in collegial dialogue or school governance?
• What do these observations teach them about appropriate social and institutional engagement?

CONCLUSION

I remember well working for a principal who exhorted us to "remember the kids," although he had little contact with them himself. He particularly raised this issue when he was requiring obedience for his latest dictum. He used our best intentions to manipulate us, but thwarted these very same intentions in the ways he ran the school. Of course, I never told him this. I learned quickly that he was the boss, that I had the best opportunity to do what I thought was right if I kept a low profile, and that dissent could culminate in a "punitive reassignment." For more than 7 years I kept a low profile in that building, making only a few friends among my colleagues, working hard to respond to the academic and emotional needs of inner-city teenagers, and constantly agonizing over whether my work was any good.

From what I have learned over the past few years as a teacher of teachers, many teachers still labor in that same isolation and doubt. There is a social tendency to sentimentalize teaching for "touching lives," but these words, like my principal's, do little to assuage the silent frustrations with which teachers live. Teachers need spaces for open dialogue and professional autonomy, so that they can speak truths about their work, name their dilemmas, and collaborate with others to find better answers.

Public schools have a mission to serve a democracy. Teachers who envision themselves as citizens may be society's best hope for reawakening democratic participation and responsibility. We have tried in this program, not to provide technical support, but to open up the dream of a democratic vision. We continually struggle with how to help teachers build alliances with parents who, along with them, constitute the population most likely to respond constructively to children's needs and interests. We must work with school administrators and the general public to create and fund working environments for teachers that respect their expertise and encourage their collaboration. As a teacher, I remember the feeling of professional suffocation. Now as a professor, I have experienced the revitalization of intellect and commitment that comes with creative room to innovate and collaborate. I want the teachers who are my students to have the same sorts of experiences. In fact, I want them to begin *demanding* them.

Children spend a great deal of time in schools and deserve to encounter adults there who are intellectually alive and stimulating, actively involved in professional learning and innovation, and acting out of a sense of professional autonomy. They need teachers who are making efforts to creatively respond to their needs and who understand that childhood requires self-discovery in the context of relationships with others. To prepare for this society, they need human interactions that are explicitly democratic. In a confusing world, our children might find great solace, hope, and direction when they recognize the promise of democratic life is not only individual freedom but also collective action toward the common good. The living, breathing example of teachers acting like democratic citizens might provide the inspiration they need to live lives of purpose and meaning while contributing to the welfare of others. This is the essential hope for and responsibility of democratic schooling, and, of course, for professional education.

4

Talking to Learn: A Pedagogy Both Obvious and Obscure

Ann Sevcik

Integrated development of innovative curriculum and pedagogy was at the core of our thinking and planning in 1992 when the program opened its doors. We believed that "Different models of pedagogy and curriculum are essential to a stimulating learning environment if it is to foster a shift from an instrumental to an intrinsic view of the worth of what is being learned" (see *Beliefs and Principles in IET Practice* in chap. 2). Differing models of pedagogy did emerge through the years; some harmonizing, remaining distinctive but blending with others like a musical chord; some deeply contrasting with others. That a variety of pedagogical forms has been presented through the years for faculty and teachers to experience, think about, debate, and study indicates the program's approach, and its commitment, to seeing pedagogy as a primary intellectual interest for teachers, both university- and school-based.

In 1992, our seven-member teaching team, five of whom were practicing kindergarten through 12th-grade teachers, felt the pedagogy that we designed in the first class of the IET program was profoundly innovative, shaped as it was by the program's transformative vision and real-world situation. Our beliefs and principles of practice along with a curriculum grounded in moral agency, epistemology, and teacher research required a collegial learning environment, energized by exploration and critique. What helped us navigate through the initial complexity and ambiguity toward a complementary pedagogy was the belief we shared that *how* we and the teachers on the program gained knowledge would be as important as *what* we came to know.

In part, how we learned included a commitment to providing opportunities for substantive dialogue. That is, through discussion we wanted to foster voice—

the *expression* of ideas and opinions, but we also wanted to foster authentic "dialogue" characterized by reciprocity—the *hearing and critique* of others' ideas and opinions. Our concept of "substantive" dialogue concerned making a conscious and coherent effort to construct justified knowledge, something distinctly different from simply talking openly and opining accurately. In his Lexicon for *Ethics After Babel,* Stout (1988) captured the rudiments of our thinking about "substantive" dialogue and suggested an important caveat as well—*"Hermeneutics* (good sense): The art of enriching our language in conversation with others; also, reflection designed to raise this art to consciousness without reducing it to a set of rules" (p. 298).

In our conception of "substantive dialogue," we saw discussion leading not only toward clarification and, sometimes, closure, but toward what seemed to us to be more important—developing insights and questions, discovering dilemmas and paradoxes, and conceiving of transformative actions. We believed "substantive dialogue"—collaboratively probing ideas and experiences—could cultivate a deeper understanding of teaching and learning and lead to improved practice.

So, along with written work, such as reflective journals, narrative accounts, and formal position papers, we were determined to provide the teachers in the program with opportunities for substantive dialogue ranging across conversation, analysis, critique, dialectic, and planning. Working on our pedagogy for talking to learn—a pedagogy that could provide opportunities for the collaborative construction of knowledge—we found that some elements of the design were obvious, but many of the details were obscure. For that reason, we planned to use our pedagogy not only as a coherent structure for dialogue but also as a framework to explore dialogic learning and then systematically study its qualities with the teachers as participants in the research, not as subjects. We put our innovative pedagogy into use provisionally, expecting to revise it based on our continuous reflection and research.

We called our design PASCA, an acronym for four phases of work—presentation, analysis, strolling critique, and collaborative argument. We felt those titles provided distinguishing and reasonably accurate descriptors for each phase of the work. As the program grew in numbers and new faculty teams were formed, other pedagogical formats were used with new classes. In this chapter, I focus on the PASCA approach describing, first, the more obvious elements of the pedagogy's rationale and design. Second, I elaborate on some of the more obscure epistemological details those of us who worked with this design encountered as we strove to understand and continuously improve the pedagogy. Third, I include a fairly detailed example of our work with PASCA drawn from the experience of one class during their first summer of study with us in 1996. I conclude with some observations drawn from the teachers' and my own reflections on learning in PASCA.

DEALING WITH THE OBVIOUS: A PRACTICAL PEDAGOGY FOR SUBSTANTIVE DIALOGUE

In addition to designing a pedagogy consonant with our curriculum emphasizing moral agency, epistemology, and teacher research, our seven-member faculty—the teaching team—had to prepare for a number of pragmatic issues arising from the program's extraordinary popularity, the intensive schedule, and the array of meeting sites we planned to use. We opened the program with a class of 143 teachers ready to work with us for two academic years and three summers. The plan was that sometimes we would work in the 3- to 5-member school-based teams, sometimes in the 25-member cohorts, occasionally breaking out into conversation groups of 6 to 8 teachers, and sometimes as an entire class, 143 people at once. The intensive schedule called for working in full-day seminars about once a month during each academic year, for 2 consecutive weeks during two of the summer sessions, and for 1 week during the third and final summer. Seminar days were scheduled in several schools as well as in university classrooms, so there was wide variation in the facilities where we planned to meet. Faced with this diversity, promoting a sense of pedagogical coherence and continuity was paramount.

The Rationale

Designing the written and oral elements of our pedagogy and developing the mutual attraction by which the elements would be held together was an exciting and challenging enterprise. Certain elements of the program's beliefs and principles, still rudimentary constructions in 1992, helped define PASCA as a framework seeking to be:

- inquiry-based, in order to promote autonomy and professional self-direction;
- built on practitioners' expressed concerns, in order to ensure that the learning agenda would be sensitive to the teachers' contextually relevant expertise;
- guided by practitioners' practical questions interacting with theoretical frameworks in the curriculum, in order to clarify and deepen the meaning of their particular contexts and provide connections with wider perspectives and additional knowledge;
- both open and purposeful, a complementarity intended to allow learning that would be emancipated and also integrated through 2 years of study;
- rooted in up-to-date adult development theory (often neglected in professional development programs), seeking to link personal and professional concerns;
- innovative in its modes of assessment, in order to exemplify the need for radical rethinking of contemporary patterns of professional development.

We envisaged PASCA as a type of dialogic inquiry, an alternative to forms of instruction that emphasize factual and procedural knowledge (skills, processes) at the expense of deeper levels of understanding. Dialogic inquiry is, also, an alternative to forms of instruction that emphasize control (behavior management models) and relevance (hybrid, naïve Progressivism). It is based on a constructivist approach to teaching and learning that incorporates the idea that learners actively connect, interpret, and develop what they know rather than passively absorb exactly what others know. The traditional telling–listening relationship between instructor and student is replaced by one that is more complex and interactive. This can feel quite liberating, but it can also complicate learning for those who practice it as suggested by Prawat (1992):

> While there are several interpretations of what this [constructivist] theory means, most agree that it involves a dramatic change in the focus of teaching, putting the students' own efforts to understand at the center of the educational enterprise. The adoption of such an approach to teaching and learning . . . result[s] in major changes in the teachers' role . . . and places greater demands on teachers (and students). (p. 357)

Working within a learning community such as we wanted to establish—an authentic partnership among school and university-based colleagues—can create an even greater sense of confusion because during the discussions everyone actively shares, exchanges, and integrates stances as teacher and as student. The blended stance is that of learner (Sevcik, 1984).

The Design

On PASCA seminar days, we scheduled four phases of work—presentation, analysis, strolling critique, and collaborative argument (see Table 4.1). The plenary presentation session offered a coherent set of ideas—a lecture or learning experience of some sort—usually with brief excursions into journal writing or conversation. The analysis session followed immediately, usually in the cohorts, providing an opportunity to clarify and begin to critique ideas in the presentation. Strolling critique, in school-based teams following lunch, was literally that, an opportunity to walk and probe the day's work so far, sometimes with a specific focus that emerged from the analysis session. The seminar day concluded with collaborative argument, ordinarily a cohort session with the aim of developing a course of reasoning to elaborate a particular issue, illuminate a question, or develop a plan of action on some point generated by the day's work. This framework became an important experiential and intellectual catalyst as we sought to develop an orderly relationship among the program's principles, its curriculum and its unusual structure.

As Table 4.1 indicates, the design provided teachers with opportunities to be collaboratively and actively learning during each phase of the work. For a full-day PASCA, each phase lasted 90 minutes. On an 8:30 a.m. to 5 p.m. day, breaks of 30 minutes, lunch, and a closing administrative session were also scheduled. Discussion about the day's material tended to flow across these

Table 4.1
PASCA Phases

Process Phase	Participants
PRESENTATION Instructor describes a body of information to cohort (25) or to plenary (all cohorts)	Take notes Listen, reflect Raise questions
ANALYSIS Cohort groups explore the content of the presentation	Connect ideas in presentation to personal and professional experience Clarify content Clarify understanding Elaborate, expand, extend content Identify additional questions
STROLLING CRITIQUE Group of 2 to 5, usually the school-based teams, walk and talk about the day's material	Further explore concepts, ideas, questions Express opinions/feelings Discover dilemmas/problems Identify additional questions Write in journals
COLLABORATIVE ARGUMENT Cohort or plenary session discussion probes aspects of the day's work	Explore perspectives Evaluate concepts and ideas Suggest changes, build theory Develop dialogic framework to probe issue(s) embedded in the day's work Describe emerging plans of action

boundaries, an important element designed into the pedagogy because we believed that informal dialogue outside the classrooms could be a vital factor in
fostering voice and authentic dialogue. Infrequently, half-day PASCAs with 30-
to 40-minute phases were scheduled when it was warranted by the material or

other situations such as guest speakers. Some seminar days—workshops for example—were not scheduled as PASCA sessions at all.

DEALING WITH THE OBSCURE: INFRASTRUCTURES SUPPORTING PASCA DISCUSSIONS

Orienting Questions for Analysis and Strolling Critique

In the course of a PASCA seminar, some questions served to orient my contributions as the university-based facilitator.

- How much diversity are we seeing in the discussion?
- How are we experiencing risk and courage (making unclear, provisional, visionary, or even mistaken comments) in this discussion?
- How are we experiencing autonomy and the urge toward consensus?
- What is our tolerance for ambiguity in this discussion?
- What meaning are we making of the Presentation material?
- What information or conditions do we need in order to form effective bridges from partial or incomplete understanding to deeper, more substantial understanding of our ideas?

As the teachers gained familiarity and expertise, they used these and similar questions to prompt their own comments and inquiries during analysis and strolling critique discussions. The questions also served to some extent in collaborative argument sessions, but we came to believe that in the collaborative argument phase of the work, a more elaborate system of support was needed.

A Matrix of Possibilities for Collaborative Argument

We learned that an orderly combination of elements—a flexible but still systematic plan—could help cultivate development of an argument—a course of reasoning. Our commitment to collaboration made developing a course of reasoning more complex, to be sure. Being schematically aware of possibilities helped us clarify our ideas, frame generative questions, and foster substance in individual discussions as they evolved.

Building on McKeon's (1944) work, an analysis of the structure of argument and development of a frame of reference for *principled pluralism*, Watson (1993) described an exhaustive *method of methods* where *method* means a structuring or ordering of what is perceived:

Every text is not only a perspective on reality, but says something about the reality from this perspective. What it says about the reality will have some kind of order or structure or form or connectedness or argument or method. The need to distinguish different ways of ordering the real appeared already in the contrast between the dialectical ordering of essences in Hegel and their ordering in independent sciences in Aristotle . . . [O]ur concern here is not with an order of the real external to the text, but with the order of the real as presented in the text. The way in which the text orders the real can be called its *method* (p. 71).

Drawing on McKeon's and Watson's analysis, we described four methods of argument—four structures—we could use for reference during our collaborative argument discussions. We did not see the four structures as exhaustive nor as absolute. Instead, people in the discussion learned to see them as possibilities that helped us interpret and productively guide that part of a PASCA day. It was important in each PASCA phase, but particularly in collaborative argument, that everyone attempt to be conscious of the collective purpose without, as Stout (1988) warned, reducing the reflection to a set of rules. In that spirit, we proposed:

An *agonistic* method of argument characterized by opposition or contention. Pros and cons were debated, but elaboration, rather than winning, was the purpose.

A *logistic* method characterized by stating a premise followed by a conclusion, and then posing the question: Does the conclusion really follow from the premise? In the case of a rule-type conclusion: Do these incidents follow from the rule? In the case of a canon: Does every example conform to the canon?

A *dialectical* method characterized by interaction between premise and evidence that generated changes in the premise (or rule or canon) until, through synthesis, the premise reflected or "fit" the evidence.

A *problematic* method characterized by getting things in a functionally useful order, as in the steps of a plan.

As did McKeon and Watson, we further characterized our collaborative argument methods by *reciprocal priority* and *constructionism.* That is, no one method stood as primary or foundational to the others, and furthermore, the methods were constructions intended to aid in the interpretation of the discussion, not to account for or explain what was being said. Like Watson, we proposed that in terms of rational construction the four methods we described included basic forms for argument. Also like Watson, we emphasized that the interpretive function of the methods meant that more than one method might emerge as a possible and justifiable structure for a particular discussion. The four methods served to orient us toward the occurrence of dialogic method and to alert us to noticing additional possibilities.

So, hoping to foster and perhaps expedite coherent critique and inquiry during collaborative argument in PASCA, we envisaged discussions this way.

Agonistic Collaborative Argument. A collaborative argument (CA) could be framed around *developing pros and cons* so that leading questions would look something like: What are the advantages and disadvantages, opposing interests, tensions, or issues in the situation or incident we are discussing? We expected some pros and cons would be immediately apparent while others would emerge from the dialogue. Outright debate might develop but winners would not be established.

Logistic Collaborative Argument. A CA could be framed around *testing the truth of a belief or claim* that might be either a premise or some conclusion drawn from the premise. Leading questions in logistic argument would look something like: Is this belief or claim true, accurate, or justifiable? In discussion, evidence would be gathered, carefully examined and used to confirm or refute the belief or claim. The extent and quality of the evidence would determine whether or not (or to what extent) the belief or claim reflected the truth, or was accurate or justifiable. The quality of the evidence would be central to testing the truth of a belief or claim, but the key in this method—in recognizing and developing this perspective of a dialogue's structure—would be that the claim itself would not change. If the collected evidence suggested that the claim needed to be changed in any way, the discussion would shift to a dialectic structure. The purpose of a logistic dialogue would be to notice features of the belief or claim that had been obscure or even hidden before having the discussion.

Dialectic Collaborative Argument. A CA could be framed around *gathering perspectives and synthesizing premises* so that leading questions would look something like: What are some perspectives concerning a particular premise—a belief, situation, or question? How can we synthesize and transcend the perspectives and/or the premise to reach altered, presumably enriched insights? In addition to accomplishing synthesis, we would expect to discover obstacles to developing a fit between premise and perspectives or among perspectives. So, along with some synthesized, enlightened premises and perspectives, this method could generate valuable unresolved dilemmas and paradoxes between premise and perspectives or among the various perspectives.

Problematic Collaborative Argument. A CA could be developed around *solving a problem* so that leading questions would look something like: What is the most productive way to frame this problem or task? What steps shall we take to act on this problem or to carry this task forward?

The necessity of everyone consciously monitoring and maintaining a sense of structure during CA was vital to productive discussion. Naturally, this happened at different levels and with differing emphases for people in the discussion, and also quite naturally, consciousness of the discussion's structure remained a puzzle for some people.

While exploration provided the milieu for CA, working toward some purpose clearly identified and deemed by the group to be worthwhile provided the vitality for this end-of-the-day discussion. For PASCA's other phases—presentation, analysis, and strolling critique—participants' responsibilities and intentions became more or less second nature. Sometimes, CAs developed a sense of natural flow as well, but even then, in order for CAs to reach their potential, the facilitator and the discussants needed to periodically ask themselves and each other: Where are we going with this discussion? and Is where we are going worthwhile?

AN EXAMPLE OF ONE COHORT'S EXPERIENCE WITH PASCA

During the 1996 summer session, the first summer institute for the class of '98, Sarah Kaeser, a middle school teacher and graduate in the first class of the program, joined me as a co-facilitator for the discussion sessions. We designed a research project intending to document a cohort's PASCA experiences, beginning with their first sessions and following them through to their degrees. For a number of reasons, our 2-year research plan was curtailed, but for that one summer session, we did record material and write our reflections and puzzlements, mainly via e-mails each evening.

For 8 of the 10 days of the summer session in 1996, Sarah and I worked, separately or together, with Cohort 3. By way of reviewing our data, we wrote a research memo in August and, when the program resumed in the fall, we presented that memo to Cohort 3, asked for the teachers' responses, and invited them to collaborate with us on the research. What follows, drawn from that research memo, captures something of what teaching and learning in full-day PASCAs was like for those particular teachers and for Sarah and me.

The First Week

To launch the teachers on their journey, Monday was framed as an orientation to such activities as journal writing, working in teams, and collaborative learning. On the first PASCA day, Tuesday, July 16, the presentation concerned "taking a moral point of view" and "using moral language." During the first 15 minutes of analysis, items the cohort put on their discussion agenda included questions about agency (To what extent can we actually take up these moral issues in our schools?), about autonomy (How can we bring autonomy to the state-mandated curriculum?), and about the relationship of morality to religion and social rules. The discussion of rules prompted me to suggest that, during strolling critique, the school-based teams could try to rephrase some of their school rules using "moral language." Following the lunch break, and strolling critique, the group came back to CA, apparently after strolling with other teams in the cohort to ask immediately as the discussion opened: What . . . exactly . . . does "moral language" mean anyway? As we talked, it became clear that the cohort's primary interest at that point was to clarify the notion of "language," expanding it to include more than vocabulary; however, the whole term—*moral language*—was used throughout the discussion.

In a fairly straightforward way, the cohort constructed a logistic argument. Drawing on his or her understanding of concepts and practices in the presentation that day, a teacher would state a belief about what moral language means.

Other people would test the belief—challenging, elaborating, clarifying—and then the cohort would either reject it or add it to a list of claims about what moral language means. After thoughtful discussion trying to meld personal interpretations with ideas described in the presentation, four beliefs survived to describe the concept of moral language. From the point of view of the people in Cohort 3 that day, moral language meant the following:

- Speaking explicitly about and practicing virtues such as trust, respect, honesty, care, fairness, and courage.
- Recognizing assumptions and accepting conventions about seeing people as persons rather than as categories (learning disabled, gifted & talented), about the nature of children (as knowers rather than as "blank slates," as active rather than passive learners), and about the necessity of taking a stance as inquirers.
- Having artifacts and gestures such as placing chairs in a customary way and listening attentively.
- Having a community that recognizes and maintains these various aspects of "language."

The following morning (Wednesday, July 17) during analysis of Hugh T. Sockett's stance on "The Pervasiveness of the Moral," it was apparent to Sarah and Sharon Gerow (a member of faculty who joined Sarah that day because I was not there) that reflection overnight had generated some rumination on the question: What does "moral" mean? For some people, Hugh's notion of moral was seen as distinctly different from conventional notions of moral—that is, what the teachers called the "real" definition of *moral*, and they suggested that "Hugh should call his stuff something else." Spontaneously adopting an agonistic structure, the cohort discussed evidence for why "Hugh's material" did or did not represent an accurate view of what moral means. Reflecting in our e-mail exchange that day, Sarah and I thought the difference might be rooted in understanding moral in its conventional, *prescriptive* interpretation rather than in the *descriptive* mode that anchored the presentation.

In their discussion, the cohort had reviewed ideas from the presentation that moral could mean a certain principle, or system of principles, of right or good conduct. They contrasted that prescriptive interpretation of moral, something closer to ethics, with moral as a descriptive way to train one's eye on the world. That is, rather than looking to a rule to decide right or good conduct in a situation, a person taking a moral point of view looks at and is able to describe aspects or elements of a situation such as complexities concerning relationships among the people or ideas or incidents involved, none of which is seen in isolation. In taking a moral point of view, some actual rather than hypothetical situation is the center of attention, and that situation probably requires some action or decision. In taking a moral point of view to understand situations and guide actions, there is a careful search for good reasons (Fenstermacher & Goodlad, 1997), a sense of struggle, and also an awareness that, because the outcome is uncertain, continued observation and reflection are warranted.

In our e-mail exchange that evening, Sarah noted that the teachers harbored various interpretations of the distinction between the prescriptive and descriptive modes of moral. Some teachers took the differing notions of moral as an expanded insight. Some puzzled over the difference as a dilemma—a choice they would have to make. Some saw it as a paradox—an idea contrary to "common sense" but at the same time perhaps "true." Some continued to see the distinction as a mistake. Sarah and I passed on to the teaching team our impression of the cohort's discussion of "moral," and in a subsequent plenary discussion, the concept of "moral" as having descriptive and prescriptive modes was revisited. The distinction continued to be a point of discussion and debate.

From Sarah's and my point of view, these PASCA sessions—the logistic CA on Tuesday and the agonistic analysis on Wednesday—are examples of how identifiable discussion methods can emerge and develop, leading the discussants to construct knowledge—justified, true beliefs, including knowledge of dilemmas and paradoxes. We feel it is particularly important to note also that the sessions demonstrate the flexibility of PASCA and its capacity, as pedagogy, to build on the teachers' expressed concerns as learners. We think the examples demonstrate how identifying the structure of these discussions not only helped us elicit and hear the teachers' perspectives on reality, the discussions also suggest to us something about the reality the teachers perceived. We believe they show how what was needed to form a bridge from the cohort's partial or incomplete understanding to a deeper, more substantial understanding of "moral" and of "language" was fostered by substantive dialogue—that is, conscious and conscientious reflection. Finally, the agonistic session in particular shows how a vibrant discussion in PASCA can foster a variety of thought provoking outcomes, not simply winners and losers.

For strolling critique that same Wednesday, July 17, Sharon suggested that the cohort work on a question from the coursebook: What are you morally responsible for in the classroom? From their strolling came the apparently collective question: What . . . exactly . . . does it mean to be "morally responsible" and "morally accountable?"

Sarah's and my observation that the question was "apparently collective," emerging from the team conversations during strolling critique, needs a bit of elaboration. Apparently, at the end of strolling critique, teams in Cohort 3 regularly met with other teams from the cohort to compare ideas about the day's work before returning for CA. Sometimes the whole cohort, except Sarah and myself, met at the end of strolling critique for discussion outside on the grounds of the school. We began to believe this was happening because the group would come into CA and immediately someone, in a spokesperson mode, would put what appeared to be a community-based question to us. "We were all talking earlier," the cohort spokesperson actually said once, but usually the cohort's mutual interest was just implied. Someone would say, "Here's what we don't understand—here's what's troubling (or puzzling) us now."

Neither Sarah nor I had experienced this phenomenon with other cohorts.

Often, other cohorts' CAs began with teams briefly reporting outcomes from their strolling critique, and we would orchestrate the teams' issues and suggest questions for discussion. It was the type of dialogue that Cohort 3 seemed to be having on its own initiative, and it suggested that they were already beginning to work as a learning community. Of course, they might have gathered to gripe and their discussion just accidentally turned into a highly functional pre-CA session. Another possibility is that they might have taken seriously—actually anticipated—the conventional opening Sarah and I used to begin each session: "How is it going? . . . As learners, what do you need now?" We don't know what prompted this recurring phenomenon in Cohort 3, but it was noteworthy, and Sarah and I decided to ask the cohort for their view of the matter. The cohort was surprised to learn that their spontaneous collaboration seemed noteworthy to Sarah and me. We did not seek an explanation that day. We felt making the observation and raising the question was, at that point, sufficient.

Returning to Sharon's suggested question for strolling critique on Wednesday, July 17—What does it mean to be morally responsible or accountable?—the CA that emerged centered on teachers' perspectives about how they could or could not be morally responsible (or accountable) while working with their state-mandated curriculum, whose content was not, they felt, related to moral issues. It was an engaging, apparently *dialectic* argument. Perspectives were gathered that led to some insights about "moral life" and the curriculum, but the gathering of perspectives also led to some important, previously unrecognized dilemmas and problems that arise when one tries to connect moral responsibilities with official curricula. In their e-mail messages to me that evening, both Sharon and Sarah commented that the value of what the cohort had discovered and constructed—the insights, problems, dilemmas, and paradoxes—did not seem to be appreciated by them. In that sense, both Sarah and Sharon felt that the CA had not been very satisfying from the teachers' point of view.

This CA that did not satisfy the teachers' expectations is important to cite because the predicament that emerged from the discussion suggested that making the discussion's dialectic structure visible, particularly its capacity for illuminating valuable dilemmas and paradoxes, could contribute to the cohort's work as a learning community. Sarah and I decided that at the first opportunity, we would discuss with Cohort 3 the structural differences between Tuesday's satisfying and Wednesday's unsatisfying CA. We planned to point out that Tuesday's *logistic* argument about moral language might be expected to lead to agreement and equilibrium whereas Wednesday's *dialectic* argument about moral responsibility and the curriculum might be expected to expose what had been hidden, including some disturbing elements and, possibly, to create a certain amount of disequilibrium, depending on the cohort's tolerance for ambiguity.

Thursday, July 18 was framed as a workshop for the teachers' individual qualitative research projects rather than as a PASCA seminar. The week ended on Friday, July 19, with a *problematic* CA. It was characterized not by trying to figure out meanings and implications from the presentation material as the cohort had done on the previous PASCA days but, rather, by trying to figure out how to do something. The presentation that day was concerned with helping children move from being passive receivers of knowledge to being active inquirers. In their CA, Cohort 3 proposed to focus on the question: How can we transform *ourselves* from being passive learners to being authentic inquirers? To describe various approaches to achieving that transformation, the cohort decided to describe and critique each person's rudimentary plan, worked out the day before in the workshop, for a qualitative research project with children in his or her classroom. The differing structure of this discussion, centered on figuring out how to accomplish a task rather than figuring out what something means, was clear and apparently invigorating. As the first week of summer session in 1996 ended, the teachers said talking to learn in PASCA's pedagogy had left them exhausted as well as exhilarated.

The Second Week

As the week began, the teachers centered their analyses and strolling critiques on searching for clarification of the increasingly complex moral issues in the new presentations. In their CAs, they experienced various structures, using substantive dialogue to great, if not particularly conscious, advantage. The presentation on Monday, July 22, on trust, honesty, courage, and care led to an interesting *logistic* argument in the CA that day. Among other things, the cohort was interested in discussing how children might be *taught* to trust, to be honest, to act courageously, and to care. The idea that those qualities could be discussed, practiced, and actually taught in school as "virtues" puzzled many people, so Sarah began the session by telling a story about how she had learned to value and practice some of those virtues. The teachers added their stories, but the stories they told did not involve school experiences. We suggested they shift to telling stories about curricula and pedagogy that they believed to be, however vaguely, important to them. When a teacher's classroom story seemed to involve encouraging children to practice one of the virtues, Sarah or I made a claim that it did. "In that story," we might say, "I think Nancy is teaching her children to care about the quality of their work. Here is one reason I have for saying that. . . . Do you agree or disagree with my claim? What are your reasons?" Teachers began to offer interpretations of the stories, and that helped expose how children could be, indeed already are, taught to value and practice particular virtues— and some vices, as well, such as cheating and deceiving.

The *logistic* structure—stories followed by claims followed by evidence and reasons—continued through three or four narratives by the teachers, and then a more complex, extended example was offered by a high school algebra teacher. Drawing on her story, teachers provided evidence to test various claims that in this teacher's pedagogy, students were learning to be honest, to care, to be courageous, and to trust each other and their algebra teacher. Her colleagues in

Cohort 3 went on to make and support their own claims concerning the striking absence of deceit (and how children could so easily, often inadvertently, be taught to deceive) and the equally striking integration of intellectual and moral learning that was apparent in this woman's approach to teaching algebra. Adopting a logistic structure for this discussion seemed to help us systematically and collaboratively look for and see elements of our teaching and learning that had been obscure and sometimes even invisible using more casual approaches to discussion.

The presentation on Tuesday, July 23, concerned interviewing techniques. Discussion during analysis that day gravitated toward clarification of some of the terms, strategies, and rationales used in qualitative research, and during strolling critique, the teachers interviewed their own team members. During CA, each team reported to the cohort on the problems and issues they had encountered during the strolling critique interviews. The discussion's structure emphasized sharing rather than critique and did not seem to energize the group. In their written responses to the day's work, teachers indicated they thought their indifference—their "sluggishness," as one teacher put it—might be largely because they had already shared their thoughts with other teams during strolling critique. Sarah and I noted in our e-mail reflections that night that, unlike the CA that day, discussions having authentic arguments—courses of reasoning that lead to figuring out meaning or figuring out how to accomplish something—have important qualities that contribute to ending PASCA days energetically.

On Wednesday, July 24, the PASCA day offered a presentation on "Moral Beliefs and Behavior Toward Children." The first question put to the cohort after strolling critique—again apparently from a spokesperson for the whole cohort—was "What does using moral language mean?" That is, what does it mean to take a moral point of view and act on phenomena in moral terms? Drawing on their work the week before with questions about the meaning of moral language and moral, the cohort focused on specific issues concerning how children in their schools are treated. Relating professional experiences, teachers described school policies or classroom situations and, taking a moral point of view and using moral language, the cohort attempted to discuss each policy or experience. A *dialectic* CA was developed by gathering perspectives, and then imagining the experience in a different way or synthesizing the policy, trying to restate the example in terms of the moral concerns inherent in the policy or experience. A variety of situational examples were proposed, four of them becoming particularly energetic dialectic discussions lasting about 15 minutes each. As the cohort discussed each of the four topics described here, Sarah's and my main function as facilitators was to keep the discussion on a single topic until synthesis was accomplished or the topic was specifically changed. Even with that advantage, as we talked the cohort had to struggle to hang onto our purpose of gaining synthesis and insight, but we did succeed:

1. During the cohort's strolling critique, someone had apparently proposed that giving extra time or help to learning disabled (LD) students amounts to "discrimination." In CA, the discrimination idea was called into question. The teachers explored the practice of giving extra time to certain labeled children. Some people found it problematic because, they felt, every child should be eligible for time and help as his or her particular needs dictated. As a community, using the concepts, assumptions and conventions, artifacts, and gestures of moral language, the cohort probed the time-and-help example. They framed a rationale and reframed the policy and their intentions for practice to include ways every child could get help, not just the labeled children. They stated their synthesized policy this way: "Our obligation is to discover *every* child's needs and help him or her according to those needs." Many of the teachers, but clearly not everyone, applauded the reframed policy and behavior toward children.

2. A related example about a school's behavior toward children during a grief event helped illuminate the belief that every child should be helped according to his or her predicament as an individual. Unlike the LD labeling example, the theme of "taking a moral point of view" on children's responses to death was immediately apparent, but still, one teacher asked why, in this type of event, we allow disruption by inviting every child to go see the grief counselor during school hours. Many people shared her concern, but a teacher with experience in grief counseling observed that it is appropriate because "we can't take the chance of missing even one child who genuinely needs to talk to an informed and caring adult in a time of distress." Not everyone agreed, but her point was well taken and the dilemma—the difficult choice—was exposed.

3. A discussion about attention deficit hyperactive disorder (ADHD) did not allow us access to a moral point of view. The cohort discussed the topic using the language— the concepts, and assumptions and conventions—associated with ADHD. As one teacher pointed out, when interest in the topic began to wane, the group seemed to be stuck in a bureaucratic-technical, rule-based point of view, making their behavior toward children labeled ADHD at best amoral and at worst immoral where the interests of children were concerned. Another person pointed out that ADHD was the type of language that frequently shapes and limits discussion about administration, curriculum, and educational research.

4. During a discussion about assigning letter grades to a child's work (and often to the child as a label), once again, the cohort found that the discussion did not take a moral point of view nor was it characterized by moral language used to justify grading behaviors toward children. Bureaucratic-technical language dominated the entire discussion, which centered on the teachers' beliefs about how and why letter grades had to be retained. The method for this part of the CA seemed more agonistic than dialectic with people expressing more rigid beliefs about the necessity of using or not using letter grades to describe assessment. The discussion closed not with a "winning" position, but with a teacher observing that the discussion had not moved toward stating what alternative assessments might be like. Others noted the way in which paradox had invaded the group's observations about assessment. They were making statements that were "true" in terms of the bureaucratic-technical language of letter grades, but those statements appeared to contradict the moral beliefs illuminated by the cohort's

discussions during the past 2 weeks. Also, to some extent, the statements were contrary to what by that point in the summer of 1996 seemed like "common sense" about what moral behavior toward children would be. The whole cohort—the teachers, Sarah and I—looked forward to having a problematic discussion at some point about designing and practicing morally and intellectually enriching modes and signs of assessment and accountability for children—and for themselves.

The next morning, Thursday, July 25, during analysis, some teachers noted the extraordinary difficulty of the previous day's *dialectic* CA. They said that taking a moral point of view and using moral language to explore examples of behavior toward children had taken the group up one alley and down another. It had been difficult, one teacher said, to get a sense of where the discussion was going. Another teacher observed that Sarah and I had not given clear, consistent indications of when people said things that were "correct" or "incorrect." A glance between Sarah and me confirmed our agreement that, in our roles as facilitators, we were trying to figure out the examples along with everyone else in the cohort. Sarah said, "I really couldn't distinguish 'correct' and 'incorrect' points as I might have done in a 'discovery' type lesson in my classroom."

We told the cohort about how, in our e-mailed reflections the previous evening, Sarah and I had discussed the confusion, and we shared with the cohort our idea that the confusion could be interpreted as evidence that synthesis was occurring. Emerging synthesis tends to create situations in which people cannot tell which comments or ideas will lead inexorably to a meaningful synthesis. Compared with the agonistic, logistic, and problematic CAs about the meaning of moral (July 17), moral language (July 16), using moral language (July 22), and becoming inquirers (July 19)—discussions that had clearer but certainly not absolute outlines—the dialectic discussion about moral beliefs and behavior toward children was much more recursive and complex, even when the separation of topics was carefully marked and maintained.

On the final Friday of the summer session, July 26, Sarah and I shared our emerging ideas about dialogic methods. We pointed out to the cohort that, in our view, the differences among the PASCA discussions of the previous 2 weeks, particularly the CAs, could be described in terms of each discussion's structure. Our rudimentary descriptions of the methods and of our evening e-mail reflections on the various discussions during the summer of 1996 seemed to interest the cohort and provided an opportunity to talk together as a learning community. We described how the cohort—teachers and facilitators together—might begin to recognize and purposefully develop dialogic methods in future CAs. For example, the group might recognize a confused and ambiguous session as, in fact, an opportunity to focus on dialectic argument. On another occasion, the group might recognize the need to clarify or describe a concept or situation in detail, and we could decide to frame a logistic discussion. Or the cohort might see an opportunity to lay out a plan of action. Sarah and I felt we had—

somewhat hesitantly—opened what we hoped would be a continuing dialogue with Cohort 3 about the theory and practice of PASCA.

We closed our memo to Cohort 3 by stating three observations that emerged from our preparation of the research memo. The first concerned ambiguity, seeing it not as a problem but as an opportunity. Linking the summer's practical experiences with Stout's caveat about wanting to "raise this art [of substantive dialogue] to consciousness without reducing it to a set of rules," we commented on the ambiguity created by that approach, and on our renewed appreciation for the importance of learning from ambiguity. For example, sitting in the seminar discussions, Sarah and I learned that the four methods of argument (agonistic, logistic, dialectical, and problematic) clearly have reciprocal priority. We definitely did not have to do an agonistic CA before doing a logistic session, and so forth. Furthermore, we learned that any of the four methods of argument could appear in any PASCA discussion, not just in CA. For example, agonistic structure tended to occur during analysis, and its spirit often seemed to pervade strolling critique as well. The teachers noted also that sometimes they saw logistic and dialectic elements in the faculty presentations. While developing the memo, reflecting on each discussion and beginning to see them as even more complex, ambiguous, and interesting than we had thought at the time, we could see that more than one method could be a tool for interpreting a particular dialogue. Working with PASCA methods in live discussions and in reflections reinforced our belief that the methods should not become hard and fast expectations, and it also gave us new insights into the opportunities ambiguity can afford.

Second, the methods generated two types of dialogic experience: figuring out meaning (agonistic, logistic, dialectic) and figuring out how to accomplish some task (problematic). An additional type of experience that arose during the second week from a session suggested a structure we called *reporting out*. Returning for their CA, each team gave a summary of its strolling critique discussion. Reporting out came in two varieties: reporting with and without critique by the cohort. When critique accompanied the reporting out, the discussion environment was more energized, but many people said they thought it was quite unpleasant. Reporting without critique—a straightforward round-robin sharing of views—appeared to be a very dull, actually enervating way to end the day's work. Collaboratively constructing knowledge—figuring out meaning or figuring out a plan of action—provided the most energized end-of-the-day sessions by far.

Third, the evidence suggested to us that to become conscious of the structural possibilities in discussions and their implications might contribute to the cohort's work in two ways: to help produce coherent inquiry and to help people value outcomes of the discussions that are traditionally undervalued. That is, outcomes that simplify and clarify or lead to a sense of closure tend to be valued whereas identifying complexities such as developing counterintuitive insights and questions, discovering dilemmas and paradoxes, and conceiving of transformative actions seem to be undervalued.

The research memo was distributed to Cohort 3 at their September 1996 seminar during the administrative session at the end of the day. The teachers, again, were invited to become our collaborators in the research project. Unfortunately, formal research and intensive critique came to a halt, but from time to time throughout their 2 years of study with us, teachers in the Prince William class of '98 informally offered their impressions of particular PASCA experiences, and sometimes they spontaneously commented on the pedagogy in their written responses to the day's work. Halfway through their journey, during the summer session in 1997, we did specifically ask for their comments on PASCA.

REFLECTIONS ON TALKING TO TEACH AND LEARN

The teachers told us that, usually, PASCA was an acquired taste. Their candid, often anonymous reactions told us that some loved it immediately: "I feel like I'm dancing in these discussions," and "I feel like a sponge—first, I soak up the ideas, then I wring them out and look at them again." Others felt uncomfortable: "I'm awash in new, unfamiliar ideas . . . drowning." Sometimes teachers got used to feeling uncomfortable—"Disturbed by the lecture [presentation] today, confused . . . but agree that PASCA discussions help." Most of the teachers told us that they acclimated to and eventually enjoyed the lively, intellectually challenging discussions. Some indicated that they remained puzzled. Some said they remained aggravated.

From teachers' written responses, which we collected and discussed continuously, and from the teaching team's ongoing reviews of the work, pitfalls in the pedagogy became apparent. As we expected, questions and problems emerged once we had actual experiences to discuss. For example, early in her experience with PASCA, a teacher articulated a pitfall that was salient to the teaching team as well. "Analysis," she wrote, "sometimes feels like we're going down the same path as collaborative argument." In response, we made a concerted effort to articulate, develop, and consciously work with our epistemic assumptions and practices.

In the long run, time and experience helped everyone—teachers and the members of faculty who explored PASCA—understand and acclimate to PASCA's pitfalls and peculiarities: "Strolling critique is better this [second] year. . . . Finding topics and questions is easier and probing them seems more effective." With time and experience, the teachers' expectations for discussion clearly increased: "We need to explore more deeply;" "We get stuck on topics;" "We raise questions but we're not adequately discussing them." Some teachers said that returning to the active, substantive learning experienced in PASCA was actually a relief because, after getting used to PASCA, they found passive learning experiences to be quite unsatisfactory.

Most of us developed favorites among PASCA's phases. Strolling critique—

the discussion in school-based teams—was an immediate hit with most of the teachers. Many continued to favor the relative privacy strolling critique provided, claiming that for them, it fostered some of their most productive learning. For others, "Cohort meetings [analysis and collaborative argument] rule! Either time or improvement of my voice has made [the teachers in my cohort] accessible. It's wonderful to begin to talk with y'all away from my previous 'in authority' vantage." My own favorite was analysis where I had a chance to hear how the teachers were interpreting the presentation and which ideas they were struggling with or puzzled by. Hearing their perspectives, I could get a sense of where we were as a community of learners.

A teacher graduating with the class of '98 wrote about what being involved in PASCA was like from her point of view. Her comments resonate with what many of our graduates have told us in their reflections at the end of the program.

My last serious thoughts about the program are the affirmation of the critical nature of dialogue and the wonder and awe I have of [hearing] multiple perspectives. The PASCA process, working in a collaborative team, involvement in the Cohort experience—each sphere added to and intensified the sense of learning community as various perspectives and issues surfaced each year. I was in constant amazement at each level and consider those series of experiences to have been some of the most rewarding, not [so much] because I learned a lot but because I thought a lot. . . . I just found involvement in them fascinating and the discourse immensely satisfying. I learned by myself, with a small group, and then in a larger group. It was the first time I had really appreciated the word "collaboration." It really wasn't until the second year, during the second Summer Session that I fully understood the nature [and] complexity of what was happening.

From my own point of view, complexity is surely a defining characteristic of this pedagogy for substantive dialogue. In each phase of PASCA, we learned to be conscious of three orienting concerns as we talked:

- Create a friendly, professional discussion environment characterized by mutual trust and the individual honesty, courage, care, fairness, and practical wisdom of persons in the group (Sockett, 1993).
- Develop epistemological assumptions and practices that foster substantive dialogue and coherent, justified action (Fenstermacher & Goodlad, 1997).
- Maintain an awareness, through reflection and research, of the complexity expressed in emerging phenomena, evolving beliefs and provisional practices.

These orienting concerns are not rules or stages or phases that follow in any order. They are continuous, concomitant concerns, priority being determined by the situation in any particular discussion. In that sense, all three serve as standards for the substantive dialogue we sought to develop in PASCA seminars. In this chapter, I have concentrated on the epistemological standard—assumptions and practices in discussion that are often invisible and, consequently, unexamined, but I don't mean to put it forward as a priority. Nor do I mean to put

PASCA, in particular, forward as any sort of absolute, indispensable reality. Attending to the orienting concerns helped me find and shape the ethos of discussion while the framework and methods of PASCA helped me organize my thoughts as the talk proceeded and afterward, in reflection. The valuable result was that I began to see, examine and act on what had been invisible to me before.

Our experience with PASCA helped us understand how talking to learn—substantive dialogue—could be taught in university classrooms. But in addition, we found that it was not limited to teachers trying to work out an innovative pedagogy for their own use. Through the years, many teachers working in the IET program adapted PASCA to their primary, elementary, and secondary classrooms, building on their learners' natural inclination toward talking to learn, and discovering, sometimes, a prodigious capacity for it (Sevcik, Robbins, & Leonard, 1997). Conscious of the art of conversation rather than the rules of discourse, but at the same time developing appropriate epistemological structures, teachers helped children toward moral as well as intellectual growth and also toward a new understanding of what classroom discussion can be like.

5

Teachers in School-Based Teams: Contesting Isolation in Schools

Sharon J. Gerow

"Individuals benefit from working together and learning how to do so." This was the first statement in the "Work in Teams" section of our 1995 *Beliefs and Principles in IET Practice* document (see chap. 2). By the time we wrote the document as a faculty team, we were growing and feeling some pain in doing so. We hoped that the document would serve to maintain the innovation and vision of the program while creating the essential positive interdependence among the faculty members that would allow us to continue to create a meaningful and worthwhile master's program. "Working together is complex, difficult and requires considerable energy and dedication," the second statement, reflected the difficulties and challenges in our struggles.

Research on collaboration has an extensive and rich history that evolves from the fundamental premise that two heads are better than one. Group dynamics theory has spawned an impressive body of research since the 1980s in educational arenas (Johnson & Johnson, 1989; Slavin, 1990, 1991). Although the notions are not new, a synthesis of the research demonstrates a wide and rich variety of benefits for collaboration: improvement in human relations, increased persistence on challenging tasks, greater success in problem solving, better psychological health, improvement in interpersonal skills, greater productivity, greater sense of responsibility toward peers and colleagues, and greater use of higher reasoning strategies and critical thinking (Johnson & Johnson, 1989, 1990; Slavin, 1990, 1991). Research about teachers working in teams is sparse, but what exists suggests that teachers working in teams discover new roles, develop new relationships, discover more opportunities for political decision making with implications for the whole school, and develop the courage to challenge colleagues and administrators who may resist their efforts or present obstacles (Gerow, 1996; Wooten, 1993). The exception exists when teachers lack the knowledge base necessary for successful collaborative work (Gerow, 1996; Rowland, 1993). When this occurs, teachers have little effect on educational change, school culture, and reform efforts (Gilbert, 1992; Jordan, 1993; Maeroff, 1993).

The teaming and collaborative issues inherent in our multidisciplinary faculty team created an academic and real-life tension as it was juxtaposed with our requirement that the teachers apply for the degree and work in teams for the duration of their studies (see chap. 12). When I became a member of the IET faculty, teacher research and collaboration in teams were part of my teaching practice as well as longstanding research and academic interests. I knew that conflict would be a significant part in the work, and began immediately to create ways to help the teams develop in order to get the maximum intellectual benefits from collaboration.

I assumed the role of team developer and conflict mediator for the teacher teams even though there was no coursework associated with the training and despite the fact that originally team development was not recognized as essential. I knew from my previous work that it was necessary, and I was excited and challenged by the prospect. I resisted at all times the notion of team development through a "one-shot workshop approach" in favor of ongoing reflection, interpretative encouragement, and substantive feedback. I rejected the myth that adults must be naturally inclined toward collaboration. I winced when I heard, "He's just not cut out for teaming" knowing that many such people have become excellent collaborators through training. My colleagues were more than happy to have me take teams that were engaged in conflicts. Because I was fascinated by the challenge of empowering teachers to resolve conflicts in order to work productively, it was a happy arrangement. Thus, we juggled teams among the advisers so that I could work with the "dysfunctional" teams.

For 6 years, I collected and analyzed data on the teachers' work in teams as part of my dissertation research and continual reflective practice. I wanted to understand the dynamics operating within the teams in order to maximize team development. I also wanted to understand how the team cultures might foster professionalism and challenge the culture of isolation within schools. There were many variations on a theme as other faculty teaching teams developed their own approaches according to their own academic interests and expertise. However, across the board, cohort and team structures were part of the work with varying degrees of intensity and focus.

Periodically and regularly, I invited teachers to submit written reflections that focused on their contributions and skills related to their teaming. Interspersed with individually written reflections were collaborative team reflections that were written and signed by each team member. An unofficial syllabus provided a calendar for submission and a series of questions based on the stages of team development. The length of time between reflections decreased as teams became more sophisticated and confident in their collaboration. I read and responded to each reflection offering encouragement, support, and suggestions for growth.

Teachers were aware that the written reflections were studied as data, and I shared my analyses and interpretations with them after each set. Responding helped teachers see collaborative skills as difficult but worthwhile, and problems as challenging but not insurmountable. Understanding that other teams were sharing similar issues both successful and problematic helped them to consider how they worked in teams and to resist the human tendency to hide the conflict—a tendency more acute for those who work in cultures of isolation (Gerow, 1996).

In this chapter, I examine several important issues that are part of the fabric of teams. First, I discuss the formation and organization of teams, the development of early conflicts, the significance of environment and time to creating a working team. Second, I examine some moral issues arising from team relationships, the development of team identities, and some examples of destructive patterns of behavior. Finally, I examine the difficult matter of individuals accepting mutual responsibility and accountability.

THE EARLY DEVELOPMENT OF TEAMS

Because the requirements for collaboration changed over the course of the degree, the stages of team development were not always chronological. The significant shift in the way that teams worked in the second year, for example, often triggered a return—although less intensive—to the stages associated with newer teams. The teams in our program created and developed cultures that nourished the development of teachers as researchers, learners, collaborators, and professionals. Thus, studying the teams with an anthropological approach provided a more complex picture of the vibrant interwoven, dialectical dances among the different contexts: personal and professional lives, coursework, research, teams, and schools. Although some cultures developed their transformative abilities and ability to critique traditional practice more quickly, richly, and powerfully, no team was devoid of growth or some degree of constructive change by the end of the program.

Formation and Organization

Although the motivation for a teacher to join a team to pursue graduate study varied widely, no consistent pattern explained or predicted how a team might construct its culture or to what extent it experienced success or difficulties. Some teachers sought collaborative partners through schoolwide announcements. Others persuaded friends to join them in the pursuit of the degree. Graduates of the program frequently encouraged colleagues to form teams by engaging colleagues in stimulating conversations about practice, readings, and research findings. Occasionally, witnessing compelling changes in the teacher's voice and practice interested a colleague of a teacher in our program.

In some cases, principals encouraged teachers through schoolwide announcements. A few principals "strongly encouraged" teachers to apply—an approach regarded as the "kiss of death" because most teachers (and faculty) assumed the individual would be entering the program reluctantly. However, continual team development addressed these issues and most discovered meaningful professional and/or personal friendships that supported their study. One teacher described the value of team development in light of the inherent difficulties in her team's formation:

Considering that the principal strongly encouraged us to work together, it's easy to understand why we had so many problems. For the first six months, I used that as an excuse for my bad behavior. . . . But with the team development sessions and reflective writings, I can honestly say that it's made all the difference in the world—especially the writing. . . . When I realized that my finger pointing wasn't getting us anywhere because their finger pointing was targeting me, I stopped blaming them and the principal for putting us together. . . . When I reflect on our "growing pains," I see how inflexible I was as a team member.

Differences in age and experience also caused initial concerns that team development dispelled. A young elementary teacher described it this way: "It's hard to believe that almost one year has passed since Sally, Jo, and I were thrown together. I was very hesitant not being able to choose my own team members; I feared I would not be able to talk to [them]. I'm much younger, and they've taught a lot longer. I didn't think we would have anything in common. Now, I'm fearful when I am not with them." In later correspondence, she added, "I value their experience and insight so much, and they tell me that my energy and new ideas are renewing them."

Once the teams formed, they all began to create normative structures to sustain their work. They experimented with finding a mutually convenient meeting time and location. They struggled with the need to "unload" their frustrations or joys in the daily experience of teaching. They created agendas and began to discuss what to discuss. These early meetings were places to discover what worked and didn't work. One middle school teacher described it this way:

I think we're beginning to gel. We had a number of gripe sessions in the beginning. We knew it wasn't good, but it felt good! We're starting to be a little more organized now. Annie brings an agenda and we start with that and adjust it as we need to. We've talked about whose [sic] going to keep our records and remind us of due dates. . . . We talked with other teams and got some ideas from them. [The electronic conference] gave us a couple of ideas.

Most teams shared similar experiences although not necessarily at the same rate or in the same way. Some teams experimented easily from the beginning, some worked too long without organizational structures, and others locked into ways of working that later proved difficult. Those who were friends when they entered the program appeared to "settle in" more easily initially. Those who joined with strangers were more tentative.

Even for teams forged through friendships, the difficulties in working closely with others over significant time came as a surprise. Following a team meeting, one high school teacher expressed a frequently heard comment when she remarked, "We were friends before this program, but nothing like we are now."

Although teachers were unaware of the changes that would come, these friendships with colleagues were enough for many to enter the program. One teacher expressed it this way:

I worked with both Sally and Marian on grade level stuff. We even team taught in some areas. It helped to move into the team because I knew them and cared about them. It did *not*, I emphasize *not*, prepare me for the way I would come to know them and care about them through this work. It's not only that, it's that I've come to respect them as bright and intelligent teachers committed to their profession. This surprised me, but I think that it shouldn't have. . . . I think now our relationships were shallow.

Prior friendships helped create the commitment but did not insulate a team from subsequent difficulties. In reality, sometimes friendships created an initial comfort that became problematic. One high school teacher described it this way:

I see now that our friendship fooled us in some ways. We thought it would make things easier. . . . That's a crock. Our friendship became the focus of protection—don't get honest because you want to keep the friendship. I know it's not really a friendship, but I couldn't see it then. . . . It was when you came to our meeting and asked each of us specific questions about our collaboration that it opened the flood gates. We either had to risk our friendship or move superficially through the program. We chose to risk it. I'm sure glad that we did.

Thus, teachers constructed cultures in a variety of ways, but no particular way explained the nature of their difficulties or the conflicts that would emerge as a result of the intensity of the work.

Early Conflicts

Conflict is a natural occurrence in any organization where people must collaborate. The issue is not whether there is conflict, but whether it forms from creative and intellectual forces or from unhealthy personal events. The former can be stimulating, and understanding it as such benefits all. The latter can become poisonous to the individuals involved and to the work.

Although initial agendas, times, and locations were set easily in the first meetings, it did not take long for the teachers' busy lives to create problems. As the year got underway, teachers negotiated time, energy, and commitment between their professional and personal lives. The teachers who were committed to extracurricular activities such as coaching, club sponsorships, or membership on special committees forced the team members to negotiate different priorities and commitments. Others espoused the principle that families and children came first, which they shared in principle but not in reality. The priorities changed and shifted over time. Unmarried, divorced, and childless team members discovered through the frequent renegotiating of schedules, arbitrary endings to meetings, and a growing sense of differences in commitment to the work that the principle of "family first" needed adjustment. Until teams made adjustments, resentments grew with the assumption that those with fewer family issues were more committed. One young, dedicated teacher explained her frustration: "Just because I'm single, I'm seen as the one with the most time. It's like the kids; they think that when I leave here I go home and just grade papers or something. No one considers that visiting my parents is important to me. That's my family." A more experienced, unmarried high school teacher extended the notion of what constituted "family" for her: "They didn't understand . . . they thought that family was the only real issue. For me, my friends are my family. I work hard in those relationships. I need them because my blood family is far away."

Eventually, with encouragement, many with resentments articulated their concerns, sometimes with anger and tears, sometimes with more reasoned arguments. The team members with families initially regarded their concerns as added pressure. Some team meetings became emotional with the married team members breaking into tears and the unmarried members holding their ground. Polite practices, which traditionally sustained avoidance within the school and served as protection for cordial relationships, began to crumble. Many found the statements, accusations, and choices of words hurtful. However, the members with families began to negotiate their domestic responsibilities with spouses, sons, and daughters. Sometimes spouses or older children increased their share of the household responsibilities; a couple of families hired a maid or a babysitter. Unmarried team members regarded this appreciatively and became more supportive and sensitive about their teammates' commitments.

Resistance to sharing honestly often dissolved as teachers learned to express concerns more diplomatically. The teachers who sought and followed my advice on how to handle difficult issues generally described it as productive as well as a relief. In addition, once we discussed an issue, the teachers expressed surprise at the common sense of it. For example, instead of directing anger at the less productive work of a teammate, they began to inquire with compassion about the problems a teammate might be having and ask how they might help. Instead of preaching or telling a teammate to shape up, they engaged or invited the teammate to share the problem in order to receive constructive encouragement. Instead of making a teammate defensive with righteous solutions based on their own personal ways of solving problems, they asked if they might offer some suggestions for consideration. One teacher sent me an e-mail describing how this worked for her team:

We came to you reluctantly thinking that we were tattling if we told you [the problem]. But, we were so frustrated with the problems that we knew we couldn't go on. I was seriously thinking of dropping out. I wanted you to know that [our teammate] was not only open to what we had to say, but it opened the door for her to share some of her concerns about us which was also contributing to the tension. It went very well, and we all said afterwards that we were relieved that we had talked more openly.

Trust emerged from their honest negotiations—an essential element of successful collaboration that sustained the teachers through the difficulties of subsequent researching, writing, and studying.

As the team members struggled to become productive collaborators, teachers' assignments in schools contributed to misunderstanding and conflict. The regular classroom teachers who carried the greatest number of students on their rosters sometimes resented what they regarded as the lighter loads of teammates in resource positions such as special education or library services. In some cases the resource teachers reacted with anger and began, often defensively, to justify their professional roles. Diplomacy and tact generally failed to mediate this conflict. Over time, team members came to appreciate the special perspectives of resource personnel and their unique contributions to understanding individual students and other issues. Furthermore, they came to appreciate and understand the greater potential for their own use of the special resources. Conversely, the resource teachers came to understand better ways to communicate and work with classroom teachers—a problem that often had been a continual source of frustration. One regular classroom high school teacher said it best in her final individual written reflection: "I really didn't have a clue. I thought I did. I thought I knew what she did. I also didn't think much of it. . . . Now that I understand, our conversations are much richer. She provides a perspective on children that I often never considered." The resource person to whom the above quotation refers wrote independently at the same time: "I have worked in many classrooms over the last seven years. I thought most of the partnerships went well. I assumed that. I think now that they were pretty superficial arrangements."

A more sophisticated understanding and appreciation of the contributions made by regular teachers and resource personnel did not emerge through casual discussions. Rather it emerged as teachers engaged in the intense, difficult, and deep professional work requiring significant investments in time around the development of individual research questions related to practice. This work necessitated lengthy discussions in which teachers grappled with ideas, considered the relevancy of the research question to practice and described individual classroom issues and student populations. The weaving and interweaving back and forth of professional concerns with personal interests and passions and stories about students helped all members to understand the concerns and passions explicated by the research foci. These conversations went beyond listening with empathy and offering suggestions. Individuals learned and understood how a colleague's research in practice created connections and related to their own classrooms and to schoolwide issues of concern.

Environment, Time, and Individual Roles

Overburdened teachers skilled in cutting corners and skimming intellectual surfaces characterize traditional school cultures. However, the relevance of the research questions to classroom practice, the deep and respectful intellectual work, and collegial-shared understandings and interests created—without immediate appreciation—a need for significant amounts of time for critical work—a serious challenge to the traditional school culture.

Moving outside of the physical school building played such a significant role in helping teams to become more productive that I routinely encouraged it with subsequent classes. The following description from my field notes on one team meeting typifies the problem in school environments:

The teachers sit slouched in orange, plastic chairs. Misarranged desks and various wads of paper and gum wrappers litter the floor. The announcement system interrupts three times. No one smiles. Sandy accidentally brushes an article off the desk. When she retrieves the pages, she brushes off grit from the floor. A 13-year-old boy with red, curly hair rushes in and says, "Oops! Mr. Jackson, you were going to give me my book back today." Mr. Jackson excuses himself from the meeting to attend to the boy.

Finally, I insisted that they seek another location and later written reflections reflected the positive changes:

We really wish now that we hadn't taken so long [to leave the building]. We meet at Joe's house. Each of us has our own chair at the dining room table. We can spread everything out. Joe's wife comes in occasionally to see if we need anything—food, coffee, etc. She takes wonderful care of us, and we think Joe is extremely lucky to have her. We keep telling him. It's so different from school.

One large, successful elementary team moved from a small conference room off the principal's office to a large, family home decorated tastefully and neatly in the soft blues and yellows of early American decor. The spacious kitchen offered convenient snacking and the plush, pale blue carpeting in the large, sunny livingroom invited the spreading of research documents and large sheets of paper for analyzing data. One team member commented, "I think better outside of school. When we met in school there was only part of me at the meeting. I'd be thinking about things I still had to do in my classroom." Another teammate responded quickly, "Oh, I know what you mean. I did that too."

By the beginning of the second summer, all team members who met outside of school emphatically declared that it significantly improved the quality of their work. They described more laughter and joking about the rituals and artifacts of researching: high fives, silly cheers, trips to a local pub, dinners together without serious conversations, special coffee cups, comfortable chairs, an old sweatshirt worn during a winning football season, and chocolate in most any form. By late spring, all successful teams left behind school sites characterized by frequent interruptions and the remnants of the day and exchanged it for environments that nurtured the body, mind, and soul.

The movement away from school sites accompanied the identification of special talents and roles in collaboration. During my visits I heard the following: "Jack is our organizational guru; he keeps us on track"; "Joanne brings our perspectives together at the end; she's our summarizer"; "Marie's a questioner and really pushes us to question more"; "Jim really helps us when we get stuck; he's our problem solver"; "When things get tense, Elsie knows how to bring us together again"; "Sandra is our techy guru; she helps each of us learn the technology and get through the barriers in using the laptops." Some teachers also noted what would not work: "You'd never want me to be the keeper of the calendar"; or "I would never turn that laptop on if Louise didn't sit there and hold my hand."

Although some teams formally named positions in the beginning, increased knowledge about collaboration eliminated the need for formal roles. As the teachers constructed their team culture, their personal and professional lives intertwined more tightly. The early, formal roles became less visible and team members took on more complex and frequently overlapping roles driven less by planned organization and more by emerging needs based on the teams' work. Their growing knowledge of one another informed their choices as they articulated a growing awareness of the importance of shared responsibility. Three teams referred to this experience as synergy and the word began to pepper their reflections.

MAKING TEAMS MORAL COMMUNITIES

Through the research process and the creation of collegial friendships in teams, individuals also became aware of personal changes within and among themselves (see chap. 10). They also began to form distinct identities and were prey to various kinds of behaviors destructive to the team and the creation of its moral identity.

Evidence that teachers were expressing an awareness of personal and professional changes came periodically throughout the program from observations by all members of the IET's teaching team, teachers' written reflections, e-mail messages, and technological conferences. Four remarks were typical: "I've changed so much I can hardly believe it myself"; "My family notices how much I've changed"; "My teaching is changing so much I don't recognize myself"; and "I have so much respect now for what my students tell me about their own learning."

The work in moral professionalism informed the work in teams. Teachers expressed their growing awareness of deepening professional and personal relationships embedded with the moral virtue of care through comments such as, "[She] has come to mean so much to me as both a colleague and a friend, and

I don't know where one begins and the other leaves off." They expressed their awareness of the relationship between researching their practice and working with teammates in comments such as, "I run to them all the time. I cannot imagine doing this work or any other without them." Finally, they expressed surprise, not about their ability to care for others, but that others cared for them personally as well as for the quality and depth of their practice and research. "In 10 years of teaching, no one has given me as much as these three people have in the last 6 months." And, "I've never truly believed that my fellow faculty members really cared about me—not like this." Finally, "I'm reeling from thinking about the implications of [team relationships and work] with kids who are at risk and don't have friends."

During the early months of team development, I asked team members to tell their teammates how they liked to be cared for. This simple exercise deepens relationships rather quickly and when teammates respond at later times with gestures showing this care, the teacher is always deeply touched. Sadly, it is not unusual after this exercise for someone to say, "No one has ever asked me how I would like to be cared for." Such statements are deeply disturbing to me as they are yet another manifestation of the bureaucratic character of schooling within the dominant paradigm (see chap. 1).

In addition to care, the literature on collaboration identifies the moral virtue of trust to be at the core of every successful team (Johnson & Johnson, 1989). A reciprocal relationship exists between care and trust and the quality of inter-actions and research. For example, one teacher confided in me about a serious, personal problem. At the end, she described well this relationship among caring, trust, and work when she added: "I'm usually very guarded in what I share with others—especially other teachers. I've never had much trust, but there I was last week spilling my guts to my team. I didn't plan to, but they knew something was wrong. I could see that they were concerned, and that's all the encourage-ment I needed to tell them everything. . . . I really want to repay them by helping them produce the best research they can."

Many teachers expressed surprise at the depth of their active commitment to the success of their colleagues' research, which transcended any notions of ap-pearance or pay raises based on work completed. One high school teacher wrote, "If you had told me a year ago that I would be almost as curious about Joe's research or Pam's as I am about my own, I would have laughed in your face." Close analysis of my data sets revealed that the personal and professional in-vestment in their colleagues' research developed through interactions such as discussing, questioning, debating, critiquing, problem solving, and responding—all understood and interwoven with acts of caring and trust. One teacher wrote, "I found myself waking up at night with ideas for my teammate's research." And another reflected, "Sometimes, I couldn't wait to get to the meetings to hear what Susan had discovered in her data." Several teachers confessed to early morning inspirations: "I'd get an idea about my teammate's research and rush to the computer at 2 or 3 in the morning to be sure I didn't lose it. . . . Once she was on the computer sending something to me at the same time. What's happening to us?"

Teachers repeatedly confirmed the relationship between coming to know one another better as professionals and the quality of work. Additionally, they linked the depth of commitment and care also to their growing knowledge of each other on a personal level. Team members began to support one another through illnesses, family difficulties, and personal triumphs. They shared while meeting for meals, drinks, or antiquing, offering advice on friendships, rearing children, and marriage. One teacher noted, "[I'm] much happier . . . working here. I can't imagine now, and yet I did it for 8 years, working in some superficial, artificial environment. I mean this is real stuff—the grit of teaching!" She added later, "Maybe it's a lot of hooey when people say, 'I keep my business and personal lives separate.' I mean, maybe they shouldn't."

Teams that described themselves as successful and thriving increasingly shared personal stories: the loss of a beloved pet, difficulties in marriages and families, or illnesses. The list was extensive. Our faculty often received messages in which a teammate confided that another teammate was experiencing a personal problem or celebrating an event so that we might understand a problem in the work. However, in working with teams that described serious tension and difficulties in their collaboration, personal stories were noticeably absent. Furthermore, no teammate in these teams contacted me for the benefit of another teammate. In fact, I received instead messages with serious complaints and negative descriptions of their teammates.

Thus, self-described successful teams established environments through their collaborative work in which it became increasingly safer with careful steps to risk sharing more and more of their personal lives. Their commitment to the work accompanied by their deepening personal relationships with one another illuminated the links among personal and professional lives embedded in cohesive cultures. Trust and care were observable moral virtues.

Developing Team Identities

Halfway through the first year, the productive teams constructed cohesive cultures and began to describe themselves with unique identities. The descriptions coincided with a movement beyond the organizational issues in new teams and were associated with recognition of the complexity, authenticity, and excitement embedded in collaborative learning communities. The following series of unique descriptions illustrates the variation in identities: "Our team is very intense. We can really battle it out, but when were done, we're off to get drinks together. . . . We're having so much fun, it's hard to know when we're working and when we're not. Our laughter gets speckled into everything. . . . We're the team with humor and, girl, that takes care of a lot of problems!"

This teacher offers a more extensive portrait of intellectual work and social relationships and characterizes the team culture with the metaphor of a family (united with a common goal): "I can no longer tell where my research ends and my teammates' [research] begins. I'm just as anxious to see what they find out as what I find. More than one of us has called or e-mailed late at night about ideas or thoughts related to the others' research. . . . My team is starting to feel like a family too. . . . If one of us left, we'd feel like it was a divorce."

These team members used a food metaphor to explain the way that they cared for one another while implying that thinking and researching require nurturance:

We're the food team. Everything we do is around food. Now, we have jokes about it. Food for thought. No food, no thought. We're always chewing on some new piece of data or digesting some new insight. . . . The junkier the food, the deeper the research— now figure that one out. Our teeth will rot. We'll be dying from malnutrition, but our research is going to be good!

In this team, every meeting began with the ritual of preparing the table. They insisted that they could not work without food (although I noted a movement toward healthier food near the end of the school year). Their good nature, humor, and focus on nurturing one another moved every conflict easily toward resolution.

The absence of conflict and tension is not necessarily a sign of a successful team. In fact, "getting along" may mask the quality of the collaboration. One high school team formed quickly and cohesively while appearing to get along extremely well throughout the study. I observed in meetings that they greeted one another in friendly ways, discussed issues without tension, inquired about one another with genuine interest, and described their team as highly successful. I questioned the apparent ease with which they functioned; they agreed with my observation. In probing what seemed "too good to be true," they explained their goodwill toward one another as a reaction against the school's culture—an outside enemy. One team member said: "I think our team is a safe haven. Things are so bad in this school that we don't want any conflicts here. . . . I suspect we may be a little too nice to each other, but no one wants to walk into our team meetings carrying even the slightest hint of our school environment."

However, their self-described cohesion came with a cost, for it did not accompany in-depth inquiry or deep intellectual work. Their united desire to embrace all that was harmonious prevented them from working on more than the most superficial levels. That they liked and cared for one another was obvious, but their commitment was to harmony not to deep intellectual work or personal growth. It was not until the second year collaborative research project that they perceived harmony as "their problem" or entertained notions about holding one another accountable as a feature of commitment. By the time they embraced healthy conflict, they recognized what they had lost. After graduation, they expressed sadness and embarrassment that they had missed something intellectually important.

Destructive Behavior Patterns in Teams

Behaviors that damaged team collaboration took several forms. Although serious destructive behaviors were minimal, analysis of such behaviors proved informative. Teammates became frustrated and angry if one member consistently came late, missed meetings, came unprepared to meetings, or missed team-determined deadlines for phases of work. Teams described these individuals as uncaring and uncommitted. Furthermore, they viewed the actions as deliberate violations of trust. A middle school teacher explained in her reflection: "We are not working well because we keep dealing with our frustration over Jill's chronic tardiness and lack of preparation. . . . She doesn't care about her work, and she doesn't care about us."

Another problem stemmed from behaviors that teams commonly attributed to personality or style. Team members described these individuals as obnoxious, dominating, obstinate, argumentative, or manipulative. In general, they viewed the situations as hopeless. One teacher expressed the common unquestioned conclusion that "Some people just aren't cut out for teaming." Another teacher said, "Some people prefer to work alone. That's just the way it is."

My fieldnotes and interviews with the "destructive" individuals indicated that teammates consistently misinterpreted or misjudged their behaviors. In such cases, I visited teams more frequently and engaged in longer e-mail or personal counseling sessions. In one example, a teacher's fear of being seen as inadequate caused her teammates to accuse her of being uncaring and uncooperative. Understanding the true issue helped her teammates to confide their own fears and encourage her participation in less threatening ways. In other examples, earlier negative experiences within the school itself carried into work in the program. The depth and the length of these conflicts, coupled with the maturity and dedication to collaboration on the part of all involved, influenced the ability of individuals to forgive in order to grow. If a teacher never became part of the team, the team continued to express discouragement that limited the quality of their work.

Although some teams struggled throughout the program, even those that experienced the most difficult, destructive behaviors and conflicts described learning and growing from them. One teacher midway described her struggle this way:

I can't wait until this is over and if I had it to do over again, I would never join a team with Denise. But, I have to admit, it's made me more aware and sensitive toward my students. I see more issues involved. I understand their reactions to other children better. I understand the *other* children better too. I used to tell them—very impatiently—to stop it, or I'd say, "Think about this at home tonight, and don't let it happen again." [She shook her head and looked away before continuing.] I'm able to help them more now too because I'm learning patience and understanding. . . . I'm learning to scrutinize my own behavior. I'm amazed at my stubbornness. It's really strong! I just want to scream sometimes and say, "I'm not doing another thing until you get your act together." I fight against it because I see that some of this relates to different learning styles . . . and age differences . . . and race differences. Oh, I've learned a lot all right.

By the end of the program, these teammates spoke openly about their feelings for one another. They described and behaved with care and respect although without the benefit of personal friendship. They could laugh at their difficulties, agreed they would never want to work together again although they knew they would succeed if they did. They recognized that each had grown and benefited personally and professionally from the ordeal, and they were grateful.

Growing awareness of the impact on collaboration of specific constructive and destructive behaviors replaced the original notions about the ease of collaboration with a growing realization that deep and meaningful collaborative work requires continual examination and reflection. Early reflections, posts in the technological conference, and fieldnotes foreshadowed this understanding. For example, after 2 months of working together, one teacher wrote about the importance of listening and concluded, "We have to listen to each other, but I have come to think that this is going to be a lot tougher than I imagined." The same teacher demonstrated a far more sophisticated view just 9 months later:

Trust is the basis for this work. On the one hand, I can say that I *am* a better team member than I was in the beginning. I know that facilitating discussion, piggybacking on ideas, supporting and challenging others (I could go on and on) have made our team something I cannot live without. Then I realize that I can still be better at facilitating discussion, piggybacking, and especially challenging someone's thinking without making them defensive—it's very, very complicated. . . . I am comfortable working in a team now—even see it as essential, but I'm always thinking about how I'm interacting. . . . I am beginning to suspect that you don't ever really get this perfectly right.

After the first year in the program, the teams that struggled the most continued to meet and work together, although both the quality of their research and their satisfaction with the experience remained questionable. However, no one dropped out of the program and all continued to learn. By the end of each program, all teams were productive and sophisticated in their ability to collaborate. Such teams were devoid of visible warmth and enthusiasm, but a noticeable quiet respect served them well as individuals and professionals.

A SEMINAL EVENT IN TEAM ACCOUNTABILITY

Responding to the written research drafts was a seminal event in team development. Although teachers described numerous experiences and insights into how their teams created productive cultures, no aspect of the team experience had as much power or influence as the final step in the collaborative research process: responding in May of the first year to the written drafts of the research studies. I required that all team members sign a statement affirming their belief that the study was now the best it could be in terms of the quality of both the research and writing. This experience decimated most of the remaining barriers in collaboration in deep and important ways. It challenged the teachers who were still favoring polite conversations over authentic collaboration. "It upped the ante," wrote one teacher. The strong feelings of fear and inadequacy that would otherwise go unnoticed in the traditional school culture of isolation were exposed here as this moral demand for individual accountability was presented.

Even teams that had shared papers routinely noticed that writing response created the opportunity for practicing critique and emphasizing team accountability. One teacher said, It "raised the stakes." Another teacher explained, "I think our oral discussions were softer. It was that signature on someone else's research that heightened my sense of responsibility. . . . I love my teammates, but I suddenly questioned whether or not I was qualified to respond to their writing."

Now teachers worried about their ability to write. The required signature forced them to focus on the carefully structured thoughts of their colleagues' research approach, interests, writing styles, organizational and formatting preferences and ways of thinking. The writing of the study exposed other new issues for individuals. Most teachers confessed that they were embarrassed to have teammates read their writing because they considered it inadequate. Even the teachers who said they were confident in discussing their research and sharing data found this moment formidable. One high school teacher wrote, "I've always liked to write and thought I did well. For some reason this was like stripping." Some teachers described writing several drafts (5 to 15 were reported) before they gained enough confidence to share their writing with team members. Knowledge of writing response, information about previous experiences in other classes, and the support of advisers did not have much influence on the depth or power of their emotions and avoidance behaviors. Many expressed anger for the signature requirement. One teacher told me later, "I wanted to wring your neck."

After the experience, their perspectives changed. This teacher described it best: "It was wonderful learning. My team members felt the same concerns about their [own writing.] In addition, they told me that I could write well. [With each draft] my confidence increased. As my confidence increased in my work, I began to feel that I could be of some assistance to my teammates after all."

The reading of the drafts created a paradox. Similar to their early concerns about their ability to research, many teachers, particularly those who believed that they were inadequate writers, hesitated to respond to their teammates' drafts. They described feeling comfortable pointing out editing issues such as spelling and punctuation but uncomfortable dealing with higher order matters such as the flow of ideas, the adequacy of the evidence to support findings, or the relationship between the evidence and the argument in the paper. Ironically, their fears were largely unfounded even if their experience and knowledge did not inform the responses as much as they could. Although they were hesitant, restrained, and thoughtful, most probed in the margins of drafts or in their dialogue with such observations as "I'm not sure I follow you here," "I think you need more evidence for this section," "Maybe this section could go up front."

In teams where insecurities and fears about their ability to respond to one another's research and writing translated into silence, the problem of passivity and silence emerged when teachers who needed more response suffered in their work. Although their responses reflected the tentative stances that one would expect when learning new skills, their limited responses were still reasonable and sound considerations. When I returned the final studies with my extensive written responses, the problem of silence became even more poignant because in most cases my remarks expressed similar or identical ideas, thoughts, and concerns about the study. At this point, several individuals expressed both regret and self-satisfaction, regret in realizing that they had seen things that they could have reported, but didn't; satisfaction that they possessed more knowledge than they realized. An elementary teacher described the problem best:

One member of my team had to rewrite her research study. I felt that as a team member I had let her down. Many of your comments to her were on problems I had suspected, but neglected to mention because I did not trust my own judgement. . . . We then spent several hours questioning, cutting and pasting, and reorganizing her study. I think her final revision is wonderful research. Rather than lead her astray, I chose to let her down.

Although these situations triggered strong "group guilt," especially when their own studies were received well, they also appeared to strengthen the cultural bonds as they surrounded the member with profuse apologies followed by "emergency" collaborative work to resolve the problems.

Subsequently, the teachers expressed more confidence in their knowledge, judgment, and ability to contribute to the work of others. The majority of the teachers now espoused the view that collegial response to their work was essential. This view contested descriptions of isolation in their school cultures. One high school teacher expressed the importance of response by joking, "I won't leave a note for my husband without getting a read-around first." In addition, the second year of study with its nine-credit-hour collaborative research project was now greeted with increasing confidence in their ability to engage in the larger, more complex, research study.

Based on evidence from this study, my colleagues began to require reading and responding in their courses from the beginning of the program. When this occurred, the signature in my course took on less significance, for they had already developed more confidence in their abilities to respond critically to the work of others.

CONCLUSION

In my experience, the greatest obstacles to successful collaboration are the unquestioned assumptions held by teachers and academics alike that just by the nature of being an educated adult, everyone should be able to team. If adults have had successful teaming experiences where the conversations and decisions emerged with little difficulty, they often assume that all experiences should emerge as easily. If they have experienced unsuccessful collaborations where individuals embraced rigid positions and lacked important collaborative skills, they view conflicts as irresolvable. However, the former case is frequently a happy accident. The latter case is often the result of stubbornness or ignorance.

The research data I collected informs me that the teaming aspect of this program was one of the most powerful aspects of the program in challenging the traditional cultures of isolation in schools. Yet, unless faculties accept that team development is necessary and must be continuous, teams will hide their problems and skim the surface. Even programs with cohort structures as the only collaborative structure benefit from expertise in actively creating and nurturing collaboration. Because the literature and research on collaboration and teaming is extensive, no program needs to work without support. Finding experienced faculty with this as an academic interest may be more difficult. Relying on the occasional consultant to run a team development workshop as the only means of support will not address the issues in adequate ways.

PART II

IMPROVING CHILDREN'S LEARNING

The task of improving children's learning is common both to teachers and to teacher educators. Indeed, its achievement perhaps should be the central criterion whereby all programs of professional development are evaluated, especially innovations such as this. Once one moves away from the simplistic notions of the dominant paradigm, this ideal presents difficult, complex, and unexplored issues within a moral paradigm with which no one, including IET, has yet struggled effectively. For the moment, therefore, it is a matter of gathering together differing perspectives necessary to identifying the ways forward to this ideal, in this case those of faculty and classroom teachers.

In chapter 6, Elizabeth K. DeMulder, Ann Cricchi, and Hugh T. Sockett as teacher educators describe some familiar challenges, controversies, and moral complexities teachers face and begin to trace a potential path of support and professional development that appear to empower teachers to transform their practices in ways that enhance children's learning. They outline the forms of support that *Beliefs and Principles in IET Practice* (see chap. 2) provide to teachers transforming their practices, with a specific emphasis on the adoption of an ethic of care (Noddings, 1984). They then explore how teachers in the program (1) adopt a moral paradigm for the political context, (2) undertake continuous reflection and classroom research, (3) use the support of their learning community, and (4) develop a profound understanding of an ethic of care.

This provides a backdrop for the two chapters in which teachers describe an ongoing collaborative process of reflection, action, and discovery as they work to envision and to create stimulating and enriching learning environments for children. In chapter 7, Rita E. Goss and Kristin S. Stapor seek to have very young children experience life and interpret it from "as many vantage points as possible." Kindergarten and first-grade students, they say, empowered them to give back the control of learning to the children by deciding to look through the eyes of our children and allow this new view of learning to help them better understand how our children develop skills in literacy. In chapter 8, Deborah Barnard and Deborah Courter-Folly describe how middle school children constructed knowledge in their classrooms through storytelling, reflection, and autobiographical narratives, as well as what they learned intellectually and morally in the process. They use a fourfold epistemological frame that includes experiential, practical, and propositional knowledge, but also the notion of presentational knowledge that describes students linking their tacit experiences with content.

6

Complexity in Morally Grounded Practice

Elizabeth K. DeMulder, Ann Cricchi, and Hugh T. Sockett

How do teachers' experiences in the program affect their classroom practices and student learning? To grapple with this question, we first describe briefly the familiar challenges, controversies, and moral complexities that influence teachers' lives and their students' learning. Second, we outline the forms of support that *Beliefs and Principles in IET Practice* (see chap. 2) provide to teachers transforming their practices, with a specific emphasis on the adoption of an ethic of care (Noddings, 1984). Finally, we explore how teachers in the program adopt a moral paradigm for the political context, undertake continuous reflection and classroom research, use the support of their learning community, and develop a profound understanding of an ethic of care. We use teachers' written work from the classes of '97 and '99. This includes individual and collaborative research project reports, anonymous end-of-program evaluations, "exit papers" in which teachers were asked to describe their professional development experience over the 2 years of the program, and other reflective pieces written over the course of the program. (We have not discussed our experience of teachers attempting to develop learner-centered classrooms, as this topic is dealt with in chap. 7 and 8.)

CHALLENGES, CONTROVERSIES, AND MORAL COMPLEXITIES

Teachers who attempt to acknowledge and confront complexities, uncertainties, and inequities in schools risk being labeled as inefficient, ignorant, incompetent, or unrealistic. Acknowledging complexity can be said to undermine efficiency and clarity. Admitting uncertainty threatens to expose ignorance. Privilege is too often blinkered and can be blind to inequity. Problems become too great, constraints too binding, and, in any case, the costs are too high. Specifically, there is much more rhetoric than reality in the professed social commitment to an "ethic of care" and to the value of each individual as a standard for educational practice (Gilligan, 1982; Noddings, 1984). Many teachers struggle with such commonplaces of educational institutions alone and in silence. Others turn their backs.

A paramount *challenge* to those who struggle is the range of unexamined assumptions and simplistic notions about learning. Teacher effectiveness research, for example, tends to assume a linear model of simple, direct relationships between specific teacher behaviors and student learning, narrowly defined (Tom, 1984). The stress is on the commonalities and similarities of classrooms rather than differences of context, classrooms, and the child's individual learning situation. Such assumptions embody the "one-size-fits-all" solution, exemplified in staff development programs focusing on specific strategies and techniques to be implemented. Administrators and politicians are convinced, or at least hopeful (and often desperate), that they will "work" to raise test scores, increasingly the primary measure of school quality.

Second, teachers struggle with *controversy* stemming from the major paradigm conflict (see chap. 1). It appears in (a) the general conflict of educational purpose: What should children learn? (b) the concept of learning: What constitutes learning and how should it be assessed? (c) teaching method: How should teachers teach? and (d) matters of motivation: How do they learn best? These are not simply technical issues debated in the research literature, that later crop up in school board rooms, schools, and communities across the country. They reflect differing political, social, and economic priorities.

Increasingly dogged by calls for accountability, many teachers also struggle with the *moral complexity* of reconciling differing views about how and what "all" children should learn with their own practical wisdom in regard to the particular cognitive, social, and emotional needs of the individual children in their classrooms. Delpit (1995) cautioned that "Teachers who view creating relationships between themselves and their students as central to the teaching task may be misjudged by assessors expecting to evaluate their knowledge of and involvement with content" (p. 140).

Although this program seeks to equip teachers not to turn their backs, but to begin serious moral reflection about their students' learning, it adds to the teacher's moral complexity. For example, it can become a real threat to the institution in which the teacher works if the subsequent actions are different from those prescribed by the administration or school system.

Reflection in action is both a consequence and cause of surprise. When a member of a bureaucracy embarks on a course of reflective practice, allowing himself to experience confusion and uncertainty, subjecting his frames and theories to conscious criticism and change, he may increase his capacity to contribute to significant organizational learning, but he also becomes, by the same token, a danger to the stable system of rules and procedures within which he is expected to deliver his technical expertise. (Schon, 1983, p. 328)

But it is not merely reflection in general. As a teacher's reflective practice grows, and he or she gains confidence to take actions in his or her classroom based on his or her knowledge, experience, and practical wisdom, active and passive resistance from administrators (and even other teachers) usually marginalizes the teacher. A morally grounded practice, therefore, faces a context of immense moral complexity, requiring courage and determination in the face of many different challenges, specifically for a teacher driven by an ethic of care. For the challenge is especially threatening to the institution when the focus is on the individual, rather than the individual as merely an instance of, say, a third-grade child. Each individual child in the context of an ethic of care requires time and resources that are not afforded to him or her, for reasons that often seem to the teacher superficial and bureaucratic. "The student," as Noddings (1984) put it, "is infinitely more important than the subject" (p. 20). Teachers in the program, however reflective, articulate, and philosophically acute and committed to such an ethic they become, invariably have to face these characteristic challenges, controversies, and moral complexities, which in different ways sap the idealism with which they began teaching (Farkas, Johnson, & Foleno, 2000).

BELIEFS, PRINCIPLES, AND AN ETHIC OF CARE

Familiar as these problems may be, they are important to reiterate. Like other IET faculty, we provide learning opportunities for reflection, school-based teacher research, a mutually supportive learning community and morally grounded practice (see chap. 2), but we emphasize an ethic of care. We also adhere, like others, to a learner-centered, constructivist model of learning, as espoused particularly by Dewey (1902/1990) and Bruner (1996; see also chap. 3). Teachers, as this book demonstrates, bring their knowledge and expertise to the program. They then develop a familiarity in this new learning environment and acquire the tools to construct new understandings that influence the way they approach their teaching role and interact with their students. When teachers are supported to transform their practices within a moral frame as the paradigm (see chap. 1), we believe that student learning will be enhanced.

Unfortunately, measuring "effectiveness" is difficult enough. We believe we must try to connect the improvement of students' learning in classrooms to the experiences teachers have in the program. We are thus struggling to find ways that we can seriously evaluate what we do and also take into account the complexity of children's learning. Teachers are generally satisfied with the educational experiences (research, reflection, teaming, etc.) they receive while in the IET program. We celebrate the voices of teachers who work with us, we trust their intuition, and we are deeply rewarded by their sincere appreciation, yet we need to find ways to acquire a deeper, more sophisticated understanding of how the program affects practice, especially children's learning.

Our approach to this problem of establishing the link between our teaching and the improvement of children's learning in classrooms has so far been only through reflection. We have a long way to go to figure out how to do this. But, as our account of moral complexity makes clear, reflection by teachers in the program is often about moral values and the moral imperative of a situation fed by their research in a learning community of two (or 200). Research opportunities, readings, reflection, dialogue, and collaboration, seem to enable teachers to explore new ideas and different perspectives, and to grapple with fundamental epistemological, cultural, and developmental issues. Developing teachers' reflective practice (Schon, 1983) moves them away from the traditional self-concept of "teacher as technician" (see Sockett, 1993). They begin to embrace the novel and morally resonant idea of "teacher as professional" (Sockett, 1993, chap. 1), which, for us, incorporates the ethical reality of the teacher as the "one-caring" (Noddings 1984, chap. 2). Teachers in the program, we hope, then begin to reflect on the moral dimensions of their teaching, find the courage to question, engage in dialogue with others, and change their (often longstanding) attitudes and behavior in their classrooms. Noddings (1984) indeed insisted that "there is a double requirement of courage in caring: I must have the courage to accept that which I have a hand in, and I must have the courage to go on caring" (p. 9). Teachers report that insights they gain through reflection and critical dialogue lead to greater sensitivity and responsiveness to children in their care.

We believe not merely that moral virtues are central to a teacher's role in helping students to develop, but that the relationship between teacher and child plays the central role in children's cognitive, social, and emotional development (Noddings, 1984; Sockett, 1993; Vygotsky 1978). Teachers support children's development and learning, we believe, by fostering caring relationships with and among students that emphasize trust and respect, which itself encourages active participation and open communication. Morally grounded practice thus permeates all aspects of a teacher's work.

Very personal challenges, inherent tensions, and a sense of vulnerability are involved when caring teachers work to develop a reflective orientation toward their students' learning and when they struggle with the one-caring dimensions of their teaching roles. In order to develop an authentic, reflective moral practice, they must be able and willing to face the political context we have described, which includes being publicly accountable for children's learning. They must also tolerate ambiguity and open up both to honest self-appraisal and to the ethical reality of the ones cared for. Developing the art of reflection as moral professionals, teachers gain new perspectives on teaching and student learning that frequently lead them to make critical changes in their classrooms.

Yet the one-caring is not an isolate. With a supportive learning community teachers can find reflection and classroom research more public and constructive (DeMulder & Eby, 1999). Teachers, together, can muster the courage to share their questions, concerns, and confusions with others; recognize themselves as less than perfect; and learn from the knowledge and experience of others. Teacher educators, as well as principals and administrators, need to hear and listen to teacher voices. For us to understand the ethic of care, however, we need to hear these voices filtered by the framework (criteria is too strong a word) that Noddings established for the "one-caring."

Although we recognize the significance she gives to reciprocity between the one-caring and the one cared for, we here choose to listen primarily to the voices of the one-caring (the teacher) and hear the voices of the ones cared for (the students) through their teachers. We believe that much more extensive work of the kind we have begun here is needed if we are to understand the full implications of Noddings' account of caring, which articulates a profound and dramatic change in what would have to become the self-concept of the teacher. We make a start in this chapter by using a simplified version of her rich account, which we expect to make more complex as we use it to interpret teachers' voices and thereby improve our own practice as teacher educators.

The following features of the teacher as the one-caring are significant for us.

First, action is insufficient. Mere action cannot provide sufficient evidence for the one-caring. "If we can understand how complex and intricate caring is, we shall perhaps be better equipped to meet the conflicts and pains it sometimes induces" (p. 12). It follows that caring is not simply a matter of doing things that others can observe. It demands specific kinds of commitments, such as engrossment.

Second, engrossment in the one cared for carries with it the severe risk that the attention shifts to the one-caring. For a teacher committed to an ethic of care, the "burdens and worries" may make the one-caring more concerned about him or herself than about the ones cared for, especially in the context we described in the first part of this chapter.

Third, and more difficult still, is the one-caring who wants to be credited with caring and, in so doing, searches for an adequate substitute for caring. For teachers beginning to adopt this ethic and not yet facing up to its demands, some of the caring actions are synthetic. Adopting this ethic demands constant self-criticism as a defense against this weakness.

Fourth, there can be no fixed rules, as the caring situation is dependent on the perspectives of the one-caring and the one cared for. An ethic of care is, fundamentally, an ethic of ideals, not of principles—which creates an interesting tension for the program's attachment of beliefs and principles, a subject for another paper.

Fifth, the "fundamental aspect" is a "displacement of interest from my own reality to the reality of the other" (p. 14). Yet once we realize the possibilities of caring for others (relieving their pain, helping them to learn) and that caring is sustained and public, we are also caring for ourselves, for our "ethical self."

This is not, however, that easy: "apprehending the other's reality, feeling what he feels as nearly as possible, is the essential point of caring from the view of the one-caring" (p. 16). And that, as Noddings illustrated, means trying to understand what it is like to hate mathematics, not simply wanting the child to love mathematics as I do.

TRANSFORMATIVE INFLUENCES ON STUDENT LEARNING: TEACHERS' VOICES

Despite (or in some cases, because of) the challenges they have faced, teachers report that many of the changes they have made in their teaching as a result of being acquainted with IET's beliefs and principles have had significant influences on their students' learning and development. This seems to us to be a complex hermeneutic process evolving in circles of multiple, reciprocal influences. The path of influence includes the classroom teachers' initial knowledge and experience; the teachers' encounters with the curriculum; changes in teachers' knowledge, understanding, and reflective practices; changes in teachers' classroom approaches; changes in students' attitudes and behaviors; and changes in student learning. Teachers travel up and down this path throughout the 2 years, sometimes with a sense of clear direction and a clear goal in mind, more often with a sense of exploration that includes frustration and confusion, sometimes resulting in great insights. Perhaps we may even be able to construct eventually a path of development a teacher might take in the process of adopting an ethic of care, which will incorporate improvements in children's learning.

Building on this conceptualization so far, we can construct some intimations. They are too complex to be called hypotheses. Student learning, we suggest, is enhanced by teachers who

1. adopt a moral paradigm for the political context,
2. undertake continuous reflection and classroom research,
3. have the support of a learning community, and
4. develop a profound understanding of an ethic of care, defined as the "displacement of interest from my own reality to the reality of the other," including the sense and ability to care for myself as an ethical self, but with a special concern for

   a. an engrossment in the one cared for, leading to self-absorption, and

   b. the mistaken use of substitutes for caring.

We now turn to the ways that changes in teachers' practice have influenced their students, as documented by the teachers themselves through the four main categories of intimation we have iterated. These categories are not, of course, discrete, but interwoven in the subtleties and complexities of the ethic of care Noddings described. (In many cases, teachers also provided documented evidence of positive changes in student learning—including evidence from students' work, classroom observations, student journals, and test scores—that they attributed to changes they made in their practice.)

Adopting a Moral Paradigm for the Political Context

Teachers who adopt a moral paradigm in the context described earlier are almost inevitably faced with the politics of classroom, school, and school district (division in Virginia).

When the dictate came down from the School Board and the administration that kindergarten would no longer receive art, music, or physical education, the kindergarten teachers and I went to our principal and argued that, if we followed the mandate, we would take away our 5- and 6-year-olds' greatest chances to be successful. He agreed that we could write a waiver. We put that together and were allowed to continue with our programs at Mullen Elementary . . . I felt that I had moved up a notch as an educator and in the eyes of my peers.

This reflective comment raises a significant problem in the development of teachers in this program. First, in the politics of the context, the teacher has made her perspective heard, her self-confidence as a professional has been enhanced. She has refused to be marginalized. But second, we have noticed that becoming reflective often proceeds in an individual from simple description, through self-justification, and only then to authentic self-critique. It is a process we ourselves struggle with as we search for self-critique, so we note the element of self-justification here. Finally, accepting that the program often leads to a new self-concept and that self-esteem is important, this victory is conceptualized within the oppositional politics of the old paradigm. This illustrates that the overwhelming dominance of that paradigm can co-opt a teacher's commitment to reinvention as a moral professional and that just being a graduate student in the program provides teachers with a certain protection and privilege they may not be able to sustain when they finish.

However, politics can be very local. This teacher, who taught children with learning disabilities, described her growing confidence and her determination to make decisions based on the best interests of her students, apparently trying to resist co-option by the politics of the local environment, the school:

The awareness that the adaptations that I implemented could be effective, coupled with the support of the data I had collected, led me to the conclusion that I needed to be more assertive in determining the course of my students' program. I realized that, within the full inclusion model, I was able to implement strategies and approaches that positively affected my students' growth, even if it was not what the program or the regular teachers felt was the best method. I found that, as long as my students were making progress and I felt justified in what I was doing, then the decisions I was making were working toward helping my students achieve their individual goals and objectives.

Nor is the adoption of the moral paradigm always as exhilarating as it might be: Indeed, as we suggested earlier, it need not be a comfortable experience.

The experiences I have had over the last 2 years have caused me to constantly rethink, in relation to my teaching practices and my students' learning styles. The IET program has successfully held me to a high moral standard in regard to my teaching. Possibly, the only drawback to this high standard is the increased frustration I have felt as a teacher to not meet the expectations I have set for myself. However, I strongly believe that, just as we set high standards for our students, we must set high standards for ourselves or we run the risk of becoming stagnant.

Frustration is commonplace, of course. For us, there are dangers implicit here if we interpret Noddings correctly. Although we may be formally pleased with this teacher's convictions, we can worry about whether they might conceal a high-standards ideologue, a person who could get out of moral balance between "standards" and other virtues of moral importance, notably in caring. What are standards here? Moral ideals, or quasi-bureaucratic norms of performance?

Standards embodied in mandated standardized tests force changes in curriculum and pedagogy. If the continuation of art, music, and physical education is a victory, the struggle is not over. One research project reports a student saying, "Mrs. Kaminsky, I really understand why you had to run class this way for the past 6 weeks, but could we PLEASE go back to the way it was before!" And the rest of the class cheered in agreement. The report continues:

We now believe that when students see the connections of content to their own lives in an atmosphere of strong interpersonal relationships, they engage with their learning. On a broader scale, we are challenged to use the findings of our research to develop innovative ways to wed individual learning to Virginia's Standards of Learning [SOL] mandate. As teachers and school divisions seek ways to raise students' SOL scores, our voices will need to speak out loudly that the curriculum is meaningless to the student until he sees its relationship to his own life.

The struggle for the teachers here can be interpreted as just a clash between the political and the professional, or between different views of educational purpose. Significant for the development of the moral paradigm is the teachers' determination, as they see it, not to surrender their educational principles and ideals, but to work to preserve them by setting the student as a learner as the touchstone of judgment and understanding. We recognize, again, just how difficult such an ambition is and how the context of oppositional politics, once again, is impossible to avoid.

Undertaking Continuous Reflection and Classroom Research

In contrast with the teacher who spoke of high standards, others look to themselves as the source of ethical reality.

By teaching as a reflective practitioner this year, I feel that I have developed the tolerance for internal contradiction that Belenky et al. wrote about (p. 137). It is impossible for me to look critically at my daily performance as a teacher without constant doubt and frustration. Reflection is difficult and often painful, but I am realizing that with reflection comes the key to becoming a moral professional, becoming a teacher who might make a difference.

The ambition to make a difference is apparent in the most common feature of reflection, which can lay the ground for the reciprocity of the one-caring and the one cared for, for it seems to create in teachers an explicit awareness that both teacher and learner are *learners*.

[I began to wonder] how my attitudes affected and sometimes antagonized the undesirable behaviors exhibited by some of my students . . . I wondered how the use of different lenses affected the students' behaviors and success. . . . Through revisiting my journal entries, I was able to see how my approach to the students had changed. . . . Students became more receptive to suggestions and began to see how their perspectives were not always common with their peers.

But this comment does not quite nail down the matter of student learning. Needed are more reports like this, with detailed evidence:

The content and quality of my students' writing improved a great deal. I attribute this to the level of reflection I was able to inspire my students to reach and by honestly sharing my own challenges about writing. I also believe it was a direct result of the wonderful diverse literature to which I exposed my students during our collaborative research project. I found my students eager to share stories, paragraphs, and poems as they responded to the literature and as they created original pieces of writing. The level of reflection and quality of the writing from some of my students was overwhelming at times.

Student learning also has to be understood, *pace* Noddings, beyond the content given: "What I found were not only improvements and changes in writing but also in behavior, attitude, work habits, and social situations."

Finally, the connections can be highly subtle. Doing research can influence those student behaviors through teachers' attending specifically to the moral complexity of their classrooms. For instance:

Through conducting this research, I feel that I have grown as a moral professional. It took courage for me to embark on something new and care to try to make a difference in my students' learning. . . . I tried to be fair in distributing my time and attention equitably to all of my students as they were learning the process skills that I taught them.

Yet the lesson learned from the practice of reflection and research may be as simple as the fact that if you listen to students, they respond by being engaged and enthusiastic about their learning and by putting more effort into their work.

The realization that my students were a valid source of information about the effectiveness of my program was an invaluable discovery. My own observations of the classroom were not the only way I could determine if a lesson was working. I could ask my students for their personal feelings and reactions. I don't know why I didn't recognize my students as a pool of knowledge from which I could draw before, but throughout my research they became a sound resource that I turned to for feedback and solutions.

It thus appears that, through personal reflection (and dialogue with colleagues), teachers explored new perspectives on their teaching and their students' learning. According to teachers, this exploration gives them courage, engenders a commitment to take ownership of challenges in the classroom, and makes them open to different perspectives. Students thereby experience stimulating new learning opportunities and are able to demonstrate academic achievement in less traditional ways (for excellent examples, see chap. 7 and 8).

There are two central difficulties for us as teacher educators, gratified as we are by teachers' voices. First, we are concerned by the halo effect of the program. That is, the program sets out to be rigorous, but teacher-friendly; challenging the practical wisdom of the teacher in a context of team and faculty support; and evoking ideals and moral commitments, but under the glare of critique. The emotional bonds formed through the program could distort teacher judgment, especially if they lack the confidence to be authentically self-critical. Second, we are continuously haunted by the need for teachers to be able to show to a skeptical professional and lay public the truth of their convictions about student learning. That will demand a mix of descriptive patterns of teacher and student growth linked to teachers' intentions.

The Support of a Learning Community of Teachers for Private–Public Reflection and Classroom Research

As teachers developed a more reflective approach to teaching (and life in general), their own experience gave them a newfound respect for the process that they often felt compelled to share with their students. Many teachers described strategies they implemented that encourage students to develop their own reflective capacities, including the use of student journals, student evaluative feedback, and class discussions to encourage critical reflection and personal insights (see chap. 8). But we as a faculty have been rightly chided (see chap. 5) for not working profoundly enough with team development. Frankly, we often forget that working in teams does not come easy, to us or to others, and we are sure this statement speaks for many more than were prepared to put it so clearly:

One of the highlights of this program is the sharing we did in discussions. Sharing the tragedies and the delightful accomplishments of students and teachers has been enlightening. At first I was very hesitant to speak up during these discussions, but as I grew to understand the people of the program and did some personal growing, I felt more comfortable giving input and sharing personal experiences. Sharing personal experiences and personal beliefs was not easy for me. I am typically not a person who opens up and talks, especially in big groups. This was a big step for me. . . . Through these conversations, I have become more aware of the differences of the cultures in society, more sensitive to the needs of every individual in my classroom, and more understanding of what it takes to be a caring teacher. These are important steps that I have accomplished because I knew I was not a very caring and sensitive teacher. I now know how important it is to be this type of teacher.

The team as a primary learning community seems to provide a constant moral influence, with important effects on the students and the teachers themselves:

Donald A. Schön observes, "Each student makes up a universe of one, whose potentials, problems, and pace of work must be appreciated as the teacher reflects-in-action on the design of her work" (p. 333). Perhaps this statement reflects the true value of our research. In order to help our students construct knowledge and become thinkers, we had to become participants in the action. We had to provide them with strategies designed to help them process information effectively and to be self-reliant, believing that they had the ability to succeed. Our journey began with the intention to change the ways in which our students think and learn. However, through this year's research process, we realized that our thinking and teaching practice was impacted as much, if not more, than our students' thinking and learning. We were compelled to reflect and challenge our own pedagogy. It was through our reflections that we were then able to help our students become more reflective about their thinking and learning processes. . . .

Students demonstrated increased self-reliance, a new awareness of thinking capabilities, an ability to make connections to prior knowledge, the ability to take a risk as they explored solutions to particular problems, and an emerging awareness of thinking strategies.

The dynamic of work in teams was discussed in detail in chapter 5. For our purposes in this chapter, however, it provides an important lead into matters of the ethic of care.

Understanding and Working With an Ethic of Care

We found a caring community is attainable. We were able to provide our students with an environment where they could learn more, both socially and academically. This is something we each felt was missing in our classrooms in previous years. Throughout the year we were able to see positive changes in our students. They developed the ability to compliment one another, solve problems effectively, demonstrate a voice within the classroom, and interact in a positive, supportive manner. The students needed direct instruction in many of these behaviors and opportunities to practice them, but eventually many did learn and incorporate them into their daily lives.

We are not sure that this sure-fire conclusion heralds a caring community as Noddings might understand it. The language here is the language of the dominant paradigm, and the existence of a caring community is therefore opaque. The problem is one of the authentic engrossment in the ethical self of the other, as opposed to new forms of manipulating children with carrots of a "caring substitute" kind. For it to be a caring community, there must be reciprocal concern for the other. Easier said than done, of course. For we face a not dissimilar moral challenge to our practice, presaged by chapter 5. Does IET practice use the team concept manipulatively? Although teachers in the program constantly tell us of the moral importance of the team—for themselves as individuals, for the others in the team, for the children they all teach—we too often fail to see the team as an organic developing center of moral consciousness. Caring for each other as colleagues is the first main step toward shifting the bureaucratic culture of the school to a moral culture.

We suggested earlier that we can use Noddings' definition of *care*: The "displacement of interest from my own reality to the reality of the other." This includes the sense and the ability to care for myself as an ethical self, but with a special concern for two traps (1) engrossment that leads to self-absorption, and (2) caring becoming so much of a challenge that the one-caring uses substitutes.

I have become more of a caring and nurturing individual because I realize what an important role I play in the lives of my students. I rely less heavily on discipline and I focus more on the positive aspects of teaching. In a forum entry from November 1997, I wrote: "When talking about caring in the classroom, I believe that caring is the virtue that can make all the difference in the world to a teacher or a student. I find this to be the case with my first grade students. It seems that when they feel truly cared about and loved, this is when they really respond to me and their learning environment. My students become eager to please and eager to learn.

The reciprocal relationship, most common with young children, is accounted for here. We are not sure how to interpret the apparent idea that caring (rooted in an idealist philosophy of moral sentiment) arises from the role (with its rights and duties). Nor would it be clear that an absence of discipline would necessarily reflect an appropriate stance for the one-caring without a much fuller description. For many children, as we will see, that feeling of being truly cared for may be no more than being listened to.

Striking the balance or simply transforming one's practice is critical, especially in learning to care for one's own ethical self, facing up to one's weaknesses, and having a willingness to be vulnerable:

Over the past 2 years I learned that I was not the caring, insightful teacher that I thought I was. Student journals showed this to me. Really listening to students and talking with them about their entries revealed so much about their lives that I would never have known otherwise. Honest student evaluations during class meetings of the ways in which the class ran caused me to reconsider practices I had been comfortable with for years. I hadn't realized that I enjoyed center stage so much. Making the needed changes to a more child-centered learning environment allowed for more rewarding personal contact and interaction with students. I am more purposeful in my observations of student be- havior and academic achievement. There have been more positive comments about school being an OK place to be. More students talk to me during down times about their personal and academic difficulties, due, I hope, to the fact that I am more open to hearing them. Stepping back and not feeling the need to fix a problem or judge, but just to listen has encouraged these exchanges. This change was harder than expected.

Reflection for this teacher has yielded authentic self-critique. Listening more carefully to individuals has been the basis for what seems a true engrossment with the ethical reality of the children, an essential requirement for the one- caring. Indeed, teachers described a process of broadening their focus to under- stand the "whole child"—the child's past experiences, individual perceptions, and life influences, as well as intellectual abilities, in order to better "care" for him or her. In the process, many teachers made greater efforts to really listen to their students. Surprisingly, as we have seen, it has been a constant refrain that many teachers indicated that, until they were involved in teacher research activities, they "never considered asking students what they thought."

That engrossment is totally absent in relations between teachers and their employers, and perhaps their colleagues. Teachers are not cared for either:

I came to this masters program with twenty-three years teaching experience. This was definitely the opportunity for me to open the doors and windows of time and air out the dust and accumulation of old ideas. I was especially touched by . . . the aspect of being a caring and compassionate educator. I had always thought of myself as a caring teacher; however, as I analyzed this concept and we discussed it within our class and our team, it began to take on broader aspects. I began to see how narrow-sighted I had become (had always been?), and once I recognized how constricted I had grown, I wanted to break out of the mold I had constructed for myself . . . I also discovered that if I asked my students for their opinions and trusted them to reply openly and honestly, most of them would not disappoint me. They were pleased to be asked their opinions and eager to be trusted and given the freedom to sculpt an opportunity for their own education. I felt fortunate to be not only a teacher but a student as well. It was through my eyes as a student that I was able to empathize and see more effectively through theirs.

Moving though these remarks are, they represent a comprehensive indictment of the management of school systems, their neglect of their personnel, and the sad barriers that have grown up between students and teachers because of the pervasive absence of trust almost inevitable in a bureaucratic system. Clearly, this teacher has never been cared for as a devoted professional giving up her life to work with other people's children. Yet we must ourselves not manipulate this teacher's devotion and commitment to fight our political battles, to get drawn once again into oppositional politics. She shows how the idealism of teachers, and with it the capacity for care, is almost always there waiting to be supported and rekindled.

Yet the caring relationship need not just be interpersonal, for a crucial feature of the ethic of care is what might be called *advocacy*. For Noddings, that might be morally expressed as helping students come to understand their own ethical selves. As teachers came to know and understand their students, they became stronger advocates for them, particularly those with special needs. This may be simply that, like the teacher seeking a waiver for art, music, and physical education (see earlier), teachers in the program feel "empowered" because they are treated as professionals and are encouraged to use their voices.

Where this is about those cared for, however, teachers help students to become their own advocates. They come to understand themselves better, to learn about their strengths and their weaknesses:

I have learned from working so closely with these three seventh graders the importance of empowering students with the skills necessary to become self-advocators. They have improved both academically and socially. Their achievement has improved as evidenced on their report cards. They have increased motivation, which can be seen in the number of assignments completed and turned in on time and in their positive answers to the final interview questions. They are able to see their progress and are encouraged to grow further. . . . Their lives and mine are forever changed by the research that took place in my class this year.

CONCLUSION

In the course of reexamining teachers' written work, we identified some patterns that help us to reflect on how we might continue to improve the IET program for teachers. Although many teachers wrote about the effects their experience in the program had on their students' learning, others did not make explicit connections. Some teachers wrote about the connection in an offhand way: "I know that the data we have collected and shared will help other teachers in our school who are looking for ways to keep children actively involved in their own learning. And of course, it goes without saying that this research will ultimately benefit the children we teach." Similarly, although teachers reported that they became more knowledgeable about the specific subjects they teach, they gained greater technological expertise, and they improved their writing and communication skills as a result of the program, these were generally not the experiences they explicitly connected to changes in their students' learning. It is clear that we need to facilitate the learning community in ways that help teachers make and articulate more explicit connections among their experiences in the program, their professional growth, changes in teaching approaches and practices, and students' learning. Greater emphasis on reflection and critical dialogue about these connections can only serve to strengthen them.

It appears to us that the real power in the IET experience is generated in the learning community as teachers build a personal and communal sense of hope and a determination to face challenges in order to create positive learning environments for children. What seems to match their idealism is not merely a concept of themselves as moral professionals, but a specific concept of themselves as carers. We need to find ways to explore that much more deeply, not merely with them, but within our corner of teacher education. For teachers, we especially need to establish more long-term supportive communities so that, after they leave the program, they can find long-lasting support as they resist pressures to alienate children in schools.

Dewey (1902/1990) wrote, "In the schoolroom, the motive and the cement of social organization are alike wanting. Upon the ethical side, the tragic weakness of the present school is that it endeavors to prepare future members of the social order in a medium in which the conditions of the social spirit are eminently wanting." Nearly 100 years later, we must not continue to turn our backs.

7

Through the Eyes of the Child

Rita E. Goss and Kristin S. Stapor

Rather than posing dilemmas to students or presenting models of expertise, the caring teacher tries to look through students' eyes, to struggle with them as subjects in search of their own projects, their own ways of making sense of the world. Reflectiveness, even logical thinking remain important; but the point of cognitive development is not to gain an increasingly complete grasp of abstract principles. It is to interpret from as many vantage points as possible lived experience, the ways there are of being in the world.

Greene (1988, p. 197)

Looking back as alumnae, the IET program left us with the hope of reading and discovering more about teaching and learning so that our practice would continue to evolve as it did during our research project. Our research clearly demonstrated that our students continued to learn even when the reigns of control were loosened and the children were allowed the freedom to make choices and decisions about their own learning. We found that when we have high expectations and get to know each child as a unique individual, then the opportunities for teachers and students to learn together were limitless. Allowing children to experience life and interpret it from "as many vantage points as possible" is an empowering experience for both students and teachers. Our work with kindergarten and first-grade students empowered us to give back the control of learning to the children. In our research, we made the conscious decision to *look through the eyes of our children* and allow this new view of learning to help us better understand how our children develop skills in literacy. When we started our research, we had both experienced our students being labeled as low achieving, slow learning, learning disabled, normal, nonmainstream, culturally mainstream, and in some texts, low-income prereaders (D. Taylor, 1993). We had wondered, as Taylor had, what all these labels really say about our children's knowledge. "What is a low-income prereader?" As teachers, we had often heard and used labels to describe our students. But we wondered whether these labels helped children or were used to simply justify why some children were not successful on conventional forms of assessment for which we are all held accountable.

As we discussed these issues, we came to hypothesize that the children who appeared deficient, and in some cases were labeled, may actually possess knowledge but were being limited by the forms of assessment chosen by the teacher. The conventional forms of assessment often ignore a child's lived experience. "Tests, workbook pages, teacher-led discussions, textbooks, charts—each of these assumes a commonality of experience that the children in a classroom may not share. Each artificially separates the process of mastery from that of individual expression" (Gallas, 1991, p. 21). In the IET program, we had read works by Dewey (1919), Belenky et al. (1986), Greene (1988), Ashton-Warner (1963), Avery (1993), Routman (1991), Hagerty (1992), Fisher (1991), Schwartz and Pollishuke (1991), and many others, which caused us to be intrigued by the prospect of finding alternative ways to assess students. Certainly with so many diverse backgrounds and levels, they could not all exhibit what they know in the same manner. Therefore, our classes became child-centered environments that revolved around the concepts of multimodality experiences, variety, freedom, dialogue, and collaboration. We knew that children needed the freedom to talk, explore, discuss, invent, and collaborate to fully learn and understand, not only the curriculum, but the world around them. We became very skilled at kid-watching and seeing the unseen or hearing the unheard. We learned to listen carefully, question in nonthreatening ways and pay close attention to the smallest detail or interaction among students. This is where the depth of our children's knowledge first was illuminated. Our classrooms became huge display cabinets where practically every wall, window, bulletin board, piece of ceiling, and cabinet exhibited work of the children in the classroom. We utilized open-ended, child-directed centers as avenues to offer alternative assessments, advance the learning, and gather invaluable data on our children's knowledge and learning paths. We also collected data in the form of work samples derived through a writer's workshop. Our classrooms became the looking glass from which to view the hearts, minds, and souls of the children we were so fortunate to teach.

Although we had many students who demonstrated knowledge as our classrooms became more child-centered, the stories involving Mark and Victoria really highlight this fact. Mark began the year labeled as developmentally delayed with part of his day being spent in a learning disability resource class. He had a difficult time successfully completing any paper-and-pencil task. In math, he did much better using manipulatives, but he still did not appear to understand addition and subtraction concepts. One day he was working in the building center with Legos. His assignment was an open-ended one. The children were instructed to build a form of housing for people, either one that existed or a new type that they created. This task concided with the first-grade unit of study on "Our Community." When we visited Mark in the building center, he was finishing up what looked to be a traditional square house. We noticed right away that it had an alternating color pattern. Developing patterns had been a concept for which he also had difficulty. We began asking him about the house and how he decided on the shape and size. In response to these questions, he began telling us step by step how he had, in effect, planned and built this house. During this explanation, he expressed his desire to make the house a perfect square and noted that it meant the sides had to have the same number of blocks. He also told us how he had accidentally made one side too long and he showed us how he had counted and figured out that he needed to remove five blocks to make the sides even. As we walked away thinking over this conversation, we realized that without knowing it, this little boy had estimated, patterned, added, and subtracted to complete his task. This meant that he was able to do several of the math activities that he was unable to do on paper. These examples contradict the common assumption that the printed word shows "all knowledge."

In another example, Victoria was able to recognize only two letters of the alphabet in September. She was observed during center time in the kitchen area involved in writing grocery lists while she looked at the cookbook. Her lists included scribble writing but also random letters. She wrote the letters E, N, A, S, J, M, W, a, d, l, and O. The letters B and V were the only two she knew when tested at the beginning of the year and these were not even written on the list. When looking at Victoria's journal, we noted that she moved from scribble writing with a dictated sentence in September to random letters that told a story that was read with her reading finger by December. At that time, Victoria was drawing pictures and putting a letter to represent the picture: A for apple and P for potatoes. During reading time, Victoria read the book *Dan the Flying Man* by Cowley (1983). She read the book by memory having learned it during whole-group reading time. The book is a predictable reader with a rhythmic pattern. As she read brushing her reading finger under the words, it was noted that she knew that the words told the story and reading was done by moving left to right and return sweep. She used the pictures to recall the story she had read. When interviewed about reading, Victoria said that she could read. She was confident that she was a reader and a writer. It was also observed one day while Victoria waited in line for the dictated sentence in her journal that she recited *Dan the Flying Man* and replaced "Dan" with names of the children in her class. When filling out a story frame in which the beginning, middle, and ending of the story are depicted in words and pictures to show comprehension of the story, Victoria was able to draw the beginning and ending actions as well as fill in two middle actions. Her knowledge of this story was amazing.

In April, Victoria was tested again on the letter and sound recognition chart. She now had mastered the names of 24 out of 26 letters. Although she still was unable to produce most of the letter sounds, she had made incredible progress while being allowed to progress at her own rate in a natural environment where there were many opportunities for engagement in reading and writing activities.

THE PROCESS OF TEACHING, RESEARCHING, AND REVISING OUR METHODS

Writer's workshop was an important element of our classroom practice. It provided us with a great deal of important data for our research. The instruction in both classes took the form of modeling on a daily basis. We modeled the following concepts: capitalization, spaces between words, punctuation, print goes with the picture, pictures tell a story, phonics, inventive spelling, sight words, elaborative sentences, descriptive words, predicting what it says, self-correcting, and other items that would come up during our discussions. We would involve the students by having them help sound out words, read words, figure out what we did wrong, and identify sight words. The students would then go back to their seats to work freely in their own journals or notebooks. Writing prompts were not used, so students were able to choose their own topic, reflect on, and write about their own lived experiences.

In analyzing the writing data taken from writer's workshop, we attempted to evaluate and assess the children's writing based on the widely used linear spelling and writing stages. For example, we used Richard Gentry's spelling stages including prephonemic spelling, early phonemic spelling, phonetic (or letter-name) spelling, transitional spelling, and standard spelling (Routman, 1991). In addition to considering the spelling stages, we utilized the writing stages and development patterns described in the Prince William County Public School Division (1995) curriculum and assessment guides. We used them to evaluate the written language samples. The writing stages are denoted by levels and include definitions of pre-emergent (scribble), emergent (functional scribble), dependent (combination), developing (restricted), independent (expanded; see the appendix for full description of the developmental writing and spelling stages). These writing stages, like the spelling stages, are part of an early childhood writing development theory that is understood and practiced by a majority of elementary education professionals. In using these writing development stages to assess children, it is proposed that a child's academic progress will be noted by labeling the child's writing with one specific stage of development. In evaluating our children's writing, we found this to be a very difficult task. More often than not, each child's writing demonstrated had characteristics from more than one stage. As we conversed with our colleagues in our school as well as others, we found that other professionals were experiencing this same dilemma. We decided to examine the samples further and analyze the writing theory further.

While evaluating our student's writing we considered whether the child developed as a writer by progressing from scribbles to pictures to letter-like forms to random letters to beginning letters to strings of letters to words to sentences as this linear model would suggest. We also wondered whether writer's workshop provided a risk-free space for students to explore because they allowed the children to "play" with the conventions of print and to draw from their lived experiences. It was clear that

the power of personal writing [is that it] connects what is significant in children's lives with what goes on in school. Personal journal writing can be a means of validating each child, of saying to each child that what goes on in your life is important, that what you think and feel is relevant, and that everyday events are the things writers write about. Children are full of stories regardless of their backgrounds, but many of them don't know they have stories to tell. (Routman, 1991, p. 197)

We did not impose a prescription of what writing is or has to be, nor did we interfere with written language that did not appear to linearly follow the traditional stages of writing. As part of our research, we closely monitored the stories and drawings of six children throughout the year, observing their individual developmental patterns. By allowing our children to write consistently about their lived experiences and participate in writer's workshop choosing their own topics, we encouraged them to not only see themselves as writers but also to develop individually and naturally as writers.

OUR CONCLUSIONS

By closely examining and reflecting on the children's writing, we came to believe and theorize that becoming a writer is not a linear step-by-step process. Rather, it is a process of development that takes each child on a uniquely progressive learning journey based on that specific child's experiences, strengths, weaknesses, and confidence in the acquisition and consistent practice of skills. On close examination, our research showed children did not progress linearly from one stage to the next but moved freely in and out of the prescribed stages. We theorized that these individual developmental journeys took place in a helix-like fashion rather than linearly. For example, Jared was a student who went from copying only the teacher's writing models in September to completing sentence starters in December. He was copying many types of environmental print, adding more detailed pictures in March. By June, he was using invented spelling with beginning, middle, and ending sounds. On the other hand, Kassie went from drawing a simple picture and orally dictating the story in September to using inventive spelling and only writing the representations of some words in December. Due to missing or incomplete word representations and incorrect word spacing, it was necessary for her to read the story orally in order for readers to have full understanding of her writing. By March she was using sentence starters and completing sentences with inventively spelled words that represented beginning, ending and some middle sounds. Then in June she was using both conventional and inventive spelling, spacing was correct, and all words were represented. However, in between each of these writing milestones, both children often demonstrated less sophisticated writing skills in their written language samples. Often, they appeared to be in a state of regression. Like most of our children, Jared and Kassie did not progress in a linear pattern, but instead they developed in a helix-like fashion. This insight led us to develop our first writing helix (see Figure 7.1).

This free movement between stages appeared to be an outcome of the child trying to satisfy his or her brain's request for more knowledge, while at the same time tempering this with caution on the implementation and application of new skills. Often, these individual patterns of progression appeared as regression because they did not fit the linear patterns set up by the widely used stages of writing. Although as teachers we were struggling with the apparent discord between theory and the student's practices, we did not attempt to alter the child's writing or pattern of development. We did not express to these children that anything was "wrong" with their writing. We continued to model, coach, and carefully watch and record their development.

Trying to evaluate and label each child's writing based on linear stages was extremely difficult. In hindsight, we are gratified that we allowed our students the freedom to develop according to their own unique patterns. We believe that if we had tried to force them to change their writing to fit the emergent writer's "mold," their growth would have been stifled and their writing development would not have accelerated. By each of us being "an encouraging teacher [we] helped bring out the children's stories and celebrate them. In doing so, we affirmed our students, built their self-esteem, and encouraged them as writers" (Routman, 1991, p. 199).

Not only was it clear from our research that students did not learn to write in a linear fashion, it was also evident that each child's development pattern within the helix was unique. Examining student writing samples in-depth illustrated that none of the children progressed in the same pattern. Each child's helix was an individual and one-of-a-kind expression of that child's brain processing and learning patterns. For example, Kassie not only developed in a helix-like fashion, her pattern was also unique in that she often demonstrated several different types of regressions in between written language milestones. Like Kassie's, most of the students' work never fit into a predescribed linear stage that encompassed all of the facets of their individual writings. We also noted a development in our students' pictures, which is not considered an important part of most predescribed writing stages, but it was clear that there was a correlation between their writing and drawings. For example, at the beginning of the year, Jared did not draw, but only wrote random simple letters. By the end of the year, when Jared was writing simple sentences, he was also drawing more detailed pictures of the central theme of his writing in a more sophisticated and colorful way.

We feel strongly that we would not have noticed these individual helix patterns of written language development if we had not had difficulty assigning

Figure 7.1
Simple Helix

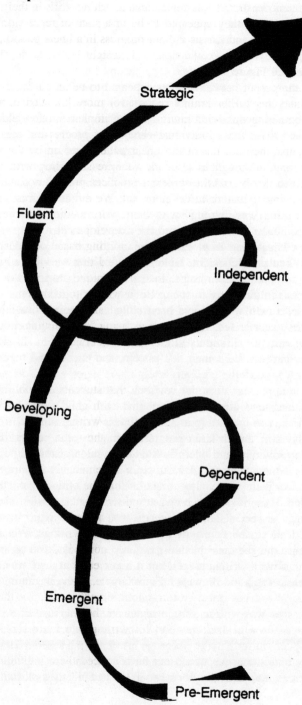

Strategic

Fluent

Independent

Developing

Dependent

Emergent

Pre-Emergent

linear stages to student writing, and if we had not spent time carefully analyzing each child's unique pattern of development. Therefore, we feel that a more appropriate way to assess children and view their writing is to not only realize that the development occurs in a helix-like fashion, but also to remove the writing labels and only use benchmark descriptors on a helix to evaluate a child's writing. Thus, we developed the second helix and what we believe to be a more appropriate assessment tool (see Figure 7.2). This eliminated the pressure to label the child's writing with a specific level or stage of development that did not completely and accurately describe all aspects of the child's writing. It also enabled a teacher to recognize and acknowledge that the relationship between reading, writing, listening, and speaking exists and is a fundamental part of understanding the child's complete language development.

We think that the helix is a developmentally appropriate tool to evaluate a child's writing progress. It allows children to have their own unique path and does not limit the benchmarks being used to describe a child's writing. It can be used in conjunction with a benchmark checklist to ensure mastery of skills while acknowledging and appreciating the child's unique path. Using different colors of pens to denote specific time frames, a child's progress can be traced on the helix to demonstrate to educators, parents, and students the unique path of development followed by a child. We believe this helix gives a deeper understanding of a child's individual patterns of thinking and learning as well as their strengths, weaknesses, and confidence or lack of confidence in the implementation of certain skills, thus further assisting teachers in differentiating instruction within the classroom.

As we have reflected extensively over our research and findings, the results left us feeling apprehensive about how our children's individual growth will be viewed and measured after they move on to different learning environments. Our research data suggests that it is a disservice to our students to look at their progress only using established guidelines and maps of childhood development. Using these predetermined guidelines and development maps may cause children to be seen as deficient and thus labeled before they have an opportunity to really develop fully in their own unique way. The special way our children acquired their language skills may not be seen as "special" at all to others. The descriptors we used, such as special and unique, may be seen as embellishments of the truth about these students' progress. We realize that not all teachers will look at our students and see them in the same way as we did. Too often, it is easier to pretend that we as teachers have all the answers. It is much more difficult and time consuming to look deeper for the truth and break out of our teaching paradigms.

This seems to be reminiscent of the storyline found in Dr. Seuss' *And To Think That I Saw It On Mulberry Street*. In this children's book, a father asks his child, Marco, to tell what he sees on his walk to and from school. Marco's first attempt ends with the admonishment by his father to "Stop telling such outlandish tales. Stop turning minnows into whales" (Seuss, 1937). Marco is

Figure 7.2
Helix of Written Language Development

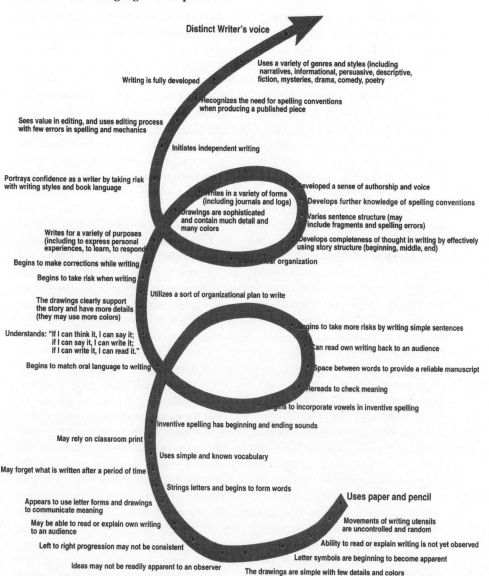

Distinct Writer's voice

Writing is fully developed

Uses a variety of genres and styles (including narratives, informational, persuasive, descriptive, fiction, mysteries, drama, comedy, poetry

Recognizes the need for spelling conventions when producing a published piece

Sees value in editing, and uses editing process with few errors in spelling and mechanics

Initiates independent writing

Portrays confidence as a writer by taking risk with writing styles and book language

Writes in a variety of forms (including journals and logs)

Developed a sense of authorship and voice

Develops further knowledge of spelling conventions

Drawings are sophisticated and contain much detail and many colors

Varies sentence structure (may include fragments and spelling errors)

Writes for a variety of purposes (including to express personal experiences, to learn, to respond

Develops completeness of thought in writing by effectively using story structure (beginning, middle, end)

Begins to make corrections while writing

Shows clear organization

Begins to take risk when writing

The drawings clearly support the story and have more details (they may use more colors)

Utilizes a sort of organizational plan to write

Understands: "If I can think it, I can say it; if I can say it, I can write it; if I can write it, I can read it."

Begins to take more risks by writing simple sentences

Can read own writing back to an audience

Begins to match oral language to writing

Space between words to provide a reliable manuscript

Rereads to check meaning

Begins to incorporate vowels in inventive spelling

Inventive spelling has beginning and ending sounds

May rely on classroom print

Uses simple and known vocabulary

May forget what is written after a period of time

Strings letters and begins to form words

Uses paper and pencil

Appears to use letter forms and drawings to communicate meaning

Movements of writing utensils are uncontrolled and random

May be able to read or explain own writing to an audience

Ability to read or explain writing is not yet observed

Left to right progression may not be consistent

Letter symbols are beginning to become apparent

Ideas may not be readily apparent to an observer

The drawings are simple with few details and colors

obviously being creative as he retells his observations, but his creativity is criticized. Therefore, when Marco walks on Mulberry Street the next time he looks for things that he thinks his father will praise him for noticing. However, his father's expectations are unrealistic, because they do not take into account the child's point of view. As a result, Marco is confused and experiences tremendous internal struggle: On the one hand, he wants to meet the expectations that his father sets for him; on the other hand, he wants to be a child who is given the freedom to be creative with, add details, and bring excitement to his lived experiences. His unique interpretations of his observations win over for a short time. Marco states:

> "I swung 'round the corner
> And dashed through the gate,
> I ran up the steps
> And I felt simply GREAT!
> FOR I HAD A STORY THAT NO ONE COULD BEAT . . ." (Seuss, 1937)

When he arrives home and sees the look on his father's face, he realizes that HIS story is not what his father wants to hear. His father is only looking for details and descriptions that match his narrow view of what his father thinks could ONLY be seen on Mulberry Street. So when his father asks, "Was there nothing to look at . . . no people to greet? Did nothing excite you or make your heart beat?" Marco responds, "Nothing, . . . but a plain horse and wagon on Mulberry Street" (Seuss, 1937). We fear that this story may parallel what happens to some children when they are only judged based on linear learning paths. We have read articles like "The Non-education of America's Children" by Wilentz (1993) and realize that there are both parents and teachers who perceive, as did Wilentz, that child-centered education is "romantic, damaging, inadequate, and daunting." However, we think our research contradicts this view. We feel that because people misunderstand child-centered theory, and because they often put blinders on when the unfamiliar arises, they develop misperceptions of children's learning and classrooms like ours. We feel, as do our students, that they "have a great story that no one could beat!" (Seuss, 1937). It may be difficult for some people to understand and value alternative perspectives. But, the caring teacher, as Greene (1988) suggested, will endeavor to see *through the eyes of the child*.

8

Illuminating Knowledge: Three Modes of Inquiry

Deborah Barnard and Deborah Courter-Folly

During our first year in the IET program, we were asked to conduct an independent research study. So, together as a school team, but separately as researchers, we conducted our own classroom research where we discovered that when students write about their art experiences and are actively engaged in their learning in science and language arts, they reveal valuable knowledge that goes beyond the course curriculum (Barnard, 1995; Courter-Folly, 1995). As the research process unfolded that year, in both projects, we became the facilitators as our students became actively engaged in their learning, started making decisions about what and how they learned, and began constructing knowledge as opposed to passively memorizing facts. Knowledge became something that students constructed—something they made. Students were "giving birth to their own ideas, making their own tacit knowledge explicit, and elaborating it" (Belenky et al., 1986, p. 217). Therefore, we were enthusiastic about working together during the second year of the program on a team research project that focused on exploring the field of knowing—What do students know and how do they come to know it? In this chapter, we describe the results of our team research project that explored how children constructed knowledge through storytelling, reflection, and autobiographical narratives, as well as what they learned intellectually and morally in the process.

Research traditionally examines the field of epistemology through an adult lens. Heron (1992) suggested an extended epistemology that includes at least three kinds of knowledge: experiential, practical, and propositional. *Experiential knowledge* is gained through direct contact with persons, places, and things. *Practical knowledge* concerns "how to" do something such as a skill or competence. *Propositional knowledge* concerns specific content such as vocabulary. *Presentational knowledge* is expressed in images, dreams, and stories. Presentational knowledge allows students to link their tacit experiences with content. And finally, *moral knowledge* helps children distinguish between what is right and wrong. It goes beyond rules governing inappropriate behavior to understanding concepts such as a child's responsibility as a citizen in a community.

Knowing in this study was explored through the voices of our sixth through eighth grade students attending a suburban, northern Virginia middle school. With more than 1,300 students in attendance, Saunders Middle School is the largest middle school in Prince William County in northern Virginia. As the context for this study, 475 students participated in four 9-week sessions of fine arts and in a full year of science and language arts classes.

RESEARCH METHODS

To study what is taking place in the minds of children in an authentic and complex sense, ultimately we found it necessary to conduct our study with subtle methods of inquiry in a participatory fashion. We began our research using familiar modes of inquiry. We used short-answer questionnaires to survey students about their knowledge and how they came to know the things they know. This approach met with confusion and frustration because the answers lacked detail. Students were unable to articulate the requested information. Our previous research on active learning caused us to wonder what our students knew (propositional knowledge), the skills they possessed (practical knowledge) and the understanding they had of the moral aspects of their learning (moral knowledge). Needless to say, the information we sought was difficult to uncover. Our challenge was to help these students recognize and share that information with us. We decided to use more subtle and engaging methods of inquiry. We observed student behavior and recorded spontaneous comments made by our students. We gradually began to ask open-ended questions allowing our students to fill in their ideas. We asked students to reflect on their experiences both inside and outside the classroom. We interviewed students and collected narrative accounts of their experiences and learning. We provided students with varied opportunities to tell what they knew in imaginative ways through expressive stories and autobiographical narratives.

As the story of our research began to unfold, we used three primary modes of inquiry: storytelling (expressive and imaginative), reflection (recall and reason), and autobiographical narrative (experience and action). With these modes of inquiry, we naturally became cooperative with our students; in fact, their responses guided the nature of our research. Reason (1994) described cooperative inquiry as research where "all those involved in the research are both co-researchers, whose thinking and decision making contribute to generating ideas, designing and managing the project, and drawing conclusions from the experience, and also co-subjects, participating in the activity being researched" (p.

326). The heart of our research was found in the stories, reflections, and auto-biographical narratives of our co-researchers, our students.

ASSESSING STUDENT LEARNING THROUGH THREE MODES OF INQUIRY

Expressive Storytelling

Storytelling is a mode of inquiry that can be used effectively to create knowledge and to make meaning. It can be used as a bridge to connect people's experiences to what they know—propositional knowledge. Although meaning exists as a result of face-to-face interaction, it may be hidden. Knowledge can be made manifest through a creative medium such as storytelling. "Meaning needs to be discovered, created, made manifest, and communicated. Stories . . . are devises with which to peer into human desires, wishes, hopes, and fears" (Reason & Hawkins, 1988, p. 80). Whether stories are told verbally or written down and read by others, they create an "empty space," a vessel in which meaning can take shape. Our students told imaginative stories and those stories created an empty space where meaning emerged. Stories that are expressive rather than explanatory "require the inquirer to partake deeply of experience, rather than stand back in order to analyze" (Reason & Hawkins, 1988, p. 80).

Art students were asked to look back through their experiences in creating art and to "tell the story" of their learning. "To understand," as Piaget (1973) said, "is to invent." Propositional knowledge is made clear in these stories as well as moral knowledge about what is involved in creating artwork.

Following a sixth-grade unit in weaving, the students worked in small groups to develop a story linking together their knowledge of weaving (both experiential and propositional) with their imaginations:

Attitude Dude and the Spider

One day Attitude Dude was walking home from class really mad that he had to do weaving in school. "I hate weaving!" Attitude Dude exclaimed, "It's girly stuff." Suddenly, a blob of fog appeared. Looking closer, Attitude Dude discovered that it was a humongous spider. He gasped in amazement. "You have wronged the art of weaving Attitude Dude," said the spider. "You—you can talk!?" Attitude Dude was stunned. "Yes. And soon, ya may not be able to!—We go." Another cloud of fog appeared and it enveloped Attitude Dude, blocking his vision. When the fog cleared, Attitude Dude found himself on a large web. "This is my home," said the spider. "Cool," said Attitude Dude. "Not cool," [said the spider]. "This is the place where you will die if ya do not pass the challenge." The spider drew out a weaving loom and some yarn. "I challenge ya to a weaving contest. If I win, ya die." "What if I win?" asked Attitude Dude. "No one ever has, but I will free ya if you do," said the spider. "Okay." Attitude Dude sat down and began to weave. The spider also wove in colors of red and orange and brown. Attitude Dude's weaving flourished. The blue, purple and green left threads blended together almost magically. His hands flew over and under the threads of the loom like lightening. Finally both the Spider and Attitude Dude were finished. Spider held up his weaving, an earth-toned masterpiece. Attitude Dude sighed, crossed his fingers and turned up his weaving. Spider cried out with fury! He could not deny it, Attitude Dude had won. "Very well, Attitude Dude, you have won. But remember, never again scorn the art of weaving," said the spider. The same smoke curled around Attitude Dude and he found himself back in front of his school. The End. Oh, and by the way, Attitude Dude got an A in weaving from his art teacher. (Alexa, Kara, Adrian)

Storytelling allows these students to revisit their weaving experience and to look at the knowledge they gained from their work. Through these imaginative stories, the students explain their clear understanding of the terms and processes involved in weaving but also their personal feelings about the work and the real purpose of the art of weaving. Storytelling becomes an opportunity for these students to invent a story about their struggle with the notion that weaving is "girly stuff." Adolescents are greatly influenced by their peers and even though two of the writers of this story are girls, they express the moral virtue of caring for the lone male in their group as they work to understand and move past gender stereotypes. The students also convey their knowledge of color and a respect for weaving as an art. They explain the difference between weaving as a functional tool to make a covering and weaving as an art form. In this story, they emphasize the aesthetics of weaving by showing an appreciation for its beauty. The spider represents the civilized cultures that carry weaving from a simple craft to a work of art. The story also expresses the children's desire to develop a "beautiful" product. These children are telling the audience (while also convincing themselves) that with the right attitude, a novice can become an expert. Finally, with the final comment about Attitude Dude's grades, the students demonstrate that they have developed a "trusting relationship" where they can openly express humor by joking with the teacher.

In the next example, a student chose to write a story about his experience with ceramics. Modeling in clay is a long process for many students. There are numerous terms and skills required to successfully complete an artwork from clay. This story identifies the student's face-to-face encounter with the ceramic process in a totally imaginary setting.

Dick Tracy was out walking on the street when he heard a bang. He didn't have a gun so he went to the art store as fast as he could. He bought a lot of clay. He wedged the clay. Then as quickly as possible made the clay into a shape of a sword. But he had a problem, he was missing a handle. So he got more clay and made a handle. He tried to connect it to the sword but it didn't stay. He got some clay slip, scored the clay and the handle stayed in place. He put his clay sword out to air dry and then fired it in a kiln. By the time all of that was done, the robber/shooter got away and was never seen again. (George)

Time and patience are factors in this story. Most students are very anxious about working with clay. The air drying and firing stages are activities that are done by the teacher and the delay is a real struggle for many students. Patience is a quality of control. For the students, the wait between modeling their piece and the bisque firing is much like waiting to open the gifts under the tree until Christmas morning. It is also an anxious time for the students because if they have failed to wedge their clay, their work may break apart during the firing and they may get back a handful of dust and broken pieces.

According to George, the opportunity to express his knowledge about ceramics in a story was not very threatening. He was able to easily use the frame of a comic book hero to describe his knowledge about his classwork. Storytelling for George was "an approach which . . . express[es] more the liveliness, the involvement, and even the passion of [his] experience" (Reason & Hawkins, 1988, p. 79).

The following expressive story was written by a sixth-grade science student. He was completing a science unit on matter.

Once upon a time there lived a little atom named Tom. Tom was an atom of oxygen. He was 10-years-old and lived in a chemistry set at Saunders Middle School. Tom loved living here because he had so many other atoms to play with. Tom's best friends were Mike and Moe. Mike and Moe were atoms of hydrogen and they were also brothers. The trio of atoms were with each other all the time, laughing and playing all over. Then one day the three of them went to a forbidden place called The Chemical Reaction Station. Their moms had told them never to go there but something happened. They all started blending together. When everything was over they had formed a molecule of water. They were all so scared and wanted to go home, but they couldn't go home like that! They had to think fast, very fast. Mike suddenly remembered what his mom told him to do if this happened. They had to go back to The Chemical Reaction Station. So the new water molecule of Mike, Moe, and Tom set off for the station. When they got there they went to the place they had blended together and started breaking apart again. They had been separated by a chemical reaction. They ran all the way home. When they were all home they promised that they would never go there again. (Garner)

Storytelling allowed Garner to express three kinds of knowledge. First, Garner used propositional knowledge about elements, compounds, and chemical reactions. He knows that elements combine during a chemical reaction to form compounds. He recognizes that a chemical reaction can also separate compounds back into individual elements. In addition, Garner creates something new—The Chemical Reaction Station. His story is an example of presentational knowledge in which Garner links experiential knowledge about disobeying rules with propositional knowledge about elements, compounds, and chemical reactions. A third kind of knowledge—moral knowledge—is evident as Garner recognizes that rules demonstrate care. He acknowledges the dangers in disobeying rules that trusted adults establish for people they love.

Reflection

Reflection is another mode of inquiry that provides a space for making meaning and creating knowledge. Reflection provides the opportunity to think deeply about a topic and to personalize knowledge. We asked our students to reflect about their learning as a form of reliving an experience.

We asked students to reflect on a chapter in the novel *Woodsong* written by Paulsen in 1991. Paulsen is running his team of sled dogs on a trail and finds a dead grouse. He finds her eggs nearby and decides to take the eggs home to his banty chicken named Hawk. Hawk raises the grouse eggs along with her own. She is very protective of her eggs and is even more protective when they hatch. She bites people and farmyard animals if they step too close to her chicks. Banty chickens cannot fly except for short distances, but soon the grouse become skilled flyers. Hawk calls to the grouse, but eventually they begin ignoring her. Hawk is furious and takes to sitting on the woodpile, watching her babies, and terrorizing anything that moves in the yard. The students reflect on the story:

I think that Hawk had no business doing what she does. She has to learn that the young get older and they fly away. If she acts that way, I wouldn't want to be her son. I know a little of how she feels that they're leaving. It's life. Kids leaving. It's the same thing with people. A child turns into a teen. Then an adult gets married and leaves. She's not going to die because they're gone. I would feel freedom to get away from her. (Sean)

This story kind of reminds me of my own life. Ever since I was little my mother made sure everything I did was perfect. It was so bad, to the point where I couldn't turn in a paper where you could see I erased something. She would be looking over my shoulder every minute. Now since she knows I'm old enough to judge my own work she never even looks at it. She raised me with a good sense of knowing what to turn in. I'm kind of a perfectionist though I have many after-school activities, friends, and a boyfriend. I still keep up my good grades. My mom isn't like that with my brother though. I guess she was just trying to make me have a bright future. (Christina)

Both students make connections between the chickens and their own families. Sean is fairly intolerant of parents like Hawk who are protective and try to prevent children from becoming independent. Christina recognizes her mother's excessively high standards, but at the same time realizes she has benefited from those standards. She even admits she is a bit like her mother. These students built knowledge through reflection by making connections between Hawk's story and stories of their own experiences.

Students were also able to think critically about their experiences through reflective writing in a fine arts class. The following reflections are evaluative in nature. Each student looks back on his or her experience and searches for what he or she feels is most important to consider in making a work of art. Many students are satisfied to allow the teacher to evaluate the success or failure of their work. In these reflections, the students are judging the key qualities they considered valuable. They are uncovering and critiquing their own values, assumptions and biases, examining their day-to-day strategies, intentions and decisions. Reflection provides students with a way of working through experiences that are both pleasant and difficult.

It hangs by a baby-blue ribbon on a wall in my mother's house. The clay is off-white. My right hand print is about half the size of my right hand now. When I rub my hand over it, it is smooth on the outside but bumpy where my hand touches. I'm glad I made it so that I can put my hand there and think back and remember when I was little. It was difficult to wait until the clay was ready. I was anxious to get on with the hand print. (Alexa)

In fourth grade I made a piece of artwork that took me 1 month to finish. It had about 2,000 triangles on it. I used four colored markers on the whole thing and it was a repeating pattern. It felt good to finish because all my classmates and teachers loved it. My teacher even decided to hang it in the hall. It was difficult to repeat the pattern over and over again but when it was done I was happy. I learned that it is hard to make something good by going fast so I learned to go slow and make it good. (Thomas)

Each reflection is an "individual contemplation" from a past experience of creating a piece of artwork. Alexa and Thomas describe their work in a personal manner with emotion and sensitivity to the way they felt about the piece more than the skills required in making it. They focus on the personal success they felt from their work.

The moral knowledge addressed in these reflections by the students is a "verbal description of the children's intuitive understandings" (Schon, 1983, p. 59). Alexa and Thomas speak about "how to use their time"; a quality of will Sockett (1988a) referred to as *control*. Thomas speaks of his struggle to work for "1 month" with 2,000 pieces that he had to place in detailed patterns. Thomas' learning experience shows carefulness—precision, clarity, conciseness, and determination—the acceptability of the ends.

Reflection takes practice and letting go of the need for the right answer. There are no right or wrong answers, just thoughts to be sorted and organized. Reflecting on one's own experiences can be very difficult; it requires effort. It requires the individual to delve deeply below the surface to find meaning. Some students have little experience with serious reflection and are uncomfortable when the teacher cannot or will not tell them the answer or what to write.

This difficulty was apparent in the last reflection exercise that we presented to a language arts class. In this exercise, we asked students to reflect on a French saying: "You forget the information you learned, but the education remains." In addition, students discussed the idea that "the point of the remark is that education is not just a matter of acquiring information, but the effect of acquiring the information is to change pretty much every aspect of your life, in ways that are typically not represented in the information you acquire" (quoted from a videotape of John Searle's 1995 AERA Conference presentation; see also Searle,

1994, p. 10). At first, students considered writing a reflection on these quotes to be an impossible task. One student remarked, "Why are you asking us to do something so hard?" Other students complained that they had no idea what the quotation meant and had absolutely nothing to say or write on the topic. We reassured them that there was no correct answer, but instead, we were interested in what their thoughts were about the knowledge they acquired in school and what education meant to them. They argued that our request was too difficult and they could not write the reflection. Again we encouraged them to write whatever seemed appropriate to them. Their reflections were astoundingly perceptive! Laura provides an example:

I think this statement is true. I forget a lot of the information we learned during the school year over the summer, but the basic ideas are still there. I also remember small details if they were taught in a funny or interesting way (i.e., Blue − Red = Acid). I also remember information that was gone over time and time again (i.e., Mayflower Compact, Preamble of the Constitution). I think that this idea means that we sometimes forget what we learned, but not how and why we continue to learn. It could also mean that we forget information, but remember skills (i.e., read, write, talk). We might forget what we read, but not how we read, or why we love it. (Laura)

Laura reflected on the quotation and thought about why education is important even if some of what she learns fades from her memory. Laura realizes that although certain teaching techniques help her remember some details and information, her education is more than a bunch of facts. She is learning lifelong skills—reading, writing, speaking. Through her education, she comes to know something about the aesthetics of learning—the love of reading. Laura claims that education teaches her how to learn and why learning is important. Through reflection, students build knowledge about the value of their own education. Reflection provides the opportunity to think deeply about a topic and to personalize knowledge.

Autobiographical Narratives

Making connections between personal experience and knowledge can assist in the construction of knowledge. However, this can seem such a simple matter of common sense that the face-to-face experiences and personal knowledge of our students is frequently overlooked. Some learning can be tied to experiences in the classroom, but indigenous experiences also provide strong influences on learning. In a research study, Campbell (1993) found that when people were asked about their most powerful learning experiences between preschool and high school graduation, few mentioned classroom experiences.

Sage, a sixth-grade student, provides an example of a powerful learning experience that took place outside the classroom. She told us about her first skiing experience with her family and friends. Her father taught her to ski at Bryce Mountain. Lessons were available, but according to Sage, her dad said, "No, you are not having lessons. I'm going to teach you how to ski." Sage explains that she was pretty nervous about learning to ski because the slopes entering the park towered above her:

There was this little hill before this big hill just as we drove up. We saw this hill and said, "Maybe we don't want to do this" [She smiles a great big smile and laughs a bit]. So we got our skis and I could barely walk on them. Dad taught me to go up the hill, and I finally got the hang of going up to the top of the hill. Dad told me to go down it and I said, "No, it took me long enough to get up here" [smiling and chuckling at the memory]. "Why do I have to go back down?" So I went down and Dad tried to teach me how to stop which I couldn't do. I just kept on going. Someone had to stop me. Eventually after I kept going down and down and down. I learned how to stop because Dad told me to jump to the side and you'll stop. I tried that and I stopped.

Once I got the hang of it, Dad told me that I was going on the big hill. So I sat down on the ski lift. Dad told me going up on the ski lift that the ski lift would push me out. There is a mound that you ski down, and then there is a flat area, and there is a slope. So Dad told me the ski lift will push you down it. I thought he meant I would just sit there, and it would push me out. So I just stayed sitting, my dad got off, and I was still sitting. It kept going up, and I was still on it. People were getting off, and I was still on it. So they had to stop it. They had to come up, lift me down off the ski lift, and then Dad took me to the hill and taught me how to snowplow.

During this adventure, Sage demonstrated effort and courage. She mentioned that learning to ski was hard and that it took a really long time to get the hang of it. Many times during our discussion she noted her doubt. She told her father and her friend that she did not think she could ski down the long, steep, slippery, and sometimes icy slopes. But she was courageous and attempted the slopes despite her fears. Sometimes she was successful. "I did fine the first time. I didn't fall at all except for the ski lift, so I figured, I can do this. This is pretty easy." Sometimes she was not as successful: "When I fell down and dragged Dad down the hill, I started panicking thinking, 'This isn't as easy as I thought.'" Sage's story also demonstrates the importance of trust. Sage believed that having her dad help and talk her through the process was an important factor in her learning experience. "I wasn't as nervous because I knew if I fell he would be there to help me." Sage talks about the importance of confidence and moves easily to relating her knowledge gained through her skiing experience to schoolwork.

After I went down the first hill I gained confidence, so it was really easy for me after that. I thought it was easy after I gained confidence. Sometimes things are really difficult and if you gain confidence in doing them then you can do them, especially in math. Math is sometimes really hard. Right now we are doing geometry and the first night we started doing it we got homework. I tried it and I just started crying, "I cannot do this." But Dad came in and started helping me. I figured out how to do it and then I could do it by myself. [Next time I encounter a difficult situation] I could remember I can do it because I went down that big hill and I could do that.

Sage is confident that once she gets the hang of a new challenge she will be successful. Through the telling of her story, Sage has built self-knowledge. "I learned that I could do something that I had never done and it was hard, but I did it. I can probably do anything if I really try." Effort, courage, confidence, and the support of a trustworthy individual in meeting a challenging situation are evident in Sage's story of her skiing adventure. This type of understanding lays the foundation for taking significant risks in the learning process. Autobiographical narrations of indigenous experiences help students recognize and share the intellectual and moral knowledge they construct.

CONNECTING STORYTELLING, REFLECTION, AND AUTOBIOGRAPHICAL NARRATIVE

Three modes of inquiry have been discussed separately as ways students construct knowledge. Consider the possibilities when they are woven together. A student has a memorable experience and in the telling of that story, imaginative or narrative, reflects on the significance of the experience and what can be learned from it. The knowledge uncovered through storytelling, narration, and reflection can be generalized and transferred, yielding even more complex understanding. The combination of experience, storytelling, and autobiographical narration with reflection can produce powerful learning. Robin, a sixth-grade student, wrote a story about her parents' divorce.

When I was 7 years old, I faced the most difficult thing a 7-year-old could face: My parents got divorced. I was devastated when my mom sat me down on the couch and told me about the divorce. I cried for what seemed like ages to me.

I used to sit alone in my room and dig up the memories my dad and I had. There were lots of them because my dad and I were very close. My dad and I used to do tons of things together. He would take me to Kline's Ice Cream, and we both usually got double-dipped chocolate ice cream cones. Then we would get a seat and exchange jokes for hours. After that, my dad would take me to a movie store, and we would purchase at least 10 comedy movies. Then we would go home, get all settled in, and microwave some popcorn. Then the fun started. We would munch on that nice, buttery, juicy popcorn and watch all the movies with an occasional phone call or fridge break in between switching the movies. Those are only a few things my dad and I shared that I will cherish forever!

Then when my mom's and dad's divorce was final, my dad moved out, and I felt like I lost my best friend. My dad and I started to drift further apart and spend less time together. My dad still visits on my birthday and on holidays and calls often, but I still miss him more and more every day when he is not with me.

Now that I am older I've accepted the fact that my mom and dad aren't getting back together. But after all this time there's always going to be room in my heart for memories that me and my dad will hopefully share for years to come!

Robin's story demonstrates the value of narration and reflection. Standing by itself, Robin's story is a moving piece, but taking it one step further, when she reflects on her own writing, Robin constructs knowledge that might otherwise go unrealized.

Doing this piece I had to do a lot of thinking. I had to put the words in just the right order. I had to make each word sound like it was coming from my heart and not my mind. I think that this will be my best piece yet, Mrs. Folly. I put all my effort into it.

I think that what I learned is that getting this story off my chest I can relax now. I also learned that I don't have to keep things all bunched up inside. I can write it into a story and relax. I also learned to respect my mom's wishes and not hold a grudge.

I think this will help me in the future because I know how to handle it. I won't let things get so bunched up that I feel I'll explode. I will talk to someone or write it down on a piece of paper.

What does Robin know through reflecting on her experiences? She knows that effective writing requires effort, and she knows that choosing words carefully gives the writing the author's special voice. Robin has come to realize that what her mom has been telling her is now possible—"Don't hold a grudge." Without anyone telling her, Robin has discovered for herself the value of being a reflective individual. She doesn't have to allow things to remain hidden inside of her, to lie dormant and fester. She knows, through reflection, that she can write down her thoughts or share them with someone she trusts and find meaning in them. Robin has discovered what the author Rodriguez (1982) meant when he said that writing gives him the opportunity to look at his thoughts.

IMPLICATIONS FOR CLASSROOM PRACTICE

Three implications for classroom practice emerged from this study. First, storytelling, reflection, and autobiographical narration can be used to assess student knowledge. Second, the data revealed a tension between the fear of difficulty and the desire for learning to be pleasurable. Third, by using and integrating three modes of inquiry, classroom teachers can facilitate the construction of moral knowledge.

Storytelling, Reflection, and Autobiographical Narratives as Assessments of Student Knowledge

We have found storytelling, reflection, and narratives to be effective modes of inquiry that can be used to assess student knowledge. George demonstrated his knowledge of the ceramic process in his Dick Tracy story. The character, Attitude Dude, identified what the student writers knew about weaving, the vocabulary and skills, as well as the social implications. Garner used his story about the hydrogen atoms, Mike and Moe, with Tom, the oxygen atom, to tell what he knew about chemical reactions. We believe our students were demonstrating a solid understanding of the material by retelling the story in their own, imaginative way.

Teachers can use reflection to assess what students understand from their reading. Sean's reflection from the novel *Woodsong* demonstrates his deep understanding of the relationship between Hawk and the grouse eggs. Through reflection, Sean identifies the larger picture of the parent–child relationship and the need for parents to give their children wings and let them grow.

In the past, when asked to reflect about weaving, students would simply give a definition. Now they reflect about everything they know about weaving, which reveals technical weaving skills, vocabulary, and moral knowledge. Expressive storytelling allows students to relate their knowledge of facts with knowledge from their own experiences. When Dick Tracy's villain escapes because the process of making the clay sword took too long, George makes his knowledge about the ceramic process apparent.

Writing imaginative stories and reflecting about their learning offer different modes of assessment for the classroom teacher. Students find these methods interesting and less threatening than traditional tests. In these types of assessments, the students' drawings and their text reveal what information was misunderstood, thereby allowing the teacher to clarify the information and improve on instruction. In the art class, stories and reflections are modes of assessment that assess creative activities.

The Conflict: Facing Difficulty and Experiencing Pleasure

From our research, we discovered a connection between facing difficulty and experiencing pleasure in learning. Sage was fearful about skiing down the "towering slopes," yet she laughed and smiled as she retold the story of her experience. Sockett (1993) addressed the issue of difficulty in learning, "All learners have to face difficulty—Things worth doing do not drop in our laps" (p. 73).

On the other hand, children must experience learning as pleasurable so they come to intrinsically value education. The negative affects of an uninspired education void of pleasure is often apparent in literature. For example Jane Gradgrind, a character in Dickens (1854) Victorian novel *Hard Times*, was a victim of a very difficult childhood. She experienced very little pleasure in her home and in the classroom with Mr. McChoakumchild. Her education was devoid of emotion and she suffered greatly. Sissy, another character in the book, grew up in the circus experiencing a life of fancy where she had opportunities to use her imagination and experience emotions. When Sissy came to live with the Gradgrinds she encountered difficulty, but her imagination and emotionality helped her to achieve a balance.

We believe that in an effective learning environment students face challenges and experience pleasure. When students encounter difficulty and succeed, the reward is great. It was difficult for Thomas to repeat the pattern on his fourth-grade art project made with 2,000 pieces, but when it was "done [he] was happy and felt good to finish it." In fine arts, some students struggle through the actual hands-on activities and then reflect back on the experience to discover great reward and accomplishment. The telling of stories, reflections, and autobiographical narratives are methods that can be used to help students overcome the fear of failure so they will risk struggling with difficult situations.

Constructing Moral Knowledge and Moral Agency in Classrooms

Teachers strive to help children build moral knowledge in classrooms. To a remarkable degree, patience, determination, commitment, and concentration are terms students in our study used spontaneously to describe the moral knowledge they constructed through their experiences, imagination, and reflection. Sixth-grade art students demonstrated patience as they waited through the ceramic process of air drying and firing. Garner recognized the dangers in disobeying rules made by trusted, caring adults.

In our classrooms, we have found storytelling, reflection, and narratives to be effective methods that assist in making moral knowledge explicit. As teachers we are facilitators, helping students use their moral knowledge to become responsible citizens in a community. This can be a difficult challenge because "Moral education is the leading of men [sic] upward, not putting into the mind knowledge that was not there before" (Kohlberg, 1970, p. 61). In a research study with adults, Reason (1988) used storytelling as a method of inquiry. The participants wrote stories and shared narrative accounts of their experiences. Following the initial story, the participants revisited the stories and reflected on them as a group, reviewing their meaning. Reason termed this follow-up reflection an *echo*. We think this process could be helpful with children to illuminate the caring, patience, self-restraint, and determination our students discovered about themselves.

CONCLUSION

According to Eisner (1985), "The more students conceive of their roles as scholars and critics, as makers and appraisers of things made, the less tendency they will have to regard the world as beyond their power to alter" (p. 35). Through this study, we found that storytelling, reflection, and narratives are modes of inquiry that create opportunities for the construction, recognition, and articulation of knowledge that evolve in the classroom. Through storytelling, reflection, and narratives students make meaning. These methods bring to the surface knowledge that is hidden. The discovery of this knowledge was exciting for the researchers as the students told them about effort and determination, courage and patience, difficulty and fear, openly and with enthusiasm.

As researchers, we built knowledge along with our students. We discovered things about ourselves as teachers and as moral agents. We found a new and greater awareness about the moral education that is occurring in the shadows of our classrooms. For teachers, showing patience and respect to students in the classroom will serve to model moral behavior. As facilitators, our role is to help students to recognize and develop their moral knowledge. "Can we dare to place ourselves in contact with children if we do not have purposes for them, if we do not have dreams for them and plans for helping them to get there?" (Sizer, 1970, p. 5).

In this study, we have encouraged our students to examine their own tacit knowledge and to build on it. When we set students loose, stepping aside as the dispensers of knowledge by allowing them to write stories, share narratives, and reflect on their learning experiences, students made choices about their learning and constructed their own knowledge. We believe that if students come to view themselves as constructors of knowledge instead of receivers of knowledge they will have the courage to tackle the uncertainties and difficulties of life.

PART III

DIVERSITY AND DIALOGUE

Despite the sweeping, totalizing language of educational reform, the real work of education dwells in the particular and the specific. In brief, contexts, personalities, identities, and lifeworlds *matter* to teaching and learning. Children and teachers enter classrooms with past knowledge and experiences, with aspirations and dreams, with fears and anxieties, and with attitudes and beliefs. The parents who send their children to public schools hold a wide spectrum of hopes and expectations regarding classroom learning. The nested communities—business, neighborhood, religious, civic, ethnic—that look to the schools for social and economic amelioration frequently demand contradictory agendas.

All of the above are further complicated by the interplay among people and cultures. Cultural experiences and perspectives shape individual consciousness and sway opinions and beliefs. So it is with those who inhabit schools or try to influence what happens in them. Issues of power and privilege seep through classroom walls and affect the opportunities of children educated within them.

Here, the moral issues that schools face in a society whose ideals demand democratic pluralism are carefully explored, specifically the intersections of individual identities with social institutions. The chapters in this part explore the too often sublimated issues of race, class, and ethnicity in public schools affecting so many lives in public education. How, the authors ask collectively, can public schools as institutions be both responsive to the needs of individuals and also encouraging of a common good? In chapter 9, Mark A. Hicks takes a close look at tensions that emerge when schools pressure children and their teachers to conform to dominant ways of being and knowing. The freedom to develop an authentic identity, he suggests, is crucial for intellectual growth and integrity. He examines this claim through: the notion of identity, specifically for professionals; the ways in which identity is affected by oppression; the requirements for teachers reflecting on and developing new conceptions of identity to transform their practice; and a concept of a multicultural self that helps us avoid the cultural clashes inherent in a monocultural view of the world. Teacher education, he concludes, needs aims coupled with how the narratives of our lives influence the epistemological frameworks we use to make sense of ourselves and the world. It also needs, he claims, a more reasonable, even democratic, process for how we know ourselves and engage others, which will take into account the process of forming an identity in full recognition of the oppositional and interlocking nature of oppression.

In chapter 10, Donna V. Schmidt, Renee Sharp, and Tracy Stephens relate their experiences as teachers working to build a collaborative culture in their schools. They portray vividly the impact of race and class on children's learning experiences and on the collaborative relationships among teachers, specifically through their own stages of development of their own mutual understanding, namely, the formation of their team and the school context of their work; the year-long project they developed together as teachers in the program, and their work as alumni leading discussions with teachers following them in the program.

Elizabeth K. DeMulder and Leo Rigsby in chapter 11 lay out the all-too-frequently divergent expectations of newly arrived immigrant parents and the teachers of their children. They capture poignantly how lived experiences, including both struggles and desires, shape different hopes for children. Students and teachers bring complex lives to contemporary classrooms. Many teachers are unprepared to reach out to students whose lives are so different from their own. Specifically, they probe arenas of conflict and misunderstanding between teachers and immigrant families, discussing the hesitation to communicate about cultural issues, the specific barriers to effective communication, and conflicts of educational values and curricular expectations. They place difficulties around these issues in the larger context of an increasing need to understand the roles of culture in school learning. Together, these chapters argue eloquently for honest and authentic dialogue across differences, no matter how discomforting and difficult, for purposes of learning from them—all for the sake of children.

9

Culture Clash: Teacher and Student Identities and the Procession Toward Freedom

Mark A. Hicks

To understand our world without seating that understanding in the subjectivity of power, life role, and status is to overlook the very nature and interconnectedness of our lives (Belenky et al., 1986; Gilligan, 1982; Hill-Collins, 1986; Miller, 1991). "What about your self" asks the abolitionist, and the slave responds, "I ain't got no self," suggesting an absence of the very nature—the identity—of the slave's being. The slave's language also indicates a lack of agency that allows for the most basic of rights: to be human and to have such respect likewise accorded. In his classic *The Souls of Black Folk*, DuBois (1903) noted that the Black man must deal with the contradiction of " 'twoness' . . . two warring ideals in one dark body" (p. 45). Indeed, the oppression of people of color, women, gay and lesbian people, the disabled, and other socially disenfranchised social groups has found a unifying thread in scholarship (and in popular journalism). One's sense of identity—who we are based on our lived experiences—cannot be underestimated, it is claimed, in the process of learning and schooling. Students schooled with a deflated, nonexistent, or "outlawed" sense of self have considerable difficulty learning, much less taking aggressive ownership of their lives and life choices. Although the rhetoric of fairness and meritocracy are woven throughout public and private life, signifying markers such as "race," "gender," "ethnicity," "sexual orientation," or "disability" still serve as additional hurdles that restrain individuals from meeting their potential.

In teaching teachers in the IET program about the development of individual and group identity, I ask them to consider the notion of "authenticity," and how one's search for one's place in life influences how we relate to each other and, of course, the subsequent implications for schooling. Vibrant discussions usually ensue. Recently, the discussion clearly left some students with deep-seated questions and others in a state of confusion. Many teachers were troubled by my suggestion that students need some sense of what might be called "identity freedom" in their lives, particularly as the process of schooling encourages conformity and monisms of many types. As an African-American gay student who struggled to maintain a healthy sense of self during my own educational experiences (from middle school through graduate school), I recognize that my worldview is extremely foreign to many teachers. That apart, many teacher responses have the effect of limiting student agency.

During the afternoon session when students were working in small groups, I explored this problem by asking one teacher to further explain her point of view. Sarah is a seasoned elementary school teacher who is gentle, attentive to detail, and cares deeply about children and education. I gently reiterated my basic points of why finding one's own voice and purpose is a crucial step in the evolution of identity development. She responded sincerely (and I paraphrase) "I have a son in middle school, and he often tells me that he does not feel as if he can respond to his teachers as he would like. I tell my son, that's the way life is, so you'd better figure out what each teacher wants, and then give it to the teacher." I replied, as I recall, "Sarah, that means that your son never learns how to express what is important to him in any of his classes . . . throughout his entire day, he *never* explores learning from his perspective . . . he never tests how his life-view interacts with the experiences and ideas of others." I continued: "such an edict requires that he never scope out his own terrain, only those of the teacher in power." Her furrowed brow suggested to me that this was a new and troubling insight for her, and my uneasiness was plainly visible, too. This experience came to represent for me a moment of epiphany. How, I thought, could an educator—deeply committed to the unfolding of ideas and the evolution of future democratic citizens—sustain such views? What, really, is her philosophy of education? What logic and life experiences inform that kind of thinking? What insight does this provide into her relationship with her own students and also her relationship with me as her instructor?

In this chapter, I explore the complexities this example raises, by examining the following:

1. The notion of identity, specifically for professionals.
2. The ways in which identity is affected by oppression.
3. Requirements for teachers reflecting on and developing new conceptions of identity to transform their practice.
4. A concept of a multicultural self that helps us avoid the cultural clashes inherent in a monocultural view of the world.

We need a radical, philosophical shift in how we conceptualize our aims for teacher education, which must be coupled with how the narratives of our lives influence the epistemological frameworks we use to make sense of ourselves and the world. We also need more reasonable, even democratic, processes for how we know ourselves and engage others. We need to understand how the process of forming an identity intersects with oppositional interlocking forces of oppression.

TEACHING, LEARNING, AND IDENTITY

Schooling is often "characterized by fear, the denial of individuality, and the affirmation of conformity, control and coercion as appropriate mechanisms for shaping what is considered responsible behavior" (Goldenberg, 1978, p. 8). The implications of this reality is daunting for students. I think of Solomon's (1992) sociological study of Caribbean youth in Canadian schools and their active decision to "not-learn" because the school refused to understand their unique perspective. Such an oppressive context demands that teachers not only serve as exemplars for the ongoing exploration of knowledge and experience, but also understand the constructions that inform how they, themselves, name the world. They should systematically consider the development of their identity and articulate how their life experiences shape their epistemological frameworks. Such introspection lessens the ideological constraints that curtail one's ability to freely think and act and is critical to teachers working with students who are themselves learning how to negotiate the world. If we underestimate the complexity and contradictory nature of the elements that shape our being, I would argue, we miss the point of our lives.

Professional and Personal Identity

Teachers have both personal and professional identities, each crafted by years of experiences that shape what they believe is true. Professionally, if the teacher is consistently poorly and unprofessionally treated by a principal because of his or her ethnicity, for example, he or she may well embody these experiences and recall when dealing with other authority figures. Through a process of self-reflection, that teacher may articulate what it means to have an identity as a "Latino teacher," and how that influences his or her epistemological stance. Such exploration includes the way the teacher teaches and relates with *all* his or her students and how he or she understands the motivation and intentions that guide his or her work. From this informed standpoint, a teacher is far better equipped to respond morally—and within the democratic framework of schooling—to the needs of children whom he or she teaches.

Yet, matters of identity and culture are matters of personhood, not just role. For me, as a person with colored skin and curly hair, I find that I do not have the choice not to think seriously about the construction of who I am and what I represent to others. I think of the age-old question most Black people deal with: What does it mean to *be* a national problem? What does it mean to walk into a room and bring to representation every cross-ethnic encounter with a Black person? What does it mean to know your language and syntax will be overly scrutinized? What does it mean if the collar of my shirt is frayed? Is he poor? Maybe a bohemian? Or, is he simply not a slave to fashion? Then, can he *really* be gay? As a professor and citizen, I want to develop a healthy sense of self in relationship with others; I must grapple head on with such realities. I may have been raised securely in the middle class and hold a doctorate degree from an Ivy League university, but I am still required as a Black gay man to determine what, which Kazantzakis (1960) meditated on, "brings me to birth and then kills me" (p. 51). As a person of color, I have found my "difference" to be both a source of inspiration and pride (tenaciousness in tough situations, the ability to forgive in the face of cruelty, creativity in problem solving, learning how to live authentically within multiple cultures) and a source of pain (being marginalized simply because of prejudging and bias). Probing one's identity as a teacher cannot stop at the role, but must go beneath it to the person.

Walker (1982) reminded us of the power of reflective practice, of taking in the minutiae of one's environment, placing it in some appropriate context, and juxtaposing it with other elements we value. In her book, *The Color Purple*, Walker wrote, "I think it pisses God off if you walk by the color purple in a field somewhere and don't notice it" (p. 203). Sarah's way of thinking, per Walker's view, would certainly piss God off. Looking closely at the events of one's life—particularly those that are out of the ordinary—and how those experiences influence one's view and behavior, can usher paradigmatic shifts. Jarvis (1992) considered, for example, the notion that one can *know* the sanctity of "peace" more fully after having lived in a war-torn country. One must mine the terrain of war—the landscape, smells, the dirtiness, torn relationships, the horror of facing death at every turn—in order to be able to speak knowingly of such an experience. One must be able to comprehend the brutality and impetus of violence to begin to understand the perpetrator.

Identity and Experience

But what is to be gained by having such experiences? Life is not a "uniform uninterrupted march or flow," wrote Dewey (1934). "It is a thing of histories, each with its own plot, its own inception and movement toward its close, each having its own particular rhythmic movement; each with its own unrepeated quality pervading it throughout" (pp. 35–36). Experiences are the building blocks on which we make meaning of yesterday and tomorrow. Understanding those experiences that are especially sensitive to the development of one's identity will lead to a more clear articulation of the procession of our own lives, the meaning of the stepping stones we cross on the way toward a more complicated understanding of ourselves, what we think, and what we value. By failing to encourage her son to undertake that journey, Sarah is mistakenly validating an unsettling disconnection in terms of our lived identities.

It is a real struggle to form an identity in a multicultural world that refuses to name itself as such. Rooted in the notion of finding an inner moral voice that helps us connect with goodness (or God, for many), C. Taylor (1991) suggested that coming to know ourselves equates with becoming "true and full human beings" (p. 26). He argued that the reified tradition, advanced by Descartes, draws us—sometimes unwillingly—into the process of discovery, of placing and naming ourselves within the dominant tradition, which is, of course, what Sarah is urging on her son. In his essay on multiculturalism, C. Taylor (1994) ties this need for naming ourselves to the "valuing" that is associated with framing identity: "identity is who we are and where we're coming from. . . . Being true to myself means being true to my own originality, which is something only I can articulate and discover. In articulating it, I am also defining myself. I am realizing a potentiality that is properly my own" (pp. 31, 33).

This process is a cornerstone of the Western experience of identity development, Taylor claimed, one that each of us considers, and with varying degrees of intensity. Yet, this dominating ideology (which some claim is a myth) complicates the "knowing" process for the multicultural person. DuBois (1903) spoke of a constant "warring" (p. 45) between what dominant society holds as important for one to achieve, and the individual yearnings that insist on some form of unique representation of the self.

Yet teachers, like all of us, have multiple identities. They have identities associated with their gender, generation, economic class, sexual orientation, and so forth. Teachers get socialized into conformity and a fear of risk-taking (Jackson, 1968; Lortie, 1975). Sarah the nonteacher parent, for example, might encourage her son to find his own way, to explore his personal interests that add pleasure and meaning to his life. On the other hand, Sarah the teacher might encourage the same son to suppress his personal desires in order to achieve success in the classroom. Such a scenario points to the deeply rooted contradictions Sarah experiences within the same body. If I were to imagine my way into a student's mind, this has direct implications for me, as her student, trying to develop the capacities needed to negotiate my life. As Sarah's student, I would argue that she is defining herself as a champion of the norm: White, heterosexual culture and cultural standards. I, on the other hand, am trying to negotiate the process of *becoming* myself, which includes balancing two or more worlds (dominant culture, i.e., schools—and my own culture). Problematic here is that my view is in contention with Sarah's, and at the end of the day, she has more power. Her belief that I, as her student, should "learn what's necessary" and assimilate into the dominant expectation trumps my need to determine the essence of my life *apart* from Sarah's expectations of what it should be (echoes from DuBois: two warring ideals in one body, whose dogged strength alone keeps it from being torn asunder). Her static, objectified, and noncritical view of the self shuts down any hope I have for finding my own way. Indeed, I know who I am by determining who/what I am *not*. This inability to name my life as my own motivates me to discover the deeper sources of my self, and to articulate those findings to both myself and others.

IDENTITY AND OPPRESSION

Indeed, power is a significant player in the equation. Those oppressed must always be involved in an internal and external battle for peace of place (Where do I fit?), and peace of mind (Why must I carry this burden?). How do I find a comfortable zone for my nascent self to develop, and how does that interplay with a teacher who wants me to live inside the box she has created for me, not merely inside her classroom but in her mind? Our needs are utterly opposed. My own need for authentic existence and the same struggle that Sarah experiences suggests, de facto, that we are both oppressed, and perhaps for similar reasons. Goldenberg (1978) argued that oppression operates on the premise that "one's experience of oneself is always contingent on an awareness of just how poorly one approximates the images that currently dominate a society" (p. 1). Witness the African-American experience! Yet the craft of teaching, at the close of the twentieth century, continued to mirror the mechanistic and autocratic structures that characterized our early public schools. Increasingly, teachers are at the mercy of bureaucrats and political pundits more invested in self-preservation (or preservation of "their kind") than educative experiences for all children. As with students, so now with teachers.

Oppression claims victims in similar ways. Young (1990) stated that oppression "consists of systematic institutional processes which prevent some people from learning and using satisfying and expansive skills in socially recognized settings, or institutionalized social processes which inhibit people's ability to play and communicate with others or to express their feelings and perspective on social life in contexts where others can listen" (p. 38). By its very nature, oppression is a silent but very present force. Just as a person who does not see a pane of glass is unaware of being constrained by that border, oppression categorizes and limits the ability of individuals to function as an agent of change for the self or Other. One may not see or feel the parameters of oppression and domination, but the restraint is present indeed. Young continued, "Domination consists in institutional conditions which inhibit or prevent people from participating in determining their actions or the conditions of their actions" (p. 38). Of course, oppression and domination are thus forces that constrain one's progress toward the good life. If schools are to be places of liberation for both teachers and students, then they must be places that "contain and support . . . the institutional conditions necessary for the realization" (p. 37) of the values we foster and cherish. The view from my multicultural room ensures that I cherish the freedom to understand and develop one's identity with full awareness of its expansions and constraints.

Let us return to Sarah and her disposition. Sarah's acculturation to the conformity, control, and coercion of schools is strikingly similar to my identity oppression as a Black gay male in White heterosexual society. The culture of schools dulls teachers' sense of agency, even while they struggle to make learning evocative for students (Cohn & Kottkamp, 1993; Goodlad, 1984; Jackson, 1968; Lortie, 1975; Sarason, 1991; Waller, 1967). Teachers are constantly derided in the popular press as unprofessional and incompetent, and their pay— America's barometer for what is valued—represents the low esteem most people hold for them as individuals and workers. As a Black gay man at the outset of the twenty-first century, I face a similar conundrum. I must be mindful of role models like the John Rockers of the Atlanta Braves, of Driving While Black on New Jersey highways, and/or of having an innocent conversation with a would-be homophobe gay-basher at a local eatery. Both Sarah and I are in constant interaction with dominant, oppressive conditions that seek to limit us from achieving our capacity as professionals and human beings.

Yet, although Sarah and I are both prejudged multilaterally, there is a distinct difference between us at the point of our interchange that afternoon; that being an active reflection on the nuance of oppression and the yearning for freedom. My voice yearns for a form of expression so as to sing the jazz of life, weaving in and out of the multiple worlds that give my life meaning. Sarah is writing a Bach organ fugue, where, unlike jazz, expectations are clearly established and little deviation from that expectation is expected or occurs.

Uncritically, Sarah might conclude that she has little ability to "author" her own professional and personal life (see Wood & Lierberman, 2000). Many other teachers who study with us—some of whom have been school teachers for 20 or more years—begin the program with a deflated sense of self-respect and self-esteem. Self-respect, Moody-Adams (1997) argued, occurs when a person places him or herself at a high enough level so as to "make [him or] her willing to contribute" (p. 252) to that which gives him or her significant honor. Self-esteem, on the other hand, is seen as a sense of "*confidence* in one's life plan" (p. 254, italics added). The distinction here is important for this discussion. Teachers who are disillusioned with their professional selves to a sufficient degree have limited capacity for contributing to their own evolution (i.e., development and growth). Likewise, if teachers lack confidence in their ability to strive for their intentions, they are also limited in reaching beyond the boundaries set in place for them. If teachers devalue their professional identity (which is not their "personal" identity), then it is likely they have little appreciation for the identity struggles of others.

The implications of this notion for teaching and learning are very significant. First, think of a nonreflective teacher working with pre- and mid-adolescent students fully engaged in their private (and sometimes very public!) quest to "become" someone important, of being recognized by a significant other. When a teacher has need to suppress the exploration of the learner's identity—regardless of the intention—it has a daunting effect on the student. I am reminded of experiences throughout my schooling where my "becoming" was suppressed by teachers more intent on assimilating me into dominant cultural standards, as opposed to encouraging me to find my own way of developing my intellect alongside my character. Second, the issues crop up in collaborative team efforts between teachers. I recently experienced a cross-racial group of new teachers who were having extreme difficulty in taking responsibility for the identities they brought to their joint project. A White member of the group, who is married to an armchair racist, has difficulty understanding why the African-American member of the team is uncomfortable working on group projects at her home. The African-American member of the group finds it difficult to understand the identity struggle of the White members of the group who don't understand her worldview. Although many issues loom large in such a scenario, the rich and complicated identities of these teachers speak to the need to confront and name the intellectual, developmental, and social justice issues embedded in the context of professionals in collaboration.

A CRITICAL IDENTITY FOR TEACHERS: A NEW SYNTHESIS OF TEACHING AND LEARNING

Moral philosophy has the capacity to pique human consciousness and challenges people to think mindfully and broadly about how they might respond to questions of oppression and teacher identity and their impact on teaching and learning. Sockett (1993) and Hicks and Sockett (2000) remind us of our need to be "moral professionals," referring to the notion of teachers being treated as moral agents, as opposed to technicians with little input into decisions of curriculum practice, governance, and accountability. One of the negative outcomes Hicks and Sockett focus on is the teacher's "struggle against their technically defined role to create humane, caring environments in their classrooms and schools" (p. 2). Needed is a context in which, given the fact that human beings create meaning from their lived experiences, a re-visioning of one's conception of the self can occur so as to honor the diversity and integrity of lived experiences, and still allow for individual freedom. In that context, teachers can redefine their roles as visible agents of transformative thought and practice, and also usher students into fuller conceptions of their emerging selves. Teachers will thus need a philosophical foundation that informs their approach to teaching and lifelong learning, enabling them to break free of epistemological constraints to moral thinking and behavior. On that base, I suggest that a new conception of identity be used to sustain teachers in their work, one that pulls both teacher and student into a relational bond—in full view of the complexity and "messiness" of human relations and growth.

Transformation as the Philosophical Foundation

Hicks and Sockett (2000) posed the notion that *reform*, as popularly tossed about, refers more to "the improvement of an on-going system without any necessary change in goals or purposes, roles, relationships or products" (p. 2).

Transformation, on the other hand, inherently requires a radical change so as to manifest new ways of thinking and being and, hopefully, all at the same time. Responding to the broadly critiqued notion of teacher-as-technician, Hicks and Sockett look at some of ontological experiences of teachers and suggest what may be a broader conceptualization of an educational aim, one that sustains the realities of contradictory thought and experience.

As an aim for professional education of teachers, Hicks and Sockett (2000) posited that transformation becomes an attempt at radical redefinition of teachers' understanding of personal and professional moral agency. Fundamental to this experience is the challenge of engaging teachers in the development of their naïve idealism, in the examination of their existing moral and professional standpoints, and in an extensive process of team-based and individual reflection. This provides for the development of new ways of thinking, some release from the chains of the technical role, and the realization that their moral autonomy can be exercised, not supplanted.

What we would want for teachers like Sarah is to become something akin to what Giroux (1988) called a "transformative intellectual." Our version calls for teachers to engage in a critical discernment that challenges present modalities of truth, considers "what is knowledge" and, finally, enables teachers to think about how their discoveries influence their intentions and behavior. The teacher becomes responsible for such analysis both internally (an ongoing evaluation of his or her own beliefs, practices, and behavior) and, also, externally: How might he or she revisit his or her practice to make sure he or she is being a moral professional who is responsible for the learning experiences of impressionable children who are under his or her care?

The New Identity

How might this be manifested in a teacher? Gently nudged into a more complex exploration of what she really wants for her son and for her students, Sarah would affirm "freedom" to explore and choose a life plan that was appropriate. However, at present, it seems her lack of critical reflection on her professional identity translates into her operating in such a fashion that contradicts her personal identity, say, as a caring mother who wants the best for her son. The transformative intellectual as a professional teacher is called on to think seriously, even in view of her own commitments and values, and consider her behavior and its impact on the evolutionary development of the student.

As one might imagine, the promise of contradiction and conflict is unavoidable. First, Sarah's identities have shaped her life profoundly; for this she should not apologize. Still, she must acknowledge and take responsibility for the facticity of her life and consider how it might influence her students. Second, Sarah (seen now as a composite of teachers I have known) must come to confront the contradictions that her "teacher" role calls into play. She may, qua teacher-self, honor sources outside her domain, but the ability to question her work authority is not contemplated. She may have an ambiguous relationship with authority, vacillating between claiming authority for herself and deciding to remain dominated by an external authority. She may be frightened of operating outside this structure with consequences for her good status as a "team player." Or she may see herself as being static, or not having a view of the world that is forgiving, where boundaries and borderlands shift according to needs or demands. Indeed, she may simply have never thought what it would be like were she to allow a student to "follow his or her authentic star." To exist outside any of these worldviews requires new forms of knowledge and insight, an epistemological shift— sustained by ongoing reflection—that includes a wider base of experience to maintain such broad thinking.

Hicks and Sockett (2000) argued, from the base of experience in the program, that a reflective process of inquiry serves teachers like Sarah quite well. Requiring her to respond to the questions, "what do I mean" and "how do I know" opens up a process of exploration that leads her to consider seriously the intentions and outcomes that result from her aims. For many teachers, teaching has never been an intellectual enterprise, and the moral aspect of working with children has not been considered as an essential aspect of their daily work. Developing identity changes intentions. A shift of intentions encourages a teacher like Sarah to move from her position of being powerless to an active role that brings authority to think and respond, and also engenders a self-initiated authorization to act on behalf of what is best for all the parties involved.

IDENTITY AND CULTURE CLASH

As she acquires this new sense of moral and intellectual authorization, what more would a teacher like Sarah need to know? The essentialist way in which we define ourselves—our identity—encourages us to frame a narrow conception of ourselves and thus others into a similar, unyielding box. The problem is *monoculturalism*, which "universalize[s] the presuppositions and terms of a single culture . . . as embodying and reflecting worthy values" (Goldberg, 1995, p. 5). A monocultural society demands that "any expression that fails to fit into its mold of 'high culture' is summarily denied access to the cultural canon" (p. 5). This insight allows us to blend the traditional school's siren's song of conformity and obedience with the modality of monistic, singular, and universal ways of being.

American schools, as monocultural institutions, function as sites that reproduce the history of this nation with particular attention to the "facts" as we know them, as well as the individuals and values that shaped that evidence (Darder, 1991; Giroux, 1992; Goldberg, 1995; Solomon, 1992). In northern Virginia, where many schools are as ethnically diverse as New York City in the early 1900s, local teachers and administrators are frantically responding to monocultural ideology at work as they did then. Current practices seem to deny what was learned earlier in the history of public schools. It is simply erroneous to claim that wholesale identities change through socialization programs. "Americanization" processes that underlie what it means to be an "American" are rich with narratives of assimilation and identity oppression (Levine, 1996; Sollors, 1996). Darder (1991) and others attested to the impact of this process on minority groups, particular in public schools. In San Antonio, Texas, for example, Mexican-American children in the 1960s and early 1970s were forbidden to speak Spanish in schools, and were monetarily fined for every word of Spanish they spoke. This effort, supported by parents and members of the Bexar County School Board, was an explicit plan to make certain that English and American values were exalted above the values of Mexican-American culture. The plan failed. The concept that multiple cultures could exist within the same dominant culture was not entertained nor, obviously, celebrated. Indeed, some parents of that era believed, as many do today, that second-order cultural affiliation led to fewer opportunities for social and economic advancement. What these parents failed to realize was what sociologists Kallen (1915) and Bourne (1916) recognized at the turn of this century; external signs of acculturation can be observed, but immigrants maintain their identities, as well as the values that give their lives meaning:

Men may change their clothes, their politics, their wives, their religions, their philosophies, to a greater or lesser extent: they cannot change their grandfathers. Jews or Poles or Anglo-Saxons, in order to cease being Jews or Poles or Anglo-Saxons, would have to cease to be. (Kallen, 1915, p. 91)

Still, the theory of monoculturalism holds tenacious sway despite the realities of human experiences. Students from nondominant groups are led to believe that they are incapable of bringing their identities into schools, or, more accurately, into the structures of meaning-making. The well-being of best-selling novelist Cedric Jennings, who attended "one of the worst schools in Washington, D.C." (Suskind, 1999, p. 191), was in danger because he dared to academically excel in his studies. According to his peers, to be "smart" was to lessen his commitment to Blackness, which according to such logic, means that Black culture cannot equate with intelligence. This expression rings true for middle-class African Americans also. As a dean of Columbia College, Columbia University, I had many long and tearful conversations with students of color from White suburbs who, now entrenched on a multiethnic New York City campus, were in turmoil over their ethnic identity. Many had been so deeply ensconced in White, suburban culture, they had no experience of other Black students as scholars, or the realization that one could be "real members" of both Black and White communities within the university. As one student said, "I speak 'White' but I don't look the part . . . where do I fit?"

These problems lead me to believe a different modality of identity needs to be conceptualized, what is being called a *multicultural self*. Denying the tenets of monocultural thought and practice, this new way of being encourages the individual to develop a conceptual framework that legitimizes his or her experiences from a historical, intellectual, and social standpoint, and also serves as the grounds for critiquing the conditions in which those experiences take place. Moreover, this conception works to demystify the fallacious need to live life dualistically: as either Black or White. The conception of a multicultural self allows individuals to think of themselves as being both "White" in terms of literacy in dominant discourse, and Black in terms of cultural literacy, and straight in terms of sexuality, and Catholic in terms of spirituality, and a New Yorker in terms of geographical origin, a Republican in terms of politics, and so forth. Such a conception reflects the interlocking nature of who we are and what we represent, actively denying the myth of monoculturalism. Such an interlocking conception of the self, which resists "either–or" dualities in favor of "both–and" possibilities.

Recognizing a need to become intelligible to oneself holds great benefit in that it promotes the idea that the world was created by humans, and can be likewise dismantled. Indeed, the philosophical foundation of significant social constructions such as "race" and "gender" are unmasked as what Minnich (1990) called "faulty generalizations." Appiah and Gutmann (1996) and Blum (1998), for example, call into question the notion of "race" in society (i.e., rac*ism* may be real, but races are not). De Beauvoir argued the same being true for women (not born, but *becoming* a woman). Gay and lesbian scholars (e.g., Browning, 1996) join that chorus by affirming that, for example, the identity of gay and lesbian persons is a recent phenomenon (i.e., homosexuals may have existed throughout history, but they had no "gay" identity as we know it today). Each of these notions undergirds the empowering agency embedded within us as humanly constructed beings. The facticity of our lives may not be changeable, but our *response* to the facts of our lives is well within our making.

The implications of this notion of identity are powerful for teachers, for in it lies the opening for a new possibility to emerge. The transformative intellectual—the teacher—who considers actively his or her identity is more likely to come into an understanding of the social and intellectual reality of his or her world. Thinking about new openings for identity as a collection of fluid cultures allows one to see every encounter with a student as a "dialogue" (Bohm, 1996), a chance to be changed, to learn something new about oneself and the person(s) with whom one interacts. Each encounter with another person, idea, or situation requires solid skills that enable us to listen, hear, and respond to Other in a way that is respectful and honest, yet still leaves room for disagreement and imaginative dialogue. As a student, I would have cherished such qualities in a teacher. As a teacher, I seek such experiences with my students. I have an urgent need to engage them holistically and seriously, taking into account the life experiences that have shaped the disposition of their cultural selves and how they, in turn, relate to others. How do I, for example, respond to a teacher who accuses me as a male of being sexist? Or, what happens when a student makes an offensive homophobic remark in class? Should such situations be cause for closing doors of understanding, or for opening up new, evocative contexts for learning about our selves and the selves of others?

Thinking of self-as-multicultural encourages the teacher and student to frame a dialogical way of being that recognizes the limitations and possibilities of both of their lives. The self as multiple as opposed to singular allows, a priori, for many variations to exist. The *expectation* is that difference is present, and that the job of the teacher is to come to understand the character of that difference, and put that into an operative motion of discernment. Singular ways of thinking about oneself or the problems that arise out of contradictory identity experiences (i.e., speaking the literacy of "whiteness" within the context of Black culture) is not an allowable option. The multicultural self as dialogically framed denies the supposition that one's culture is static and unyielding to external or future influences. Al Gore's recent admission, for example, that his views on abortion changed over his political career suggests a change in his identity: from a fresh-man senator from Tennessee to a vice president exposed to a world beyond Tennessee. It is a realization that his identity is in a constant state of both agreement, contradiction, conflict with who he is, and who he is becoming. "I am what I am not yet," as Maxine Greene put it. Therein lies the core mechanism of our dialogical, contentious selves: we do not stop the process of becoming until we no longer exist. Teachers responsible for ushering students toward deeper understanding of themselves should be present to this idea.

The multicultural self also demands reflection. A person engaged in mono-cultural ways of knowing and being has little inclination to reach outside what is known. By its very design, monoculturalism refutes all things not normative; it gains its power by resisting the extraneous. Hence, if only one culture exists, it follows that there is no need for contemplation of or valuing other cultural perspectives. The act of reflection changes this by encouraging a shift in the point of reference for what the teacher counts as valuable. Reflection demands that one be accountable for what we know and do, it asks us to delve beneath the "crust of conventionalized and routine consciousness" (Dewey, 1954) that keeps us in the business-as-usual mode of being.

Finally, the construction of a multicultural self suggests a yearning quest for freedom. Here, freedom is the search for understanding the facts that bridle one's sense of possibility and threaten separation from that with which one is in re-lation. The multicultural self is born of the paradoxical that is oppositional and seeks to understand what often is mystifying or daunting. For both the teacher and student, the need for freedom is evident on multiple levels. Intellectually, freedom for the teacher may represent the student's bringing the subject matter to life, or the will to craft new approaches, or a fresh analysis of a subject. It might also encourage the teacher to loose the bonds of hierarchy and learn from the student. Clearly, the student's experience of freedom is similar, but from his or her perspective.

But, there is more. Most important, the search for freedom represents the loosening of ties that lead to a constrictive conception of the self. It is a motivating passion for knowing what is on the other side of the matter, to see the paradox that renders what is familiar to be strange, unjust, oppressive. If one cannot identify the paradoxical in one's life, repressive views have the potential to act boldly and thwart one's ability to name oneself and one's world. This search for a place of freedom, however, leads the multicultural person to an "in-between" space, a nether-world that allows for a coexistence of paradoxes in full view of each other. That which is reasonable, contradictory as well as audaciously hopeful, all dine together at this banquet. Indeed, like the inner workings of the transformative intellectual, the multicultural self is always in the making, questioning the parameters of identity and the knowing thereof, reaching out, challenging selves, while in dialogue with Other.

In summary, given the working nature of dominant institutions such as public schools, we need to be mindful of how these institutions and those who people them shape the identities of future generations. The interlocking nature of oppression ensures that those without agency revisit oppression on each other in subtle and overt ways, killing potential, closing off present and potential, and ultimately reaffirming discriminating views and practices. The outcome of such experiences not only dooms another generation of students to a life of bland experiences, but suggests to them that, indeed, that is the most for which we can hope. The principles that guide schools must be rooted in a form of critical dialogue that requires each of us to move beyond the limiting boundaries of what we know and have experienced firsthand, and to do so with the courage to become who we are not yet.

10

No More "Making Nice"

Donna V. Schmidt, Renee Sharp, and Tracy Stephens

> For the kinds of changes necessary to transform American education, the work force of teachers must do three tough things more or less at once: change how they view learning itself, develop new habits of mind to go with their new cognitive understanding, and simultaneously develop new habits of work—habits that are collegial and public in nature, not solo and private as has been the custom in teaching.
>
> —Meier (1995, p. 140)

Change how we view learning? Develop new habits of thinking? To entertain this ambitious agenda and to accomplish these goals, it is necessary to go beyond superficial relationships, thinking, and action to achieve in-depth collaboration. "Making nice"—saying and doing the polite things that sustain superficial harmony—keeps us from making important changes in our teaching practice, developing authentic collaboration, and developing a critical culture. Our experience in IET taught us that it is imperative to give up "making nice" in order to accomplish the goals Meier proposed.

We came as a teacher team to the program from Cora Kelly Elementary Magnet School in Alexandria, Virginia. In this chapter, we describe and comment on three stages in the development of our mutual understanding through the following:

1. The formation of our team and the school context of our work.
2. The year-long research project we developed together as teachers in the program.

3. Our work as alumnae leading discussions with teachers following us in the program.

We begin, however, with our individual and interactional biographies to ground our discussions.

LOOKING INWARD—THE INDIVIDUALS

We are three teachers with very different backgrounds. Although both Donna and Tracy came to the program as kindergarten teachers, their prior education and experience varied greatly. Tracy, with 4 years of experience, had a bachelor's degree in secondary education with an emphasis on history, geography, and political science. She had previously taught emotionally disturbed children in Grades 3, 4, and 5 and a half-day talented and gifted (TAG) program. Donna received her degree in early childhood education in 1971. Before teaching kindergarten, she taught first, second, fifth, and pre–K classes. Renee, now considered a special teacher, received her elementary education degree in 1973. After spending 14 years in the classroom teaching third and fourth grades, her interests led her to apply for and become the computer lab teacher, where she worked with students ranging from Grades 2 to 6. Later she moved into the position of network resource teacher (NRT) for the school. As NRT, she has an opportunity to work very closely with all staff members.

Each of us was interested in furthering our education. For Donna and Renee, up until this point, the right program had not come along. Traditional master's programs in education were not inspiring. Donna was looking for a graduate program with substance, which would not be a repeat of her undergraduate courses or of lessons learned from experience. She did not want to leave the classroom for administration. In retrospect, she realized she was looking for an environment where she could delve into her own thinking about education, schools, teachers, children, society, and culture. None of the coursework she had taken during her teaching career had excited her or made her feel like she had grown professionally. The emphasis was on content areas of education and activities to do with students. What she needed were opportunities to reflect on an already established career—to consider what she had been doing, why she had been doing it, and how she might reach children better.

Renee was looking for a program that would help her affect change in public education. As an African American, she lived daily with the fact that the current system was failing children of color. She worked with teachers whom she believed were genuinely interested in educating all children but, by default, were continually perpetuating a system that was not working. Her classroom and lab experiences limited her view of education to issues that directly affected her. The position of NRT, however, allowed her a more global view of educational practices at the school. Everyone had struggles and bringing everyone together to create effective change became a major focus for her.

Tracy was interested in furthering her education to raise her status as an educator and to reap the financial benefits that would accompany an advanced degree. She still considered herself a beginning teacher. Each year her ability and confidence grew, but she relied on the guidance and support of her mentor and more experienced teachers. Most of her attention was focused on her own classroom and issues that grew from that environment. With little time to communicate with colleagues, she was unaware of larger issues that impacted teachers, her school, the community, and public education in general.

LOOKING INWARD—THE TEAM AND THE CONTEXT

Bringing our own ideas and expectations, borne of our differing professional stages and experiences, we entered the program and began work as a team. The program promised opportunities for critical reflection, critical reading of educational theory and imaginative literature, dialogue within a community of interpretation and critique, and teacher action research (see chap. 3). The first 2-week summer session awakened our curiosities. It was an intense immersion into a different learning structure that respected the experience teachers brought with them but pushed them to think in ways beyond the traditional. The varied readings, discussions, presentations, and reflective activities engaged us intellectually. We found that teamwork, collaboration, and dialogue were integral components of IET and that mastering the intricacies of these were significant in building professional relationships (see chap. 5).

Development as a Team

In the early stages of our team development, we learned we had to give up "making nice." In a team discussion about *The Power of Their Ideas: Lessons for America from a Small School in Harlem*, we all agreed strongly that "There must be some kind of combination of discomfiture and support—focused always on what does and does not have an impact on children's learning" (Meier, 1995, p. 143). This began a passionate but difficult discussion of race and its effects on us as people and teachers as well as on the children we teach. Renee, an African American, wrote in her journal, "This led us to a discussion of issues that are rarely discussed in an educational setting and almost never in mixed company. They all dealt with race and class." Donna, a Euro-American, expressed her caution in discussing charged topics with African Americans (e.g., the racial makeup of TAG classes) because of the potential risk of being labeled a racist. Tracy's discomfort was obvious. Race was not a topic she had discussed outside her Euro-American family. Tracy and Donna initially "made nice." Then, the discussion turned to racial images portrayed in our society. There was a lengthy discussion of why it is important to be aware of the lack of racial diversity on television and in positions of leadership and power. "Making nice" was no longer possible. We had to persist even though it was uncomfortable. Tracy made the comment "I don't see race." She honestly believed that "not seeing race" was as unprejudiced as one could be. She was resistant to accepting that this was a form of racism that denied others' heritage and cultural identity. Renee probed Tracy's thinking to awaken her to her embeddedness. "How can you not see race? When you go in a store, when you watch TV, when you read the newspaper, how can you not see race?" It was obvious that Renee was becoming increasingly frustrated by Tracy's lack of awareness. However, she continued to make the effort to challenge assumptions without causing Tracy to retreat from the discussion. Tracy had great difficulty seeing any reason to consciously notice race—acknowledging race would be wrong and would make her a racist. To Renee, "not seeing race" meant denying who she was. Finding common ground was a struggle. But their discussion continued—each grappling with ideas that challenged her thinking. Donna's level of participation varied. She understood where Tracy was coming from and had some personal experiences confronting racism. She moved in and out of the dialogue, drawing on her life experiences, in the hope Tracy would make connections that would clarify what Renee was saying. Tracy worked hard to understand the new perspectives she was hearing. This was the beginning of many discussions about race and diversity. Renee's persistence and willingness to talk made it possible for our team to move beyond "making nice" and heighten our awareness of issues of diversity. Tracy's openness to new ideas and theory enabled the team to broaden understandings and place these understandings in context. Donna's talent for drawing on her life experiences and teaching practice helped the team focus on the needs of children and schools.

Teachers enter IET in teams and can quickly learn, through experience, the benefits of collaboration. As our team developed, we faced other challenges that are inevitable in group interactions, which can be worked through by open, honest dialogue about sensitive issues. We learned to appreciate the cultural and experiential differences of each member and to rely on these to construct and deepen our knowledge and understandings. Yet we were encouraged to maintain our individuality within the team and felt appreciated for the individual strengths and knowledge that we brought to the group.

With a common goal—to create the best possible learning conditions for children—we developed team values that helped to sustain us. Communication, flexibility in roles, sensitivity and mutual decision making were key. We worked diligently to balance our own introspection with the ideas of others. We were nonjudgmental, but questioned each other in depth to broaden our own thinking, moving out of embeddedness and encouraging understanding and change. We approached sensitive issues cautiously, but with complete honesty. Responding to body language, we learned to interpret each other's feelings. We knew when to continue to probe and when to move on. Our roles varied with the task at hand, allowing each of us the chance to lead, to follow, and to sometimes act as mediator or interpreter. This flexibility aided us in reaching consensus and meeting deadlines. We had created a safe, nonthreatening environment in which we could test the development of our own voices.

These relationships were a source of strength to each of us. They are also critical in breaking the isolation that is embedded in the teaching profession. But the development of our relationships was not a natural or accidental occurrence, for our professional experience is that collegial relationships are too often superficial. "Make nice" politeness stands in the way of open, honest discussion about deep educational issues. We had to work very hard to reach beyond this superficiality and take the necessary time to dialogue and build our team. We struggled to listen to and understand one another. We developed trust and respect for one another. Time for meaningful dialogue had been essential in this team building process.

Built into this dialogue is the process of reflection. From it, we learned to examine our daily practices critically from multiple perspectives and to uncover our beliefs, values, and biases. Reflection, we believe, helps us to understand ourselves and our practice better so that we can constantly work to improve. We learned to uncover our multicultural selves (see chap. 9) and to understand ourselves as individuals. We were often reminded that, "reflective practice demands individual contemplation and collegial dialogue" (Atwell-Vasey et al., 1995, p. 5).

We were on a journey—as one. Our dialogue and reflection had served to build a sense of unity. We learned to appreciate our differences and use them to the advantage of the group. We offered each other new ways to interpret information. We were forced to discover the roots of our own ideas. We remained determined to transform our classrooms and our schools.

The Context

During the 1996 summer session of the program, we felt strongly that the concepts we were addressing in IET were important to our fellow teachers. By the 1997 session, we felt it was important to open dialogic spaces for our colleagues. We believed it was imperative to rebuild the fragmented sense of community at our magnet school and to open communication in order to strengthen collaboration. This need stemmed from the different programs existing within the school and the many administrative changes that had occurred since March 1995.

Over the years, Cora Kelly Elementary Magnet School had developed three different programs. The magnet students, chosen by lottery, entered a strand of multiage classrooms. This became a school within the school because the children stayed in the same classes together through the third grade. Also, these classes were predominately made up of middle-class and Euro-American children. To provide this type of opportunity for neighborhood African-American and Latino children, two teachers began a separate multiage classroom. But the majority of neighborhood children were in self-contained, straight grade classes. The school had three different faces—strand, multiage, and neighborhood—

which led to fragmentation of students, teachers, and parents. Each face had its own needs and wants.

Between March 1995 and June 1997, the School Board appointed two interim principals, two assistant principals, and a principal. It was difficult for teachers to adjust to the widely varying styles of the individuals filling these positions. This frequent turnover in the school administration also affected efforts to reorganize the school. In an effort to begin unifying the instructional program, teachers made proposals to restructure the school. However, the central administration would not allow program changes to be made until a permanent principal was hired.

At the close of the 1996–1997 school year, the staff was fragmented, isolated, and frustrated. Teachers felt powerless and unable to make changes toward improvement. Furthermore, no forum existed for teachers to come together to consider the school from a global perspective, leaving us more fragmented and isolated. In order to bring all of the school together, our IET team felt an urgency to open dialogue among teachers—to begin the healing process, to reduce the feelings of isolation we felt existed, and to improve collaboration.

In the spring of 1997, a new principal was hired but would not officially begin his principalship until July 1, 1997. In June, he met informally with staff to hear our hopes, dreams, ideas, and goals for the school. Staff members were encouraged to "think outside the box." He listened to, and heard, teachers' ideas. This gave us an opportunity to turn to our experiences in the IET program, for we, too, were part of the school staff and experienced the difficulties of this context.

EXPANDING COLLEGIAL DIALOGUE

During the summer of 1997, we began one of IET's major assignments: a team-based research project. We sought to design a research question to address the unfavorable conditions that existed in the school. Transformation for us meant a renewed feeling of excitement about our work as teachers, a sense of commitment to one another, a strong sense of empowerment, and a deeper commitment to the children we teach. We recognized the skills and knowledge we had gained through our work in IET, which enabled us to see past the difficult realities that existed in our school; we could now imagine possibilities for the future—a school where teachers participate in meaningful dialogue and seek ways of strengthening professional relationships. We wondered how we might bring our own transformation experiences, and our vision, to a research project designed to build collegial community.

Transformation of our school's staff had to begin with dialogue, as it had within our IET team. The dialogue would initially focus on building collegial relationships in which every voice mattered and was heard. It was our hope that, out of this dialogue, a new vision of our school would emerge. We also hoped that a sense of empowerment, gained from strengthened, nurtured relationships and from dialogic experiences, might stimulate individual teacher's agency to initiate change. The major difficulty, we knew, would be to spark the interest of teachers and to create the time and space for dialogue.

Yet we also needed to understand the conditions contributing to a teaching environment that was less than the school we imagined. We speculated that the problems were to be found within the school structure and that the teachers themselves were either isolated or marginalized within the social context of our school, hence the lack of collegial relationships and meaningful dialogue. We each had our own ideas about isolation and marginalization—how these were defined, what they looked like, how they affected our school, and, most importantly, how we might challenge them. They are obviously disadvantageous for teachers, individually and collectively, and for the children they teach.

We came to focus on this question for our research project: "How do opportunities for reflective dialogue among teachers generate new perspectives and insights about teacher professionalism?" We intended to use some of the learning experiences we had in the program in the creation of a research strategy.

The Research Strategy

First, we began our research by asking the faculty to participate in a reflective writing and discussion activity during a faculty meeting. After this, fliers were placed in teachers' mailboxes inviting them to an organizational meeting the following week. Out of 60 teachers, 14 were interested in participating in reflective practice groups and attended this meeting. We wanted the teachers to make the decisions about the structure of the group because we felt strongly that teachers should take ownership of their learning. We shared our own ideas for reflective practice groups: an online conference space, a reflective journaling group, and a book discussion group. They were interested in all of these ideas, but could participate in only one of them due to time constraints. We wanted the group to be meaningful for the participants and practical in terms of their schedules. The consensus of the teachers was to meet every other Tuesday an hour before school opened and discuss a chapter from a book at each meeting. We constantly emphasized that this would be their group.

Second, they asked us for literature suggestions. We wanted a book which would evoke critical thinking and provoke dialogue. We proposed *Other People's Children: Cultural Conflict in the Classroom*, by Delpit (1995). We hoped the group's discussions would transcend the typical daily conversations of teachers and open dialogue about the larger issues of education. This book discussion group met six times, from October 1997 through January 1998. We videotaped the discussions and used the tapes for data analysis.

Third, we were participants in the discussions that followed and tried to strike a balance among these priorities: participating in the group, studying it, and recruiting new members. We were concerned that the group was predominately White and female. One team member regularly invited African-American and male teachers to participate in the discussion group. These teachers occasionally attended. But this lack of diversity continued to concern us throughout our research.

Attendance at the meetings varied but averaged 10 teachers, not including our team members. The other teachers were aware that the discussion group was part of our research project. All teachers were reminded of the meetings through e-mail, fliers in their mailboxes, signs on the outside doors and at the sign-in sheet, personal reminders, and notes taped on their classroom doorknobs the morning of the meeting. Four times, we asked teachers to write reflections on participating in the discussion group. We sent two e-mails asking for reflections and twice asked them to write during the meeting—once at the end and once at the beginning.

Fourth, we wanted to investigate the school's social context to better understand isolation, collaboration, and dialogue within the context of the school, about which we had our own beliefs, perceptions, and assumptions. We speculated that several factors caused isolation and affected collaboration and dialogue: lack of time, differing schedules, physical structure and room location, differing grade levels, teaching assignment, and length of time on the staff. We designed interview questions to probe each of these areas, in order to confirm or disconfirm our assumptions, and to gain a sense of the staff's perceptions.

During a 6-week period beginning the last week of October, we interviewed 16 teachers, approximately one-third of the staff. We felt it was important to hear a variety and balance of teacher voices that were representative of our teaching staff. To determine which teachers to interview, we analyzed the makeup of the staff and used grade-level assignment, gender, ethnicity, length of time on the school's staff, age, teaching experience, and location of classroom to choose interviewees. Initially, we had planned to reinterview all of these teachers at the middle and end of the project. Instead, we conducted a focus group that provided data on how dialogue affected the teachers' perceptions of collaboration and their classroom practice. In early March, we conducted interviews with three teachers. We asked them how they felt about the discussion group, if and how they thought the group affected teacher collaboration, and how participation in the group influenced their own teaching.

Answering the Research Question

"How do opportunities for reflective dialogue among teachers generate new perspectives and insights about teacher professionalism?" When we started to confront this question, we grappled with our own assumptions about the working conditions of teachers within our school, about our beliefs in the need for meaningful dialogue and strengthened collegial relationships among teachers, and our expectations that few opportunities existed for teachers to work toward improved collaboration.

First, our assumption that teachers were isolated and marginalized was, in most instances, supported and then rendered more complex by the stories, experiences and observations of the teachers who participated in our work. Through their voices, we were able to deepen our understanding of the relationships among teachers in our school, and to realize their frailty in the absence of meaningful dialogue.

However, we changed our belief that these isolating conditions were the result of circumstances, which were particular to our school and the teachers who work there. We came to understand how teachers had been coerced into isolation by the hierarchical and bureaucratic structure of schools in general. We also came to realize that many of the marginalizing conditions were the manifestation of the ills of the larger society (e.g., racism) that had permeated the school walls.

Second, dialogue was liberating and transforming. Teachers developed a collective voice and felt empowered toward action. They developed a sense of agency to challenge the hierarchical and bureaucratic structures, which kept them isolated in their thinking and in their practice. Discussions were candid and probing with dialogue focused on culture and race and how these affect teaching practice. The teachers were willing and eager to discuss topics such as silenced voices in schools, language diversity, and illiteracy in our society. We were struck by how willing our colleagues were to share personal connections they were making to their reading. During the November 5 discussion on literacy, we observed this. As the teachers reflected on their reading of Smith's (1995) "Overselling Literacy," they were able to examine literacy through their own experiences and the experiences of others. All present were touched when Tricia became emotional as she shared a story about her own husband, whom she considers to be quite successful. However, he struggles with his own inadequacies in the area of reading when it comes time to read with their children. Tricia's openness created a sensitivity in others that may not have existed previously. Monica and Denise commented about how their own children are not motivated to read for fun because of all the reading they have to do to complete school assignments. Beth talked about her son, a recent college graduate. He took an hourly wage job, rather than pursue a job in his field, in order to have time to read the many books he could not read for pleasure while he was in school. After critical reflection, Beth posed this question to the group: "What does this say about this issue, which is the structure of the instructional system in our culture? What are we *doing*?" These teachers all made connections, constructed knowledge about the more global issues related to literacy, and then began to question the system as it exists within education.

They regularly discussed how they could change their practice to address these problems and help the children they taught. One teacher responded after a discussion of Delpit's (1995), *Other People's Children*:

Reading this book made me more aware of how I speak to the children and my observation of others. I listen to the demeaning remarks and tones of voice from teachers and want to cringe. I can feel the energy being zapped from the children. . . . I see the differences in the treatment and feel sad. If only they knew and realized the effect on the children.

Another teacher commented, "I worry that we can become like the White establishment teachers that Delpit talks about. The ones that are deaf to other voices. Cultural biases are extremely difficult to overcome." They had let go of "saying and doing the polite things which sustain superficial harmony."

Third, dialogue enabled us to reconceptualize teacher professionalism. We realized that, in addition to conventional definitions of professionalism, there existed the need for a sense of unity and belonging. The dialogic space became a caring place, in which concerns and ideas were listened to and where teachers could become part of a professional community. They became unified through their shared concerns, ideas, and frustrations, and felt a sense of validation among their colleagues. Teachers came to appreciate the opportunity to draw on the knowledge and experiences of others to envision new ways of thinking.

Fourth, dialogue challenged teachers' thinking and awakened their imaginations. Teachers were encouraged to think about larger educational issues. The readings, which preceded discussions, were opportunities for individual reflection on such issues as literacy, language and culture, and silenced voices. These readings served as a catalyst for the sort of dialogue which recognized that teachers could have ideas rather than simply implement them. The dialogue heightened the attention of teachers and brought them to consciousness about real issues. It beckoned them to stop, to look, and to attend to the reality of their professional lives and to reinterpret the work of teachers.

In summary, although the circumstances and situations at our school were, of course, particular to our school and staff, such conditions are commonplace in schools. It is often the case that teachers conduct their daily work within the confines of their own classrooms and without participating in collegial discussion or collaboration. Little (Lieberman, 1990) wrote, "In large numbers of schools, and for long periods of time, teachers are colleagues in name only. They work out of sight and hearing of one another, plan and prepare their lessons and materials alone, and struggle on their own to solve most of their instructional, curricular and management problems" (p. 165).

GOING PUBLIC

Candid dialogue had enabled us to develop an expanded understanding of collaboration and teamwork, and we had come to see its transformative power in our own school. This encouraged us to accept an invitation to facilitate an IET seminar that focused on issues of diversity for beginning graduate students.

Diane R. Wood (see chap. 3) and Mark A. Hicks (see chap. 9), our GMU teaching faculty, recognized our commitment to building the kind of collegial relationships essential to meeting our goal of creating the best possible learning conditions for all children. They had been impressed by our honesty, integrity, and willingness to address the most difficult issues in order to meet this objective. Our commitment to authentic collaboration for this purpose was evident throughout our IET experience as we established team norms, engaged in dialogue about important educational issues, collaborated on a research project, and explored the intricate web of relationships that are part of schools and of the teaching profession. Our school team, they wrote, "displayed the greatest degree of professional courage and commitment in creating working relationships that recognized, honored, and eventually thrived on differences."

Preparing the Seminar

We were pleased to have affirmed what we had felt was a significant accomplishment in the growth we made as a team, and as individuals, in understanding race and racism and their impact on public education. Race penetrated every aspect of our work, sometimes because of the issue at hand, and sometimes because of the composition of our school team. Exploring racism was often painful and required courage and inner strength. The invitation gave us an opportunity to share our experiences and expertise with others and to test our newfound voices.

We approached the issue of racism from the standpoint of "whiteness." This was a new and challenging way of examining race and racism for each of us, and we began to question our knowledge and expertise and wondered how to meet the needs of the graduate students, as well as the expectations of the IET faculty. Our preparations began with critical dialogue among our team about whiteness. Asking ourselves "What is whiteness?" we approached the question differently based on our individual lived experiences. We shared our understandings and insights with each other and engaged in critical dialogue about whiteness. Tracy, a Euro-American, was the most resistant to the concept of whiteness and was, for the most part, unaware of specific examples of White privilege. She knew that she had privilege as a White woman, but had difficulty identifying conditions or circumstances in which she recognized her own privilege. Renee, an African American, was most aware of whiteness and was able to share stories and life experiences that helped the team, and Tracy in particular, progressed in understandings about racism. Donna, also a Euro-American, was somewhere in between. She realized that, although she and Renee had brief discussions about race before the formation of our IET team, there was much more she wanted to learn about race and its impact on schools. To move forward, we each had to be willing to accept that our truths would be challenged. We had to be willing to be uncomfortable—to feel anger and frustration, shame and guilt, and outright fear—but ultimately to feel empowered to make changes.

We selected articles and books to read to deepen our understanding about whiteness and in particular, about White privilege. McIntosh's (1998) paper, *White Privilege: Unpacking the Invisible Backpack*, challenges readers to acknowledge that systems of racial dominance exist and to recognize that White privilege is denied and protected by society. The idea was vital in opening our minds to looking differently at racism and how it is thoughtlessly and often unknowingly perpetuated in society and in our schools. For we often had long and in-depth discussions about race and the subtle ways that prejudice infiltrates our thinking. We were willing to bare our souls and to do the work necessary to move beyond our current thinking about race. Delpit's (1995) book *Other People's Children: Cultural Conflict in the Classroom* had helped us cross racial barriers and begin the discussion about race. Delpit's book is an insightful analysis of the imbalance of power and inequity in American classrooms that are the result of miscommunication among races. The focus of our discussions was on the impact of culture and race on the classroom and teaching.

White Privilege: Unpacking the Invisible Backpack took us a major step further. It opened Tracy and Donna's thinking to how much they and many other Whites accept whiteness as the societal norm. Donna wrote, "This was a challenge to subtle, basic beliefs that I hadn't fully acknowledged. I know that racism is something we all participate in and that I have an obligation to be aware of my thinking. The McIntosh article made me systematically unpack my 'backpack of privilege.' " The article caused a shift in Renee's thinking as well. After reading and reflecting on the article, she wrote about new insight she had gained. "Many—probably most—White people are oblivious to their privilege which makes them also oblivious to the *lack* of privilege for minorities. They see the world through eyes that tell them that everything associated with white skin is normal and right. Everything else is abnormal and needs to conform to the 'right way.' " Tracy's admission early in the discussion about *"What is white?"* confirmed Renee's assumption. Tracy responded, "I know this is wrong, but when I try to name White culture I think 'normal,' as in having a conventional family, two kids, suburbs, ballet lessons, and a dog. It's what everyone wants." In her reflection about the article, Renee came to realize that Whites have been socialized to this way of thinking; it is not necessarily a conscious choice. Her reflection and insight helped Tracy and Donna understand how this lack of awareness denies minorities basic rights and power in society. She wrote, "Everything that surrounds us is set up to confirm this lack of power."

We also critically read and reflected as a team on *Racial Healing: Confronting the Fear Between Blacks and Whites* by H. Dalton (1995) and *White Teacher* by Paley (1979). Dalton's book asserts that Blacks and Whites "need not remain estranged" and asserts that what is required to heal relations is up-front communication and risk-taking (p. 248). Paley's *White Teacher* is a personal account of her experiences teaching in a culturally diverse school and her changing perceptions about race. Each of these readings stimulated the discussion about racism and whiteness and brought us to a new level of thinking and understanding about our own racism and the implications for the children we teach. We were well prepared, but still felt nervous and fearful of the reaction of our audience. We were not familiar with these students and realized the multitude of responses they might present. We proceeded, nonetheless, trusting that our professors had laid the foundation for the seminar to be a success.

Teaching Diversity Issues

We decided to use the McIntosh paper and assigned this reading prior to the seminar. The seminar began with a simulation in which racial differences became an issue for our school team. During the simulated dialogue, Renee began unpacking an actual backpack filled with visible examples of White privilege such as mainstream magazines that did not appropriately represent our diverse society, "nude" pantyhose, and "flesh-toned" bandages. We then engaged the group in discussion around the question, "What does it mean to be White?" Following the discussion, small groups of school teams responded to the McIntosh article and brainstormed evidence of White privilege. During this segment, we each facilitated small group discussions and probed teachers who were resistant to the notion of White privilege.

Following a short break, teachers organized into three cohorts to engage in critical dialogue about White culture. Each of us facilitated one of the cohorts. A lunch reading and reflection were assigned. The reading was an excerpt from Dalton's *Racial Healing*. It described an encounter between the author and a Polish woman who is confused by the racial tensions she observes in America. Teachers reflected on the reading and considered personal and professional experiences related to the reading. We provided two questions to guide reflection. How do we get beyond superficial discussions of race? How does the lack of meaningful dialogue about race affect our classrooms and schools? Teachers came together, in small groups, to share their reflections on the lunch reading and to discuss the guiding questions. We again facilitated these group discussions. Dialogue was intense and sometimes confrontational as teachers grappled with racial issues and considered the implications for their practice. The teachers then came together as a large group to reflect on the day.

In reflecting on the day, we concluded that teachers who participated in the seminar reacted in different ways to the concept of whiteness and to the realization that, despite our best intentions, we are all racist. Some teachers were in complete denial and were either hostile or nonreactive to the dialogue. Some were initially resistant, but, over the course of the day, became responsive to the concept of White privilege. They were open to exploring the implications for schools and teaching, and began looking inward and to each other to deepen their understanding. A few were eager to begin the hard work of confronting their own racism. They began to understand that cultural assumptions are deeply rooted and invasive of consciousness. They were willing to participate in candid discussion about this sensitive issue and to consider the possibilities of such dialogue. We believed we were successful in awakening many of the teachers to the subtleties of racism.

This experience reinforced for us that patience, time and determination are necessary to develop a critical culture. It is a mistake to think that moving from "making nice" to serious reflective and in-depth dialogue, especially on topics of intense human importance, can be anything but a lengthy, painstaking process.

CONCLUSION

We have learned many things since we began our journey together. We learned that discussing our practice with each other broadened our knowledge, strengthened our pedagogic theory, and made us aware of diverse points of view. Facing conflict and not "making nice" expanded our thinking in new and exciting ways and made our collaboration meaningful. Individual passion for theory, practice, and diversity made us stronger as a team. We know that teachers need opportunities to develop their collective voice and to become empowered in order to make their knowledge public. We need to grapple with the difficult societal issues that impact our schools. As long as teachers remain isolated within the walls of their classrooms, their knowledge remains hidden—and in the end, it is children who suffer the consequences. Authentic collaboration, rooted in deep, candid, supportive and penetrating dialogue, moves us beyond our own worlds and helps to empower us to make meaningful educational change for our children.

11

Toward a Common Goal: Teachers and Immigrant Families in Dialogue

Elizabeth K. DeMulder and Leo Rigsby

Inside Me

In the past I was hurt by someone I love. I felt emptiness inside me, no one around to listen and understand. Running away, being in a gang, and just wanting to end my life—these are the things I went through.

My father died in the war before I was born. My mom was a slave in Cambodia, working in the rice field. She was scared and lonely. Nowadays my mom brings her past into me. Things she says bring me down. She doesn't understand me and my lifestyle. I'm scared I might carry her problems and mine down the line with my life.

I can't run away from my problems. They will always be a part of me. But now I have more hopes in my life, more friends that understand me, more opportunities to change my thinking about my problems.

Sometimes in life I wish I could be on my own, a free bird.

—Lyn Min, 1999
Cambodian, born in Thailand, age 21

An elementary school teacher shares knowledge of the life of her student prior to his coming to the United States:

As the school year continued, Phakob shared bits and pieces of his life with me. I was astounded by what he had seen and lived through in his short life. He told me of seeing people murdered in the streets of his town and of hiding for his life. How trivial school must have seemed to him!

Figure 11.1. Lyn Min, *Self-portrait*. Photograph courtesy of Lyn Min and the Columbia Heights West Teen Photo Project, Arlington, Virginia.

INTRODUCTION

Students and teachers bring complex lives to contemporary classrooms. Many teachers are unprepared to reach out to students whose lives are so different from their own. In this chapter, we describe some of the arenas of conflict and misunderstanding between teachers and immigrant families and probe these differences. We discuss the following: (1) hesitation to communicate about cultural issues, (2) specific barriers to effective communication, (3) educational values and curricular expectations, and (4) recognition of the importance of communicating about culture. We place difficulties around these issues in the larger context of an increasing need to understand the roles of culture in school learning.

First, it has long been acknowledged that learning takes place by fitting new ideas and information with that which is already experienced and known (Bruner, 1996; Dewey, 1902/1990; Yancey, 1998). Throughout children's development, parents and teachers provide important support to help them connect new experiences to established knowledge as an aid in their learning (Vygotsky, 1978). This support requires that parents and teachers have knowledge of and can respond to the child's individual experience and needs. There is an increasing recognition that teachers' awareness of and respect for the child's home culture and "lived curriculum" (Yancey, 1998) helps children make these important connections. When expectations, values, and experiences of the home culture conflict with school culture, children may have great difficulty in resolving conflicting expectations. Unresolved conflicting expectations can lead to frustration, disengagement, and rebellion. We believe that when the parents, the teacher, and the child can share their experiences and perspectives and discuss ways to negotiate and perhaps reconcile conflicts, this shared understanding of the child provides greater support for the child's learning.

Second, particular obstacles influence the learning experience of many immigrant children in U.S. schools (e.g., Garcia, 1997; Genesee, 1994). These include the following: (1) disconnects between the knowledge and experience the child brings to school and current expectations for learning, (2) language and communication barriers that impede children's understanding and create confusion and anxiety in the learning context, and (3) literacy and communication barriers between parents and teachers. Especially where families also experience economic hardship, schools and teachers can play a significant role in creating "collaboration in an enabling community." Through enhanced communication and support, children and parents may find a way out of poverty and illiteracy (Bruner, 1996).

Third, increasing cultural sensitivity is influencing curricular decisions and pedagogical approaches in schools (Gonzalez & Darling-Hammond, 1997), although attempts to create dialogue around cultural issues do not appear to be common, either within schools or in the wider society. McCollum (1996) identified several communication barriers between parents who are immigrants and the teachers of their children. There is an absence of mutual understanding: Language differences often leave parents frustrated or embarrassed about their inability to make themselves understood. Despite the fact that they are themselves working adults, teachers often expect parents driven by work schedules and child-care issues to be available for conferences on demand. Finally, parents may resist traditional attempts by teachers to "change" them instead of valuing them. It seems that when attitudes reflect an ethnocentric bias (the notion that one's view of the world is inherently "right"), communication, understanding, and children's learning are likely to be further limited and undermined.

Bruner (1996) pointed to a too familiar consequence of ethnocentric bias for immigrant families:

The discovery of the importance of early human interaction and of the role of self-initiated, self-directed activity in the setting of interaction was an important step forward. But it should never have led researchers or educators to so ethnocentric a notion as "cultural deprivation." Such deprivation was interpreted narrowly as the absence of idealized, American middle-class, child-centered child rearing. It left too little room for the cultural identities and particularities of the varied ethnic and lower social-class children and families exposed to it. It left unexamined the nature of human groups and human cultures and the needs human beings have for guarding a sense of their own identity and tradition. (p. 81)

This study explores the perspectives of some immigrant parents of preschoolers and teachers and cultural differences that impact immigrant children in schools. The study was based in the Urban Alternative (see chap. 1) and is part of an ongoing university–community partnership initiative developed by IET with a low-income, predominantly immigrant community.

THE RESEARCH PROCESS

The study originated from faculty reflections on teachers' writings about situations from their classrooms where culture or cultural differences affected children. Throughout one course teachers contributed to Web-based discussions where they shared their classroom experiences, particularly those where cultural differences and perspectives appeared to come into play. As we read through teachers' early narratives, we were struck by their complexity. To get parents' perspectives on some of the issues teachers raised, we established communication with parents through the Urban Alternative's Arlington Mill Community Preschool that DeMulder helped to establish. The preschool, by design, serves children from low-income, non-English-speaking families. We conducted focus group discussions and individual interviews with parents of 15 preschool children and other immigrant community members in English or Spanish, relying on notes and audiotape. We later developed a panel discussion where representatives from the two groups met together.

In an attempt to reinforce our common interest in the children's education, we started each meeting with the parent group by talking about the preschool and the preschool children. They described a variety of cultural backgrounds, educational experiences, and stressful life conditions and shared their life experiences to varying degrees. A breakthrough in our communication in the focus group came when Sonia (further identified later) began to describe her life and the challenges she experienced. Her narrative picked up momentum and the group sat riveted, sometimes asking questions but mostly just listening. Others in the group seemed to open up as they experienced her enthusiasm for telling her story. Indeed, because many of these preschool parents grew up in conditions of severe poverty, the contrast between these parents' experiences and expectations and those of typical middle-class teachers is particularly poignant. We felt that as researchers and educators, it was important to pay attention to these contrasts in order to understand how barriers of communication arise and are to be surmounted.

Preschool parents, relatives, and parents from the community included the following people. The preschool family members' names are pseudonyms, chosen to protect the privacy of the informants.

Liliana (age 33) grew up in Guatemala, the oldest girl in a family of 10 children. Liliana had many responsibilities at home—taking care of the younger children, cleaning the house, and so forth. She went to school between the ages of 7 and 12 but she "didn't pay much attention." Her mother said, "If you're not going to do well, you might as well come home and work." She came to the United States in 1989 "to have a better life because I came from a poor country." She has not been back to Guatemala and does not plan to return. In the United States, Liliana met her husband (who is from El Salvador), and they have a 5-year-old son. Although Liliana understands some spoken English, she neither reads nor writes English and is barely literate in Spanish.

Claudia grew up in El Salvador. Her mother left her in her grandmother's care at the age of 3 months and her father was killed when she was 8 months old. Her grandmother became very sick when Claudia was 2, so her grandmother asked neighbors to care for Claudia. She was not required to go to school, as it was a 2-hour walk from her village, although she did go to school sporadically for 1 year when she was 7 years old. Claudia wanted to come to the United States because she "wanted to escape war and poverty." She made three illegal attempts to get over the border through Mexico. Her third attempt was successful and she immediately sought and found work but she "felt like an outlaw." She was relieved to receive amnesty and a green card in 1991 or 1992. Claudia has two daughters, ages 5 and 3. She understands some English, but prefers to speak in Spanish.

Sonia grew up in El Salvador. Her parents did not think education was important, and her father felt that she should stay at home, even though she wanted to be a nurse or a teacher. Her mother told her she was "crazy" when she said that she wanted to study. Sonia married and divorced young and had one child.

She said she was unable to work or go to school because she had a child. She came to the United States, leaving her daughter, Myra, in El Salvador with her grandmother. Sonia worked as a maid and a nanny and sent for her daughter when Myra was 10 years old. She then "put everything into her daughter" to get her a good education.

Myra (Sonia's daughter—age 21) lived with her grandmother in El Salvador until age 10, when she moved to the United States to live with her mother. Her early experience in U.S. schools was "stressful." She felt "depressed" initially because she could not speak English and did not want to (or know how to) ask for help. However, she learned English quickly and excelled at school in English as a second language (ESL) classes. She received several grants and scholarships because she was very bright and because her mother sought out educational opportunities for her. The transition from ESL classes in middle school to regular high school classes was a "big jump," and Myra struggled and was unhappy. She got pregnant and married at age 16 but finished high school (with honors) and went on to business school with the help of her mother. She worked for several months as an executive secretary but has recently been laid off. She has a daughter, age 5. She is literate in both English and Spanish.

Carlos (Myra's husband—age 22) spent his early years in El Salvador with his father, who was a strict disciplinarian. When he was 12 years old he came to the United States with his older brother to escape the war. He graduated from an alternative high school last year and received a 2-year soccer scholarship to college. Although he hopes to use the scholarship in the future, he now needs to work to support his family. He feels isolated at his job (apartment maintenance) because his boss no longer hires Hispanics "because he says Spanish-speakers are trouble makers." Cultural conflicts are common at work (where his co-workers are mostly from a different cultural and religious group). He and Myra have one daughter. According to Carlos and Myra, each has very different expectations and beliefs about how their daughter should be raised (i.e., Carlos has an authoritarian childrearing style, whereas Myra has more progressive views about the importance of communication, respect, and warmth). They have frequent conflicts over how to raise their daughter.

Lourdes grew up in a small farming village in Mexico and was cared for by an aunt. She only went to school during the year that she was 6 years old. Lourdes said that children in her village went to school in order to learn to read and write. Like all children in her village, she worked in the fields with her family after school and, after age 6, instead of going to school. She came to the United States in 1991 with her husband in order to work and to find "a better life." She says she likes it in the United States because there is "so much more time to learn." She has three children, ages 7, 6, and 4. Lourdes speaks a little English, is not literate in English and is minimally literate in Spanish.

Jaime grew up in Ecuador. His father was an English teacher and his mother was a nurse. His father left the family when Jaime was young, leaving his mother with seven children. His uncle provided some support and his mother "believed in education," so, over a period of several years, Jaime attended private school when there was enough money. He came to the United States in 1981, finished high school here, and started college. He got married "too early," dropped out of college, and is now a single parent with two young daughters, ages 6 and 4. He speaks English well and is literate in both Spanish and English.

Other members of the group included Cesar (uncle from Bolivia), Delia (parent from El Salvador), Mercedes (parent from El Salvador), Martha (sister from Bolivia), Mahesh (parent from India), Asha (parent from India), Thuan (parent from Vietnam), Sandra (parent from Mexico), Sophia (community bilingual outreach worker), Hawa (community bilingual outreach worker from Somalia), Wilfredo (community historian from Peru), Mamta (preschool teacher from India), Todd (Urban Alternative director), Angela and Selma (graduate research assistants), and the authors.

As teachers engaged in Web forum discussions and parents participated in focus groups and interviews, it became clear that what we were learning from parents would be very useful for teachers to hear and vice versa; teachers were making judgments about the engagement and performances of children in the absence of knowledge about the home lives and prior learning of the families. It was also clear that an understanding by parents of the perspectives and expectations of teachers would have profound implications for the welfare of children. We invited several members of the immigrant community to join the teachers enrolled in the master's program. Jaime, Hawa, and Mamta talked with the teachers in the class about their cultures and potential conflicts for children in schools.

The panel discussion gave immigrant parents and teachers an opportunity to discuss their views on the complementary roles of schools and families. We explored issues that were raised in the Web-based forum and in the immigrant parent focus groups, and everyone gave written responses to these discussions. Each participant was asked to indicate whether and in what ways the dialogue was useful and to describe what they had learned, what surprised them, and what they would like to know more about.

Creating these three spaces allowed teachers and parents to talk among themselves and to each other.

1. In focus group meetings, parents and other immigrant community members described their experiences and discussed their expectations and beliefs about school-related issues.

2. The Web forum allowed teachers to explore together the cultural issues that were significant to them in their schools and classrooms, raising questions and examining their assumptions.

3. The panel discussion brought the voices together, informing and challenging some long-held beliefs.

These exchanges of perspectives revealed the barriers that challenge the relationships between teachers and immigrant parents (e.g., lack of common experience, communication problems, creating an environment of trust, and so forth). Scheduling constraints, common for teacher–parent meetings, presented problems for us, too: Although we invited several community members to attend the Saturday panel discussion meeting, most could not attend because they had work commitments or other scheduling conflicts.

Finally, it was frankly much easier for us to consider and take into account the views of middle-class American teachers than it was to capture and document the views of non-English-speaking, less literate, immigrant parents. Teachers had a forum for expressing their views in written form, whereas with parents, it was necessary to rely on discussions and interviews, with their inherent cross-cultural and language complexities that made the whole experience more difficult to document. Indeed, we were in danger of losing sight of immigrant parents' views and focusing on middle-class teachers' expectations, beliefs, hopes, and dreams because it was so much easier to collect and analyze that data.

CULTURAL COMPLEXITIES IN RELATIONS BETWEEN TEACHERS AND IMMIGRANT FAMILIES

Reluctant Discussants

Parents and teachers discussed their beliefs and expectations concerning children and schooling against the background of differences in education, economic situations, and cultural values and beliefs. They sometimes described their perspectives concerning the roles people and schools play in the form "teachers should," "parents should," and "schools should." In fact, however, differing beliefs and expectations that may be embedded in cultural traditions or differing life experiences are not commonly discussed openly. Teachers may make negative assumptions and judgments but say nothing, for fear of not being "politically correct." One teacher said that multiculturalism is a "touchy" subject, and that "Usually it's people who are considered in the majority who are confused or don't quite understand what all the controversy is about." An African-American teacher expressed her discomfort and concern with the teachers' discussion. She wrote,

I am not comfortable discussing multicultural issues because not only am I a minority in my everyday world, I am also a minority on this forum. I am having to write and read about issues that I only discuss with close friends or friends in my culture. It distresses me to read about students whose behavior does not fit into the scheme of things in your classrooms. I also have students in my classroom who are not of color who do not fit into the scheme of things. I do not even consider that this behavior is because of their culture. Are there any successes in your classrooms with the students of color? I'm sure there are minority students who come to you without the nonsense behavior some of you write about and are ready to be academically challenged. It would be refreshing to read about them.

Although some immigrant parents were willing to share their expectations and beliefs in the focus group and in the school setting, others expressed discomfort in discussing cultural differences in the group and indicated that they have not discussed any problems or concerns with teachers. When asked whether they would speak up if there were things that they didn't approve of or agree with at school, several immigrant parents said they would feel free to do that. None said they would not speak up. However, when asked about "the worst thing that had happened to your child at school," several parents responded "Nothing," suggesting that they may be uncomfortable bringing up potential conflicts. This reluctance on the part of teachers and parents to address differing beliefs and expectations may well lead to further misunderstanding arising from lack of information, lack of trust, and so forth. We hoped that the separate discussions would serve as preliminary steps to overcome this reluctance to openly explore cultural issues and potentially conflicting views. The discussions certainly reinforced the notion that differing experiences lead to differing beliefs, expectations, and values concerning schooling and the roles parents and teachers should take.

Perhaps the most fundamental issue we encountered, both among teachers and among immigrant parents, is a reluctance to talk at all about issues of cultural difference or conflict. There is a general reluctance in this society to deal with issues that can be tinged with racism or that could provoke charges of being "insensitive." Given the politically charged character of such discussions, people find it more comfortable to ignore the issues, rather than take the chance of causing hurt or anger. This reluctance to deal with issues of cultural difference exacerbates difficulties in communication between teachers and immigrant parents and contributes to communication barriers.

Specific Communication Barriers

Teachers discussed the struggles they encountered in trying to communicate with and involve immigrant parents. One teacher wrote:

I would also assume that if I moved my family to another country because I thought the education there would benefit them I think I would also make an honest effort myself to learn the language with my children. So many people talk about students whose parents do not speak English at home and that presents a definite breakdown in communication between the school and that home. I would want to know how my student was doing in school not take his word that he is good.

In contrast to this teacher's assumptions, there was a general recognition among parents that they needed to learn English. Some related their struggles to learn English, and many of the parents had attended and were currently attending English language classes through local community organizations. However, many of the parents expressed the wish that there were more teachers who spoke their child's home language, because teachers could then more effectively help their children learn English, help their children understand what is expected of them, and help parents communicate with other teachers. Both Claudia and Liliana said they often do not understand what the teacher says when she calls on the phone, but that they respond as much as they can. One preschool teacher speaks Spanish and English, and the head teacher speaks Hindi. This facilitates communication for Latino and Indian children in the classroom and between school and home.

Parents emphasized not only the need to learn English, but also the importance of retaining and honoring their home language and culture. Thuan suggested that because her children live in the United States, they need "to be in American culture," and that includes learning the English language. She wants her children to be bilingual so she teaches them Vietnamese at home and expects them to learn English at school. She expressed the view that "children are lazy," and that even though they understand English in school, they are tired after school and so object to doing homework in English, saying they don't understand it. Her child's elementary school teacher, she said, helps her to understand what she needs to do to help her child do homework.

Claudia expressed her dismay at communicating with a non-Spanish-speaking preschool teacher. Not only did they have difficulty communicating, but also she claimed that the language barrier in the classroom adversely affected her daughter. Because the child did not understand the teacher, she "didn't listen to her, didn't behave, and did whatever she wanted," and so, for a while, did not want to go to school. Myra was frustrated with her high school when she arrived in this country as a teenager speaking little English. She said the classes were "humungous" and the teachers were too busy to help her when she didn't understand. Knowing about cultural values is useful, she said, but teachers needed to have the language skills to reach the children as well.

Teachers raised issues of relevancy and power in their discussions of language differences and English language acquisition in U.S. schools.

I do not think that it is necessary to set up separate schools that are primarily non-English . . . the fastest way to learn the language is to be immersed in it. If you set up a school where little English is spoken, those students will not learn the language. Even though I believe that no one's cultural identity should be quelled, English is the official language and is what is used to get business done. Why not learn English at school and speak your native tongue at home? There has to be a point where a non-native culture must compromise in order to integrate with the larger "foreign" society.

In a similar vein, Georgene wrote,

In his book, *The Opening of the American Mind*, Levine [1996] speaks of his "twoness." He maintains his Jewish culture and celebrates it, but he also recognizes that he is an "American" and celebrates the mainstream culture. Does allowing acceptance of the cultural language only, instead of becoming fluent in the "mainstream" language, set our Hispanic population up for failure in the "power" culture? I believe this would be unacceptable to Delpit [1995], author of *Other People's Children*. She maintains that you must possess the tools of power in order to be in power. Fluency in the English language would seem to be high on the list of tools of power.

One teacher had this insight regarding ethnocentric attitudes:

I have had the opportunities to live many places around the world. I spent some time in Korea, and Germany. In Korea, communication was difficult, many hand gestures were used, I can remember smiling, nodding, and replying with YES, even when I did not have a clue what I was replying yes to. I can understand those ESOL students' YES reactions to our questions. In Europe, many Germans also spoke English; they were taught at an early age. Germans were always friendly and anxious to speak in English. Frenchmen were not, they always seemed to be looking down their nose at me. I never felt very welcome in France, I now wonder if that is how some recent immigrants feel about Americans today? The real problem lies not in the language spoken but in the perceptions we all harbor regarding those that are not like us.

Communication issues go beyond language barriers, according to some parents and teachers. Several parents said that although they felt isolated in the United States with little social support, they also suggested that communication was difficult, saying they "don't befriend people easily" or that they "need a sense of trust" or that they are "reserved from experience." When asked what schools and communities could do to help support communication and trust, one parent said that often "they don't let the families have voices—they try things but without input." When Jaime, Mamta, and Hawa met with the teachers for the panel discussion, they talked about the great respect that was given to teachers in their countries and attitudes about sharing problems. Several teachers suggested that awareness of these attitudes was essential to understand why some immigrant parents might be reluctant to get involved in schools. One teacher wrote, "I found it informative when [Mamta] spoke of how most immigrant parents hold educators in such high esteem so as to not question authority. How in some cultures you do not discuss problems outside the family circle. This makes it especially hard for me as a special education teacher."

Language studies have shown that learning a language is much easier when one is a child than when one is an adult. Furthermore, many of today's immigrant adults come from societies with low levels of literacy. Many immigrant adults are not literate in their own language, much less in English. For many groups, there is a tendency to reproduce aspects of the home culture by congregating in urban neighborhoods to support each other and to support the development of stores, churches, and services by and for individuals from their homeland. In fact, many of the parents in our focus groups did not find that it was necessary to learn English in order to live in their community (although they did want to learn English for the sake of their children). It is perhaps easy for American teachers to forget these facts when dealing with immigrant families. Placing multilanguage signs in schools is no substitute for having adults in schools who understand and speak the languages spoken in the homes of their students. Teachers' impatience with immigrant parents belies the desperate struggle of parents to both maintain their native culture and assimilate aspects of the adopted culture.

Educational Values and Curricular Assumptions

Teachers wrote in the forum that parents did not always appear to value education. One teacher, who teaches in a "very diverse school," wrote:

Where I now teach the parents are very trusting of our ability as teachers to teach their children. While it is nice to be so trusted, they do not always value education. It is very apparent when most of the year is spent addressing behavioral issues before we can begin addressing academics. We are constantly torn between keeping our expectations high and not criticizing their parent's lack of support of our high expectations. I also think that the parents expect us to keep our standards high here at school and that school and home are separate.

In contrast, in the focus groups and interviews with parents and other family members, no one expressed ambivalence about the value of education. In fact, many in the group said that they came to this country for the express purpose of creating educational opportunities for their children that they never had. For example, when Sonia was growing up in El Salvador, her parents discouraged her from pursuing education. She said that she came to this country to make a life for herself and her daughter, Myra. She looked for educational opportunities for Myra and actively discouraged her from dropping out of high school saying, "You must stay in school or forget I'm your mother!"

Cesar said his parents were "stricter about education than many other Latino and American families and that was a good thing for me." He suggested that "some parents don't care" about their children's education but that he and his sister "were raised to do the best that we can—our parents encouraged us to do well in our studies." For example, he said, "My parents did not allow me to work so that I could concentrate on school." Cesar said his parents were "definitely always proud of us." When asked why he thought his parents were strict, Cesar said, "They didn't have much education and they felt that their children could do anything if they could get a good education."

During the course of an interview with Claudia, we asked whether she planned to return to El Salvador. Claudia said, "It would be beautiful to go to El Salvador. But it would be the same. I could only work on a farm for little money.

Maybe when my children are grown up and making their own life, they are safe in their own life, I might go back to stay for my last days. Now my children in America have a chance to study and get a good career." Although the parents said that the preschool their children attend is good, several parents worried that the curriculum might not be meeting their children's needs. Claudia said, "We think that children have wasted their time doing things that are not related to "A–E–I–O–U." She said that she "only got to first grade but they had us read a book and practice vowels." When she watches her child in preschool, there are "lots of games and toys, with not so much focus on books." She said she would like to see that "they have 2 hours to drill the alphabet and then draw and paint—first they need to sit and focus." Thuan agreed with Claudia that the children did not have enough structure (e.g., there was too much emphasis on "telling stories and singing" and "too much free play"). Jaime expressed the view that "kids learn by playing." He, too, was concerned that his preschool-age child would not be prepared for formal schooling (and he got the kindergarten curriculum from the elementary school to give to his daughter's preschool teacher). He also indicated that he thought his child would benefit from a full-day preschool program.

One teacher responded to Jaime's educational views:

I was surprised to hear that the single parent was heavily involved in his children's education. Also, he wants them to learn about their culture and where he came from, but he also wants them to learn about America and the American culture. I think this surprised me because I currently work with a Hispanic family who refuses to speak English. Talk about a barrier! I guess this is a topic I would like to discuss further—what to do when a family you work with refuses to speak English. To me using a translator seems so impersonal.

One high school teacher is very disturbed by the challenges of meeting the needs of individual children, as expressed in the helplessness and perplexity teachers have in facing these problems: "Unfortunately, it is difficult for us to forge ahead as Ashton-Warner (1963) did—a teacher with a vision of how culture was related to learning and the freedom to act upon her intuitions. . . . We do not have the same freedom. Curriculum content is mandated by the school division and the state."

These data suggest that not only do teachers and parents have different perspectives on the learning of their children, they are often misinformed about each others' perspectives. What teachers observe to be lack of caring about children, conversations with immigrant parents reveal to be awestruck respect for the position of teachers. Parents in many cases hold higher expectations of their children and the learning context than teachers themselves hold. It appears that parents fail to intervene in the school context because of their lack of a sense of efficacy to intervene. Furthermore, at least for the Latino parents in these focus groups, early educational experiences were ones in which teachers commanded attention and forced learning on the students, through corporal punishment if necessary. The teacher, meantime, looks past the child to the home, wondering why the parents do not take a more active role in forcing the child to behave and to do catch-up work at home.

The Value of Communicating About Culture

Many parents indicated a desire to share information about culture. Liliana said she hoped and expected that her child would retain his home culture, and said that she teaches "in my house about my culture and other cultures." When asked whether discussion of cultural differences was important in schools, Claudia said, "Yes, you should talk that way. If you talk about differences, the children will learn about their own and other cultures and be able to compare them." Cesar, however, said he "doesn't think it matters."

Teachers indicated that learning about different cultural beliefs and practices gave them insights about the value of creating connections with parents in ways that would support children's learning.

I found it informative to hear that it is important to ask questions of the parents as to what their expectations are for their child's education. . . . In the past I have not asked questions for fear of offending someone. I had not thought of the parents' concern of not being able to communicate with the child who has decided to learn English, but not the native language. . . . The parents must be so frustrated to not be able to communicate with their child, and the child will not realize until they are grown up how much of their heritage they have missed, by not being able to experience language and traditional language through stories, rhymes, etc.—I had never thought of this missed opportunity of a culture.

Teachers also found that they had many important insights from the panel discussion and were enthusiastic about continuing a dialogue:

I realize how much I assume and take for granted. It never occurred to me that children who have never had toys would not know how to play. Doesn't everyone have toys? After today's discussion—"No." How scary it must be to come to a new country with a new language, new values, new expectations with no one to guide you through. These panel members certainly have my respect. I would like to hear more about how the children are affected by such a drastic move and how their past experiences affect their ability to trust anyone in a strange environment.

One elementary school teacher described how she capitalized on the cultural background of Saira, whose Mexican parents speak only Spanish at home. Saira had said she spoke no Spanish but corrected her on the pronunciation of an author's name.

I [was] a little surprised by her response and frankly so [was] she. She admitted then that she does speak Spanish. I got so excited and . . . told her how special she was to be able to speak and understand two different languages. Excitement began to show on her face as well. In fact at the end of the year, I had all of my students write a letter to a teacher they might have next year. . . . Saira wrote two full pages. One of these pages was about how she was special because she was a "Spanish kid" and could speak two languages.

The teacher continues:

There are several things that are important about this story. First of all, by learning about Saira's background, I was able to understand the difficulties she was having with reading in order to help her. Saira received no assistance at home with reading and was often called upon to read things for her parents and translate them! She began the school year with limited language skills and by focusing on her needs and doing a lot of "skill and drill" she finished as one of my top kids, fully armed for second grade. She was even able to recognize her own growth and was aware that by the end of the year she was a really good reader. She wouldn't put books down!

These views of parents and teachers reinforce the importance of communication about culture and cultural differences. Whether or not it is ultimately possible for immigrant families to preserve their home culture in the face of the enormous pressures from school, popular culture, and peers, it is clear that when teachers know about and can build on children's home culture, children will benefit.

CONCLUSION

Our conclusions about human experience across cultural boundaries have to remain tenuous, given the limited context and small number of informants in our study. On the other hand, we have clearly uncovered a number of issues that demand further study and deep reflection. The non-English-speaking segment of the U.S. population is the most rapidly increasing segment. The issues we have discussed here can only grow in importance.

Foremost in our discussions with teachers and immigrant parents is the stark fact that everybody is reluctant to talk about issues of cultural difference and cultural conflict. Nobody wants to be insensitive or to open themselves to charges of racism. They are interacting in a context of uncertainty that does not promote risk-taking. This applies both to the context of the research and to the context of home–school relations. Their context of interaction hides the common purposes these parents and teachers have and exaggerates their misunderstandings and differences. We believe that both teachers and parents have feelings of ambivalence about these issues. They may be uncertain about their own beliefs and unsure of the perspectives of others with whom they have cause to discuss them.

Teachers do not always recognize the difficulties many immigrant parents have in learning a new language. They often do not take into account the greater difficulty parents not literate in their native language have in becoming literate in English. They do not take into account that parents may be both intimidated by and embarrassed over their lack of English literacy. Parents understand the need to become literate in English but may not have literacy skills to build on or resources with which to develop literacy in English. Even when these parents understand the kinds of activities that are needed to support the schoolwork of their children, they may not be able to participate in those activities using English. For many of the Latino parents in our focus groups, the struggle to learn English occurs in a community environment where there is little necessity to speak English. All their neighbors and neighborhood merchants speak Spanish!

Research on language development and literacy emphasizes that language learning in the usual case comes more easily for children than for adults (Reich, 1986). This gives particular urgency to effective work with children from non-English backgrounds. This urgency in turn points to the need to build effective communication links between schools and families who do not have English literacy. Our research demonstrates the extra difficulty faced by those who take responsibility for cultivating these links.

A crucial resource for the tasks of establishing effective communication across all issues we have discussed in this paper is bilingual teachers. Of course, bilingual teachers have to be bilingual in the "right" languages. In schools like those in the area served by the Arlington Mill Preschool and the Urban Alternative, families sending children to the school speak dozens of different languages. One elementary school in that area reports that its children represent 87 different home languages. One bilingual teacher in a classroom can never solve the problem of communication between these diverse homes and the school! The guiding idea in finding a solution is to create an environment in which all children can learn. Such an environment will have to be one that fosters the understanding of different beliefs and expectations, encourages more effective communication between home and school, and responds appropriately to the diverse learning needs of all children. Such an environment will have to draw on all the linguistic resources of homes, communities, and schools.

Epilogue: Hopes and Dreams of Teachers and Preschool Parents

Parents and teachers have common core concerns for supporting children's healthy development and prosperity. "We are all striving toward a common goal," wrote one teacher. "We are all in this for the children. I feel like I must do whatever it takes to further my students' education. If this means learning the language, calling parents daily, or making a home visit—whatever it takes. Trying to strengthen the home/school connection is difficult to do alone, but if you keep working at it, then progress will occur."

Figure 11.2. Albert Hernandez, *Self-portrait*. Photograph courtesy of Albert Hernandez and the Columbia Heights West Teen Photo Project, Arlington, Virginia.

Although aware of the challenges, parents still described the United States as a "land of opportunity," and are optimistic about their children's future. They said that they hoped and expected that their children would have a better life than they had. Myra thinks that her daughter will make more of her opportunities than she did because her daughter knows the language at an early age. Her goal is for her daughter to go to college. Liliana wants her son to be a doctor or an engineer. She believes that he will have these opportunities. Liliana said laughing, "sometimes he wants to be a chef—a good chef—and sometimes he wants to be a carpenter. It is important that he is good at what he chooses to do."

Several parents said that they hoped there would be an increase in bilingual teachers in schools who would help their children learn. Thuan expressed the hope that her children "would be good kids" and that the English language would "not be too hard for them." Sandra expressed concern that her older children did not want to stay in school and she very much wanted them to "keep studying." Claudia said, "Now my children are in America, they have a chance to study and get a good career. I will not let my children forget Spanish. They must be bilingual. I will never let them say, 'I don't speak Spanish.' They learn to speak well the Spanish and the English." Later Claudia said, "The best of America is probably the real security that the most limited persons have to take care of the children."

Cesar, a young adult who came to this country as a teenager, suggested ways that schools and communities can support immigrant children, to help them feel that they belong in school: "Find out what they like—their hobbies, help them see how they could make a business of it. Push education. Help them know to stay out of trouble because who you hang with is a problem. Teachers and parents need to encourage them, find out what interests they have, some special talents."

The Urban Alternative has sponsored community activities that help children and teens develop their interests and talents. Albert, another member of the Columbia Heights West Teen Photo Project, wrote the following narrative to accompany a self-portrait. We think it is appropriate to end as we began, with the voices of the children.

Remembering

Remembering my childhood in L.A.
Living in a neighborhood full with gangs.
Afraid of following a path of drugs and violence.
Feeling trapped by my surroundings.
Worrying, would I be able to go to school tomorrow?
I was on the edge of taking the wrong way.
I was tempted. I was confused.
But, I hope that someday I would leave this all behind.

That day arrived. We left L.A.
A new life in Arlington.

Living in a community that supports me.
Less afraid of people around me.
Feeling relief that a boulder was laid off my shoulders.
Not worrying about being gunned down for stepping into the wrong neighbor-
   hood.
Now I have started a new way of living.

Now remembering all I've gone through
I wish that no other teenagers would choose to take the wrong path.

Albert Hernandez, 1999
Born in El Salvador, age 18

PART IV

FRAMING PROFESSIONAL CRITIQUE

For those who espouse the moral paradigm, an honest dedication to self-critique and a willingness to take risks when advocating for positive change is paramount. They will be prepared to reveal tensions in their professional lives, which often are not found in print as they confront norms in bureaucratic institutions. However, a dedication to continuous improvement in the context of critical cultures calls for risk and disclosure—a type of truth that can be found only in the passionate stories of people who care. The risks lie in naming problems, which many would prefer to have left quiescent.

Yet, this is not a matter of venting emotion or munching sour grapes. It is necessary to the kind of continuous improvement described by Deming (1995) and his followers from whom IET has drawn structures and advice for supporting and nurturing innovation. Continuous improvement, considered one of the common characteristics of Total Quality Management (TQM), claims that all aspects of work and business are viewed as everyone's responsibility (Kinlaw, 1992). No practice, policy, tool, system, service, or product is exempt from close inspection and change. Each person is seen as a potential source of fresh ideas and innovation. Kinlaw claimed that until reflection is viewed as normative, improvement will be a response to pain (putting out fires) as opposed to creating new opportunities, which is the most proactive strategy for improvement.

Across the whole gamut of professional life, of course, there are many ways in which reflections can be framed (Schon & Rein, 1994). Individual experience is necessarily different, of course, and subjectivity may even be generalizable, where experiences are similar. Critical to the moral efficacy of a professional culture is its ability to seek to learn from the individual experience and the frames through which events and actions are perceived. For institution and individual alike, that must include the ability to engage in honest, open, reflective dialogue, the ability to admit to mistakes, and the willingness to take risks and stand up to external pressures.

In chapter 12, Pamela C. LePage, as a member of the IET faculty, provides a penetrating critique of the IET culture as she examines the struggles the faculty face as they strive to live up to their rhetoric. She seeks to first understand the tensions a moral frame sets up for faculty inside the program, specifically in terms of the complex relationships with teachers and the interplay between the moral standards set for them and faculty attempts to meet those standards themselves. She then explores tensions outside the specific teaching context, specifically the pragmatic problems arising for faculty in their role and in the university context. Finally, she asks what motivates faculty to work through the difficulties inherent in innovative morally framed programs and indicates a way forward to address the need for improvement.

In chapter 13, as a veteran teacher, Margaret Kaminsky describes her struggles to influence policy associated with state-mandated curriculum and high-stakes testing through the Standards of Learning in Virginia. She is searching for an approach to ensuring both standards and accountability that truly supports the complexity of learning and the uniqueness of the individual teacher and student. Her journey describes her commitments to challenge the bureaucracy, seeking to care for her students over the dictates of the state, to confront the deceit in a plan that she sees as inhibiting student learning, to demand fairness and practical wisdom, and to seek to evoke the courage to confront those who, as she sees it, have lost sight of the true meaning of learning.

In the final chapter, Hugh T. Sockett, as the founder of IET and its first director, tells the story of the challenges the IET program has faced in the context of a hostile university environment. Each person takes a strong stand for positive change despite barriers they encountered in their political contexts, illustrative of the fact that transformation is not without cost. Sockett argues that the strategy for IET's growth as a structural ambition was a failure. But, he argues, we know that innovations are expensive and always extraordinarily fragile, and that the job of the university is to nurture ideas. He describes in detail his perspective on the story of the Institute. Where deliberate assaults on the innovation, which do not address its ideas, bring about the failure of innovation, there is at least a prima facie case for saying that the university's proper role has been corrupted and that such assaults are an assault on the academic freedom of the innovators.

12

Sustaining the Moral Framework: Tensions and Opportunities for Faculty

Pamela C. LePage

Noddings (1997) argued that a morally defensible mission for the schools in the 21st century "should be to produce competent, caring, loving, and lovable people" (p. 28). That demands, I suggest, that teachers and teacher educators must themselves demonstrate these qualities in a clearly defined moral frame.

That frame must first include the moral, rather than the technical, aspects of teaching. People who think education is a technical business believe there is a right way to teach and the teacher educator's job is to explain the right way. People who adopt a moral approach believe there are many choices available, none of which are perfect. Those exposed to a technical approach will spend their lives trying to figure out how to teach the right way. Those who are trained with a moral approach will spend their lives experimenting, reflecting, making mistakes, and starting over. Their focus is on continuous improvement and "doing what's right," not "doing it right" (a hopeless endeavor).

Second, the moral frame must also include a moral professionalism that focuses on interactions with students, colleagues and the community. The quality of the moral behavior of K–12 teachers is often associated with treatment of children. The quality of the moral behavior of college professors is reflected in the treatment of their students and the commitment to improve their own practice. But, moral professionalism does not just have an internal focus. It also provides a frame for examining how we treat colleagues and others outside the program in the schools and the community. Most important, it provides a basis for judging the quality of relationships within a community.

Finally, a moral approach demands philosophical inquiry. Noddings' (1997) mission opens up the opportunity for continuous dialogue and debate. What do we mean by competence? What does it mean to care? How can we teach some-one to be loving? These kinds of moral inquiries find a specific context in the work of IET. For example, how do we select faculty teams in a way that is fair and appropriate? How do we interact with a traditional bureaucracy using a moral rather than a technical epistemological approach? How do we seek input from the outside and listen to it? How do we show care for each other and for students, and, above all, how do we talk about these issues?

Since the early 1990s, IET has had mixed success struggling with moral issues. In this chapter, I describe the tensions we have experienced implementing a moral frame, while acknowledging there are many different interpretations of *moral.* Earlier in the book, morality was connected with social justice and dem-ocratic practices (see chap. 3). In chapter 5, the authors focused on care as a moral imperative in teaching. In chapter 4, Sevick contrasted the *prescriptive* interpretation of *moral,* which she claimed is closer to ethics, to *moral* as a *descriptive* way to train one's eye on the world. In the descriptive interpretation, people do not depend on rules to decide right or good conduct in a situation; a person taking a moral point of view is able to describe aspects of a situation such as complexities concerning relationships among the people or ideas or incidents involved, none of which is seen in isolation. In taking a moral point of view there is careful search for good reasons (Fenstermacher & Goodlad, 1997), a sense of struggle, and also an awareness that, because the outcome is uncertain, continued observation and reflection are warranted.

In this chapter, I advocate for democratic practices in institutions and care among colleagues, but the distinction between prescription and description is blurred. It is necessary for a community of learners to establish norms and expectations about how people will function in a community. But I also "strug-gle" to untangle the "complexity concerning relationships." I search for "good reasons" for our difficulties, and my ultimate aim is to "further reflection and refinement" as well as set policy.

For a morally based innovation to have credibility, it has to adhere to moral principles and examine where it falls short. Our most significant lapses have occurred when we try to deny that we have moral lapses and when we ignore the contradictions and paradoxes we face. Because it is impossible for individ-uals and groups always to make the right moral choice, denying the struggle indicates a serious lack of self-reflective capability, which must surely be at the center of a moral organization. Like other teacher educators, we have tried to expose our shortcomings and confront the gaps between rhetoric and reality (e.g., Macgillivary, 1997; Moje, Southerland, & Wade, 1999), a practice that we urge on professional K–12 teachers studying with us.

Although this chapter is based on my personal reflections as a faculty member, it was circulated to my faculty colleagues (and some former staff) for comment. All of us (including myself) have fallen into moral traps over the years. In this chapter, I provide a penetrating critique of our culture, while acknowledging and affirming the incredible care and effort faculty put into their work to create a good program.

This chapter has three parts. In the first part, the goal is to understand the tensions a moral frame sets up for faculty inside the program; specifically, in terms of the complex relationships with teachers studying with us and the interplay between the moral standards we set for them and our attempts to meet those standards ourselves. In the second section, the goal is to explore tensions outside the specific teaching context, specifically the pragmatic problems arising for faculty in their role and in the university context. Finally, I ask what motivates faculty to work through the difficulties inherent in innovative morally framed programs and indicate a way forward to address the need for improvement.

THE PRAGMATIC CHALLENGE INSIDE THE PROGRAM

The challenges of embracing a moral foundation rest not only in working with teachers to grapple with complex questions, but also in experiencing the difficulties ourselves and struggling with the realities inherent in this approach. Inside the program, tensions for faculty arise in the implementation of a moral frame for ourselves and advocating to teachers their articulation of such a frame, specifically in respect of the following:

1. Working with teachers to develop authentic relationships with their students and our developing authentic relationships with them.
2. Advising teachers to develop collaborative relationships with colleagues against the background of some of our own difficulties in collaboration.
3. Advising teachers in their teams to grapple with problems and imperfections and living up to that injunction as faculty.
4. Extolling the value of reflective practice against our own problems of sustaining individual reflective practice.
5. Expecting teachers to develop community at their schools against the backdrop of our own efforts to build community.

Throughout these tensions run the confusing question of faculty autonomy. In some ways, individual IET faculty members have an amazing amount of autonomy, and yet in other ways it is seriously constrained. The degree structure allows faculty teams to recreate an entirely new program with each new student group. Yet, every decision we make, every book we assign, every paper we require is by convention agreed on by a team. When faculty are working in compatible teams, the autonomy is extensive: Where there is incompatibility, individuals can feel horribly constrained by "the group process."

Authentic Relationships

The question of autonomy has not provoked interfaculty tensions on the treatment of students. The program was designed to draw faculty into the professional lives of teachers by providing a structure where professors connect more intimately with students and where they are more accountable to students as teachers and advisers. The focus on teaching has never posed a problem for a faculty dedicated to teachers, none of whom would see the quality of practice with regard to teaching as anything less than their first moral priority. Indeed, connecting moral behavior primarily to their interactions with teachers is the reason why IET faculty see themselves as people who adhere to moral principles.

Collaborative Relationships

Collaboration among faculty is another matter, with the potential for severe friction. First, in IET, we do not have the freedom to distance ourselves from team colleagues with whom we disagree or with whom we have no personal bond. Even small differences in philosophy have created problems. For example, one faculty team member might believe in re-envisioning the teaching and learning relationships between professors and teachers as "everyone learns and everyone teaches," whereas another believes in a modified traditional hierarchical relationship. Some IET faculty are anxious to preserve what they view as the nontraditional and transformative nature of the program and fear that faculty will fall back toward the familiar. Because the faculty come from different disciplines, these conflicts and misunderstandings can be amplified because members use different language to describe the same things. Sometimes there was argument when there should have been agreement. Within a team, such dissonance creates confusion with regard to the "type of community" the faculty plan to foster among teachers who will then face infuriating contradictions because of faculty team divisions. Collaboration becomes a burden, not a joy, undermining everyone's autonomy. Moreover, there is the threat that a simple difference of philosophy or style can in principle damage a career because it can negatively affect student evaluations and faculty recommendations when promotion and tenure come along.

Second, interfaculty relationships are influenced by traditional academic norms. In a team context, an "unreasonable" individual is protected bureaucratically from being treated unfairly if he or she is disliked (because this is not uncommon in academia), whereas the rest of the team is not. On the other hand, the "rest of the team" might be the "unreasonable party," working to marginalize a person who is somehow different. Collaboration problems often stem as much from clashes of style and personality as teaching ideology. Is it even possible to define "unreasonable" faculty? Anyone whose opinions were constantly in a minority could be considered problematic and unreasonable to the rest of the team. For me "unreasonable" would describe a colleague who didn't seem to understand or was not willing to engage in productive conversations about IET's ideology, did not realize the extent of its ambitions and its influence on their workload, had particular character traits that undermined his or her abilities to work in teams, or whose previous experiences turned out not to be as valuable as either he or she or the search committee thought! Whether we call the phenomenon "reasonable" or "unreasonable," this immensely difficult issue has to be faced in the context of faculty autonomy within a moral frame.

In IET we have found it difficult to live up to our rhetoric. We need to recommit to:

- treating everyone (whether or not they are liked) with fairness and respect;
- working with people who need technical assistance as teachers;
- avoiding engaging in subtle forms of harassment and marginalization;
- standing up and together against unjust practices; and
- developing assessment procedures where teaming, communication, and adherence to moral principles are somehow recognized as important parts of our program.

Because IET faculty members are perfectionists when it comes to teaching, and collaboration problems can affect program quality, faculty members have trouble accepting responsibility for a program that does not meet their standards. Therefore, we have succumbed too much to arguing behind the backs of people, perhaps even trying to force them out by subtly (sometimes unconsciously) marginalizing them. Some have disdained working with others. Some have raised concerns about the temptation of the faculty to focus too much on creating a "comfortable" space for teaching, rather than attending to serious moral issues (with any or all faculty) in the development of an innovation. Also, much like forcing the first-year K–12 teacher to take on the most difficult kids, we have considered placing burdens on certain people who should not be asked to shoulder those burdens.

Facing up to Imperfections

Yet, to address these challenges and to live up to our self-imposed moral standards, we need strategies to implement this vision. First, it is important to establish open communication where we confront our own and each other's weaknesses in open dialogue with specific references to real events and behaviors. Such communication would be a drastic departure from what most faculty experience in traditional academic settings, where publicly confronting weaknesses is extremely rare.

Academics have various tactics when facing conflict. They use innuendo, ignore the problem, or use intellectual debate as a professional façade to fight personal battles. Some cannot see the weaknesses or will deny they exist, and/

or will think a person should keep silent in any case. Conventional ways of functioning become so normative that people do not even notice them. These norms then exert both dormant and active power over others by dictating how people should act. The norms become strengthened by traditions (this is not the way things are done). Those who challenge them, or those with different moral emphases, are considered out of step, accused of making trouble, acting crazy, whining, or acting arrogant or superior. Those in the majority seek to silence these people for the sake of group harmony, or control. In a hostile climate, people will ignore behaviors as insidious as overt racism or sexism because conflict in such an environment can be so damaging. People wait for others to address relational problems because they want to avoid being labeled "trouble-maker" or getting marginalized themselves. A hostile environment is not merely one that lacks tolerance for nontraditional verbal and written styles, or promotes silencing behaviors and unspoken racist and sexist norms. It can be one where the lack of open communication (a culture of silence) fosters injustice.

Whether my colleagues would agree on this or not, problems have arisen in IET because some have dealt with confrontation in a less direct way and others in a more direct way, which itself causes friction. Some confront issues and are accused of "relishing confrontation." Some avoid issues and are accused of "avoiding open communication." Some do both. Some don't say anything until they get angry, dispatching e-mail that is more personal than professional. I certainly have fallen into this trap myself.

Installing a dialogue in IET on our imperfections is a key part of the moral frame. We must be dedicated to providing a welcoming climate for people who challenge conventions, and we have a responsibility as colleagues to create a nurturing work environment for the entire community. The first step in developing good relationships is to clarify beliefs and principles (see chap. 2) and decide together how to communicate about them.

Service and Community

Faculty autonomy in IET is also influenced by two other considerations: the conception of service within IET and the interweave of autonomy with community. First, faculty members are asked to do specialized service, such as recruiting students, fostering connections with alumni, and reaching out to the community. By institutionalizing certain types of service work (especially recruitment), the faculty is obliged to reach out to principals, superintendents, and teachers. The ivory tower is no longer a hiding place. Teachers come to us and we must reach out to them. Our hierarchical authority, by design, is diminished. The service work in IET, although unusual, does have the common theme of a focus outward to the schools and to the community. This contrasts with the view of traditional citizenship in the university where people serve on governance committees.

Such service can be a source of real confusion for promotion and tenure committees, as it is seen not as "real service" but as just a way to "sell the program." The upshot is that to continue service work in IET and prepare ourselves for tenure, we must engage in both nontraditional service to IET and also traditional service work that is recognized by the university.

IET has an emphasis on building learning communities. For the faculty, community can cover at least three areas: the faculty team, the identity of a particular group of teachers and faculty, and the faculty as a whole. In faculty teams, it is easier to develop community because it is easier to carry on conversations about specific educational issues and philosophies, given the context of a particular group of students moving through at a particular time. People learn to care for "their" students and intimately understand the complexity of their particular group. Although we have had some success building community within our faculty teams, we have had less success building community in the larger program. Some have claimed that experiencing community in a team has satisfied their need for community and they do not have time for additional community development.

The desire to build community within a team is understandable, but in some ways, it is analogous to our teacher students telling us, "Well, I can work to develop community with a few people on my grade level, but it is too hard to develop community with the entire school." So, by asking teachers to develop learning communities in their schools and not expending the energy to do this work ourselves (especially given the fact that we have more flexible time than K–12 teachers), we create a gap between what we profess and what we do. Furthermore, we are not experiencing the complexity of what we are asking teachers to accomplish. College faculty have historically been criticized for telling teachers what they should do, while at the same time not understanding the complexity of teachers' work and not practicing what they preach. We are interested in avoiding this trap.

Reflective Practice

Working to live up to our rhetoric and avoid moral traps, however, can be a source of considerable stress and requires a "managed heart" (Hochschild, 1983). Developing learning communities demands emotional energy to constantly build and reflect on our own program, while working to help teachers build and reflect on their programs. This is an acute challenge in our program. First, the same faculty works with the same group of students throughout an entire 2-year program, so individual teacher-student success is completely dependent on the dedication and competence of a few individuals. Second, learning can be a painful process for returning professionals. They face insecurities and must push themselves to learn and grow. The IET faculty shoulders some of the emotional strain that students experience. We listen, we sympathize, we push, we advise, we confront and we bluntly state the obvious. But, even at the end, when students tell us what a wonderful program we have and apologize for that one e-mail tirade or that one angry outburst in class, I still find their tears of joy and relief emotional.

Our job thus requires a managed heart and a moral epistemology of practice, rather than the traditional empiricist-positivist one with which teacher education practice is dominated (see chap. 1). Traditionally, a school relies on moral conventions and also on local laws (e.g., prohibiting sexual harassment) to govern teaching and learning with regard to interpersonal interactions. In this type of institution, bureaucracy and convention aid people in separating right from wrong, so people do not spend time to explore how "what is taught" and "how social relations are conducted" interface. In a moral innovation, questions about the institution's fundamental values and its day to day conduct surface quickly and are always on the table. Constant reflection is essential. For you cannot simply ignore complex moral issues, many of which require naming. Problems crucial in the moral model are often ignored in the empirical model. Within this new paradigm, the IET innovation is on a kind of moral expedition, trying to recover through reflection moral ground lost to the dominant paradigm. The transformative shift IET embraces is therefore one in which the moral epistemology is installed both as a way of understanding what teaching is and as a way of understanding what an educational institution is. Faculty autonomy in the moral paradigm implies living up to high moral standards as a member of a community. And that is a very different concept of faculty autonomy.

SUSTAINING MORAL INTEGRITY IN A COMPETITIVE BUREAUCRATIC STRUCTURE

When IET was separated from the Graduate School of Education, the university administration believed that for an innovation to succeed it had to be nurtured, separate from the influence of entrenched tradition (see chap. 14). Left exposed to the "dark side of the force"—the individualistic, competitive styles of traditional academics, the bureaucratic malaise that inhibits progress, and the privileged disassociation of the ivory tower, the innovating faculty would be defeated. Critique of this dark side underpins many commentaries on teacher education. "Nowhere is the imperative to shift our effort from 'my work' to 'our work' more needed than in schools of education," wrote Hugh Petrie, emphasizing the importance of collaboration (Jacobson, Emihovich, Helfrich, Petrie, & Stevenson, 1998, p. 24). A more fundamental critique (see chap. 1) also widens to faculty conduct in general. Braxton & Bayer (1999) were unforgiving in their descriptions of faculty behaviors that they labeled moral turpitude, uncooperative cynicism, and condescending negativism, to name but a few. When IET was separated from the Graduate School at GMU, clearly the faculty resented the implication that they were part of "the evil empire" who embraced the dark side of academic life.

It is important to acknowledge, however, that faculty with traditional career expectations realistically will be torn between university norms and IET's new ways. Such conflicts will include the amount of time spent in schools, how power relations with teachers are negotiated, how to get individual recognition as they strive to adhere to a collaborative mission, and how to negotiate the rewards of innovation with the conventional forms of promotion and tenure criteria. Because IET was recently moved back into the Graduate School under a new president, it is important to face up to this legacy and name the problems. They represent continuing tensions (as I see them) that stem from an innovation with a moral epistemology that is institutionally located within a traditional hierarchical bureaucracy and that encapsulate the problems for faculty I have outlined. These can be discussed as (1) politics and the complexity of deceit, (2) collaborative teaching and university evaluations, and (3) challenging hierarchies.

Politics and the Complexity of Deceit

In the late 1980s, a friend of mine (call her Joanne) worked in a special education department that provided a toy-lending library to local low-income parents of special needs kids. The toys were specially designed with adaptations for children who had trouble manipulating objects. The program caught on quickly and it was a great success. But, for some reason, the program still was not very well supported by the department. Joanne was told by one of the professors in the department that the toy library staff needed to let the department chair get credit for this program, even though she had never supported it, let alone been involved in the design or the implementation of the program. Joanne didn't say anything, but if she had inquired or protested, she probably would have been told that it didn't matter who deserved credit, the toy library staff had better start pretending.

This example is morally complex, although it could be dismissed as institutional convention. First, if people higher up on the hierarchy are trying to "steal" credit, are they morally wrong? Second, how do those who deserve the credit react? Should they give up the credit to gather support so they can reach more parents and kids? We do not have to be selfless in all cases, but in a situation where poor kids might have access to educational toys otherwise unaffordable, the moral choice seems obvious. Yet, there is still one other layer of complexity to discuss. Are we sure this is the right moral decision? With the solution offered so far, we are solving a problem under traditional norms. The fundamental immorality of the situation remains. The dishonesty behind it is accepted. The assumptions (e.g., that the bad academics have immoral motives) provide fodder for later antagonism. Secrecy is left to feed future rumors and gossip. This situation will prove divisive, leading to a breakdown in community. Accepting there is no clear answer, in a morally framed program, we need to open dialogue, rather than accept deceit.

Politics of this sort is common in higher education. That I feel constrained not to use an example of political manipulation and deceit from the IET context shows either my cowardice or how thin the ice is when one believes it important to open serious moral dialogue. To consider the morality of such a situation finds no locus within the dominant paradigm and misbehaviors are rarely sanctioned. The lack of disciplinary action can be attributed in part to people in the academy placing a high value on autonomy, thereby making administrative interventions inappropriate (Braxton & Bayer, 1999).

A second hypothetical example is a more direct instance of deceit (see Bok, 1978, 1983). Consider this situation: We don't like the work of an adjunct, but she is nice and certainly a friend, so we tell her we don't need her anymore. We tell her that we fought long and hard to keep her (when we, in fact, suggested she go). We blame the dean, the university president, or the ambassador to France, none of whom even know this person. Given a moral frame, such clear deceit must be carefully considered, but perhaps not always completely eliminable. Bok (1978) tells us that some marginally deceptive social excuses and conventions are sometimes unavoidable if feelings are not to be needlessly injured. But most people who stretch the truth do so because they feel guilty. They actually care about what people think so they often lie in an effort to please everyone. Bok also indicates that people use deceit as a way to gain and abuse power, hence its potential as a weapon for manipulation.

Under a moral frame, it would not be appropriate to mislead the adjunct because she needs to know how people feel about her work. In this situation, we are not being nice to her when we lie. We are being cowardly in an effort to maintain our popularity or to avoid an uncomfortable conversation, or we are just being lazy or selfish. By avoiding the truth, we are probably invalidating this person's own intuition, and we are invalidating the person who told her the truth last week. We will probably have to lie again when we refill that "unnecessary" position. A better approach would be to emphasize the positive, let her know we care, tell her the truth, and most important, admit that we may be wrong, for our evaluative comments are subjective.

Faculty must, I believe, struggle openly with the moral complexity of deceit. We can admit that "stretching the truth" is commonplace, even when we say we never lie and we understand and value honesty. We should feel social pressure to enter dialogue and be honest, to break free of the fear generated by entrenched norms protected by abusive power relations, and to take risks (responsibly) even if it might provoke conflict. Not rocking the boat is the motto of the status quo. If a morally framed program sticks to its principles to deal with these common problems, it often has to face serious conflict in the search for responsible solutions in the community.

In IET, we have not had much success resolving some of these types of issues. First, people must be confident to reflect on their inadequacies and it is difficult to always tell the truth (especially if someone's feelings might be hurt) and it is also difficult to hear the truth. Second, many people honestly believe it is better to avoid conflict, because they don't want to make the situation worse. Productive disagreement is so unusual that they find it emotionally draining to engage in tense discussions that they assume will be unproductive. Many people have never experienced learning through cognitive dissonance or conflict resolution so they do not understand its value. They have never made deeper connections with people by working through uncomfortable issues. Understandably, they don't like the way conflict makes them feel. Third, we are trying to change our current paradigm, while functioning within an old paradigm (both in our heads and in our contexts). We are trying to "do it differently" with very little guidance, support and time. Working within an institution that operates with different conventions and a different epistemology means oscillating between two sets of epistemological norms and moral practices. Finding a balance is hard on individuals because there is a thin line between being politically suave and politically manipulative, being deceitful and being diplomatic, and protecting yourself and being selfish. There are no clear boundaries. We must constantly negotiate these subtle distinctions.

Collaborative Teaching and University Evaluations

Team teaching exemplifies both the promise and the hazards within IET as an innovation that redefines faculty relationships as collaborative. Personally, I have learned a great deal from my colleagues. I have learned about collaboration, leadership, and group dynamics. I have been exposed to different teaching methods and perspectives on curriculum. I have learned an enormous amount of "content" from my colleagues. On the other hand, I have argued and talked and confronted and stepped in and negotiated myself to death! It is true that even where preexisting relationships, as in a Professional Development School (PDS) smooth the way, the development of the more intimate, even intrusive, form of collaboration is not straightforward (Darling-Hammond, 1994). Previously, I talked about how the desire for faculty autonomy affects collaboration. In this section, I focus on barriers to collaboration posed by university policies and procedures.

Programmatically, team teaching enhances instructional quality. It forces faculty to adhere to certain principles and standards. It pushes people who are not strong teachers to improve, as their colleagues are in constant attendance. Moreover, because the team has input into every class session, activities have a greater probability of being useful or powerful or interesting in some way. Nevertheless, there are problems associated with the challenge of working *collaboratively* within a bureaucratic frame designed to evaluate and reward *individual effort*.

Institutionally, the problem is that the university administration does not understand and therefore does not allow for assessment for nontraditional collaborative teaching in a way that is truly understood and embraced by the promotion and tenure process. In regular university classrooms, the instructor chooses his or her own syllabus, methods, and styles. At the end of an IET course the university student evaluation process demands that students complete Scantron forms evaluating each faculty member individually, regardless of the circumstances.

By contrast, IET has historically not emphasized individual faculty contributions to teaching. Teaming means that each person is differently involved at some point during every class day (e.g., as discussion leader, presenter, small group adviser, or comic relief). IET faculty members have different strengths and commitments. Some people like presenting to large groups while others don't believe in "transmission." Some are excellent leaders of discussions in cohorts, getting students thinking and talking about the material presented (see chap. 4), whereas others would prefer to have students work in small groups so the instructor is not at the center. In a team-teaching situation, everyone must negotiate how the team will interact with students, who will develop and deliver certain instruction, and what each instructor will do at any given time. People cannot always choose to teach in the way that is best for them; they must teach in a way that is agreed on by the group. These decisions are often affected by group power relations that can be influenced by gender bias, elitism, discipline-ism, ageism, politics, fear of survival, and potential conflicts of interest.

The IET student evaluation process could be described as a constant open communication with students. We ask them to evaluate every class session. We talk with them about their evaluations. At times the faculty has given evaluative responses back to the students to analyze as data. We work constantly to improve on the program, as we improve on our own teaching. So evaluation for us is viewed as a formative and dialogic process that is constant and continuous and not a bureaucratic end of the program response to determine whether it was good or bad.

Evaluations can never therefore accurately assess individual teaching abilities because no one ever develops or delivers instruction in isolation, even though this is how the university views them. The scores on these evaluations cannot thus be individual. They are obviously affected first by how other faculty team members respond to each other and how a person "compares" with other faculty on the team. Second, they are affected by whether a team sets an emphasis and a tone that is different from what an individual is comfortable with. One group may focus on identity issues and empowering teachers to understand bureaucratic barriers. Another may concentrate on teacher research and improving kids' learning. Another might emphasize intellectual challenge. Faculty will fare better or worse on university student evaluations depending on whether the team can agree on an overall philosophy and emphasis.

Third, if an individual member of faculty is a weak instructor, but surrounded by other strong teachers, the better instructors will bolster the weaker instructor. Therefore, it can help the overall program for weaker faculty to be paired with stronger faculty. And when our K–12 teacher-students start complaining to us about "bad teachers" at their schools, we ask them how they are helping those teachers get better. Of course, because university evaluations influence not only promotion and tenure decisions, but also yearly salary adjustments, this can be problematic in a situation where an individual gets a smaller salary increase because he had to invest extra time to compensate for the bad teaching of a weak professor. For some, this could also frustrate their career ambitions in an organization where individual achievement is valued over the group process.

So far I have been explaining how we seek to compromise with the dominant evaluation paradigm that we believe has little merit, which does not match our practice, and insidiously influences our interprofessional relations. What should we do? Given a moral frame, we should not be seduced by traditional, competitive, individualistic rewards as determined through unhealthy assessment instruments that discriminate between those who are really good and really bad in an effort to make things "fair." In a collaborative situation, this causes resentment and ultimately makes things worse. When stronger faculty are willing to help weaker faculty, this shows care not only for colleagues, but also for the students who will experience a better program.

To repeat, the problem is that institutionally, the university does not understand and therefore provide assessment for nontraditional collaborative teaching in a way that is truly understood and embraced by the promotion and tenure process. We thus have no formal way to evaluate the progress of a team as an instructional unit, to monitor the growth of a team, or to reward those who make special efforts or who develop new and interesting curricula. We have no way to reward teams that face more incompatibility, yet struggle to work together productively. We have no way to reward the faculty member who spends time and energy teaching, mentoring, and compensating for weaker faculty.

In short, our work has been bedeviled by the dominant paradigm and our responses have been morally confused. Faculty members have fought to work with compatible people in an effort to avoid the difficulties of teaming, which does not reduce conflict. When some faculty decide whom they want to work with, some others are left without a choice. Who gets to choose? Most importantly, by failing to grapple openly with this problem, we are missing opportunities to learn and to struggle with the complexity of what we ask K–12 teachers to do in a less supportive environment.

Challenging Hierarchies

Challenging the hierarchy is not a problem exclusive to moral innovations (Slater, 1996). Because IET encourages teachers to interact as equal colleagues, or as partners, in the public school hierarchy, we also strive to flatten the hierarchy by treating university colleagues as equal partners, no matter what their status or title. This is much easier for university or college faculty because we cannot "be fired" for insubordination and it is part of the academic culture that colleagues relate to each other as equals. Still, people in positions of power in the university find ways to "reward loyal followers" and pass opportunities by those who are not so loyal. So, challenging the hierarchy can be a risk, a fact exemplified by my reluctance here to specify cases.

The norms of a moral-democratic program (see chap. 3) conflict with the rules and norms of a traditional hierarchy. In a moral program, people constantly question the procedures. They speak their minds, demand to be informed, don't show deference, and reject the chain of command. They have nontraditional practices that break down the power of the hierarchy. Frequently, they shock people with nontraditional verbal or written styles. To them, the university is a republic, not a corporation. Believers in hierarchy and the proper chain of command within an academic setting find this unsettling, for people in democratic programs don't adhere to the conventions as the hierarchy understands them. In particular, the hierarchy loses the critical skill of predicting what these people will say or how they will act in certain situations. Therefore, developing trust across such ideological differences is especially difficult.

A program that believes in (and implements) democratic principles can face contradictions that reside within a hierarchy, especially when the program is composed mostly of women (and men) who have adopted feminist, democratic, anti-paternalist values. Paternalism is the policy or practice of treating or governing people in a fatherly manner, especially by providing for their needs without giving them rights or responsibilities. Paternalism rarely allows decisions to be made on their merits. It usually crushes or disallows innovations not led from the top and heavily relies on patronage, as in applications for discretionary funds. Fatherly leaders (men or women) usually care very much about the people who work for them and welcome the opportunity to do something to demonstrate their dedication and care. Employees under a paternalistic leadership can feel protected and as important as the good son or daughter. Such care is too often perverted, however, for it can become a weapon of control, not an authentic caring for the other. Paternalists are closed to dissent, viewing dissenters as disloyal or troublesome children, rather than helpful and important adults.

DEVELOPING A CRITICAL CULTURE AND WORKING TOWARD IMPROVEMENT

Faced with such major challenges inside and outside the program, what provides the motivation to maintain the program? The most significant reward comes through intellectual stimulation. IET is dedicated to both the intellectual life of teachers and also the intellectual life of college faculty. So, historically, those who focus on teaching and those whose scholarly interests intersect with the priorities in the program (e.g., teacher research, teaming, school transformation, democratic learning communities, etc.) can find a very intellectually stimulating community. Within the confines of the degree structure, IET also provides the faculty (in the context of teams) with the opportunity to develop an entire master's degree program every 2 years. The faculty has an opportunity to be creative with curriculum (see, e.g., Wood, 1996) and they have more influence over the "entire graduate experience" than they would in other programs.

Most importantly, the faculty are also rewarded by their belief that we are making a difference in education. Although IET professors must engage in work that is unusual for college faculty, certain program features, like recruitment, teacher-friendly scheduling, and driving to schools are not gratuitous gestures, they transform the teaching–learning experience. The following are some comments taken from a survey (LePage & Kirk, 1999) that asked IET alumni whether the program was useful to them:

- "Yes, very thoughtful program in terms of me thinking about my students, my assignments—where am I going with it all and what do I hope to achieve—I now always have these questions in my mind."
- "I learned a great deal about myself as a teacher through reflective practice. The collaborative work has been especially useful to me in my role as department chair."
- "Absolutely, I am using many of the techniques that I learned there to the advantage of my students—fewer failures, more interest. The students are as energized as am I."
- "Yes, I learned a great deal from my research. I feel confident to voice my opinions in decision making. I love to collaborate with my grade level and team teach whenever possible. I have read books by authors we read in the program."
- "Yes, it gave me the confidence to know that I could do research and be a part of a collaborative team."
- "Yes, technology was very helpful to me! Reflection caused me to rethink some of my practice."
- "The program was extremely useful in that it encouraged me to be reflective and to use my new skills to change and improve my practice. It has also broadened my view of the role of public educators and has deepened my commitment to morality."
- "Yes, I am able to view the world differently (and my students!). I am now a better writer. I am technology literate. It also encouraged me to continue taking more classes."

Such typical responses encourage faculty members, first, to be proud of their deep connections with schools. Currently, each faculty member works with approximately five to eight teams of teachers, each from a different school, so faculty works with teachers in approximately 50 to 70 schools in the northern Virginia area at any one time. Second, some faculty strive to develop other community-based work (e.g., in the Urban Alternative; see chap. 1) where one faculty member has worked with low-income immigrant families and other community members to establish and maintain a high-quality early education program that greatly informs our work with teachers (see chap. 10). Third, I have developed one of IET's original ambitions (for work with whole schools). I facilitate the George C. Round Elementary School Community Project in Manassas, Virginia, which provides a pilot for the vision of having teachers in teams graduating from the program go back to their workplace and develop a collaborative, moral community. Out of 35 teachers at that school, 12 have earned their master's degree through the IET program. Some of these alumni, as well as other teachers, are working together on a group research project to understand how the teachers, administrators, and staff in the school can work together better to improve instructional quality at the school.

Given the value of the IET innovation to teachers, can this program be as rewarding to faculty as it is for students? Will faculty be motivated to struggle with moral dilemmas? Not, I think, without continuous long-term program development that includes the constant renewal of commitment by faculty to adhere to a moral frame of professionalism and the development of nontraditional communication patterns; the institutionalization of nontraditional procedures based on feminist, moral and democratic principles; and the development of moral leadership across all the faculty.

As part of that moral commitment to the *Beliefs and Principles in IET Practice* (see chap. 2), we must somehow first institutionalize honest and open communication, going beyond these rhetorically expressed values to such questions as "What do we mean by integrity?" and "What constitutes a morally coherent fit?" And, "What happens when we have neither?" Second, we also need to have discourse procedures available to reconcile philosophical conflicts (see, e.g., LePage & Sockett, 2000). Third, we need to work harder with each other, especially with those who are uncomfortable with nontraditional communication styles or who are not used to discussing moral issues in an open forum. Fourth, we need to negotiate consequences when these commitments are ignored, for we cannot be committed to a moral base of professionalism and simultaneously be unmotivated and uninvolved.

Fifth, for the bureaucrats among us and the bureaucrat within us, it is important to establish some nontraditional procedures that govern the program. Teaching is not just moral, it is also technical (e.g., eye contact with the audience) and it is partly bureaucratic (grading). In the past, people lost trust in a paternalistic system that sought to "privilege their friends." As a result, these people were convinced that the only way to have a fair system was to bureaucratize it! So moral judgment was replaced with rules and procedures and many people forgot what it meant to make decisions about what is right, what is fair, what is moral. We need drastically to revise the model of improvement, "grounded in the view of the schools as bureaucracies run by carefully specified procedures that yield standard products (students), based on a faith in rationalistic organizational behavior, in the power of rules to direct human action, and in the ability of researchers to discover the common procedures that will produce desired outcomes" (Darling-Hammond, 1997a, p. 39). We need to import procedures that provide some structure, while also celebrating our spirit of experimentation, flexibility, and continuous improvement.

Finally, we need to welcome all faculty taking responsibility for leadership. Faculty need to set up, organize, and foster productive communication within and outside the program and help negotiate ambiguity within. Faculty must take turns providing a moral compass. All leaders in morally based innovation need to effectively negotiate different cultures in the university, in the community, and in the public schools. They must communicate respect for organizational structures not like our own, and at the same time, work to change structures they believe to be hostile to many faculty. Each individual must acknowledge his or her responsibility to do the following:

- Serve as a moral compass.
- Direct the democratic process.
- Interact in a number of different cultures and communicate effectively given a broad range of philosophical traditions.
- Work appropriately with problematic faculty and help faculty negotiate ambiguity.
- Support and protect faculty when nontraditional methods and styles clash with traditional bureaucratic university structures.
- Organize productive discussions about the vision, the philosophies and direction of the program.

CONCLUSION

Faculty in a moral innovation must strive to understand and address moral complexity. The effort to coexist with the dominant paradigm leads to taking on its more unpleasant features (e.g., manipulation, dishonesty, pushing people out, building power camps, etc.). This temptation needs to be resisted in favor of admitting and understanding our frailties, openly acknowledging our mistakes, working to redress our past transgressions, reflecting seriously on our roles and responsibilities, and working toward improvement. Hopefully, the new dedication to morality that is emerging as a major force in teacher education (see, e.g., Goodlad, Soder, & Sirotnik, 1990; Hansen, 1998; Sockett, 1993; Tom, 1984) will provide programs like IET with support, protection, and guidance. For now, it is important to practice what we preach, foster trust, develop a caring community and support dedicated, idealistic faculty members who are committed to a moral approach.

13

The Standards of Learning: One Teacher's Journey Through State-Mandated Curriculum

Margaret Kaminsky

I have always taken my professional teaching responsibilities seriously, but my experiences as a graduate student in IET helped me frame those responsibilities in terms of moral professionalism. In that program, as I researched how to develop voice and agency in my students, I experienced the added joy of developing my own "voice." The IET curriculum encouraged me to examine the pros and cons of educational reform in light of the philosophy of thinkers such as John Dewey and Jerome Bruner. I had opportunities to reflect on past and current classroom experiences and to reinterpret them, drawing on new ideas discussed with faculty and colleagues.

As insights deepened and accumulated, my professional voice grew, reaching a crescendo when the IET faculty encouraged me to participate in a presentation of papers concerning my experiences with the nationwide "standards movement" at the annual meeting of the American Association of Colleges for Teacher Education in 1999. Since the mid-1990s, the legislature in the Commonwealth of Virginia has instituted Standards of Learning (SOL) for all students, followed by a criterion-referenced testing program designed to award student credit for graduation and to determine school accreditation. Having harbored many doubts about the Virginia standards movement, I relished the opportunity to tell the story of my journey through the development of the SOL program at this national conference.

The process to develop Virginia's SOL and its subsequent testing program has been fraught with flaws and erroneous assumptions. I realized these problems early on when I began attending public hearings and meetings about the proposed program. Although members of the state Board of Education sought the opinions of practitioners, they frequently ignored these teacher voices as they established the standards and developed the tests. When Harcourt Brace was hired to design the tests, I had the opportunity to participate on an advisory committee, but the state Board of Education had already determined some significant exclusions to the tests before I attended our first meeting. I discovered that the testing company had designed questions that focused on content-specific facts, thus excluding evaluations of problem-solving skills that foster divergent thinking and the varying stages of developmental learning. The tests were all in multiple-choice format. In fact, the Board of Education released a blueprint of standards that were to be tested in the program; this blueprint excluded the testing of process learning skills such as researching, critical thinking, and oral communication.

Additionally, I was challenged as a teacher to determine how to successfully teach the tested standards to my students because of the secrecy surrounding the tests themselves. For example, teachers could lose their jobs for discussing questions on any test they viewed, and state officials released only four or five sample questions for statewide publication. Although the results from the first testing cycle were bleak, state officials continued to keep teachers in the dark about the formatting of the test and the item-analysis of the results of the tests. The opportunity to present my paper on my experiences allowed me to crystallize my stance on the SOL: The Commonwealth of Virginia appears to have implemented a series of "benchmark standards" and a testing program to measure students and schools without regard to how students learn and how teachers teach. This new testing program ignores the complexity of learning and the uniqueness of the individual teacher and student.

THE EARLY DAYS OF THE MOVEMENT

As a veteran English teacher of more than 30 years in Virginia, I have seen educational reforms come and go. Within the last decade particularly, I have perceived that schools struggle with the conflict between grounding students in basic traditional skills, while preparing them for the intellectual challenges of the twenty-first century. In the early 1990s, the Virginia legislature seemed poised to institute the innovative Challenge 2000, also known as World Class Education, a program emphasizing decision-making, problem-solving, and co-operative work, skills necessary for every individual in the new millennium. Unfortunately, many politicians viewed the controversial Challenge 2000 document, which suggested the concepts of teaching for "outcomes" and developing values, as too open-ended. Apparently, for some, Challenge 2000 was a threat to traditional education methods and values. Then Governor Douglas Wilder, caving in to pressures from the conservative right, refused to sign the Challenge 2000 program into law at the 11th hour. When the SOL movement emerged out of the ashes, I saw this, too, as a trend that would die a natural death as most seemingly political movements do. In the next move of educational reform, the

Virginia State Board of Education, supported by state legislation, planned to identify standards of curriculum content in four core knowledge areas that students would be expected to master at 3-year benchmarks. The Board also envisioned a unique Virginia testing program that would determine the awarding of diplomas and the accreditation of school divisions, thus making teachers and schools accountable. And they believed that the pressure on students to pass tests in order to receive course credit would raise the overall state test scores. Legislation directed the Board and its personnel to write sequential standards for learning in the core knowledge areas of science, math, English, and social studies.

Early on, however, I had the sense that the Board of Education did not value the knowledge of practitioners, and subsequent events reinforced that perception. Four different groups of teachers in Virginia drafted these standards over the summer, but the Board made significant changes in their drafts, particularly in the social studies area. Content was added to the lower elementary grades in a volume that was overwhelming to most teachers with whom I talked. Even textbook companies were caught off guard. They had developed no materials to cover the extensive social studies material on ancient Greece and Rome, for example, prescribed for children in the third grade. In fact, most educators regarded this curriculum as ill advised, arguing that students should know their local social dynamics before entertaining global concepts. In another instance, against the advice of teachers, the Board drafted a list of books that all students must read to add to the standards for English that were developed by teachers. Ironically, this list was later removed when the Board discovered that many of the books were so old that they were out-of-print and thus unavailable to schools.

At the completion of the SOL drafts, the Board began hearings in local communities about the scope and sequence of the content of each of the four disciplines' curricula. Apprehensive about these mandated curriculum guides, I felt compelled to attend the first set of hearings in northern Virginia in March 1995. The auditorium was overflowing by the opening of the hearing, and the agenda had been filled with citizen speakers at least 3 hours prior to the start. I was amazed at the speakers' overwhelming opposition to the entire curriculum plan, particularly in social studies. In addition to parents and teachers who spoke of their concerns to the Board, each local school division had a spokesperson who questioned the State Board of Education's direction. At 11 p.m. I had heard enough, although the hearings continued until midnight.

The next morning I remember talking with my colleagues about how the SOL ludicrously ignored how students learn. As any experienced teacher can explain, all students are not at the same developmental point at the end of each school year; some students need repeated reinforcement to master a concept; and the unique learning needs of students demand individual treatment by teachers. I brushed the entire plan off as political "muscle flexing" by those who were entrenched in a sentimentalized, perhaps mythic, past about "the way schools used to be." I remember remarking how I was sure that the voice of reason would prevail at the state level, that these standards were a conservative political backlash to the earlier, more liberal Challenge 2000 plan. Surely the educators in charge would see that the standards plan was unreasonable! I was completely taken aback when little or no changes were made in the standards despite the hearings. In July 1995 the Board of Education approved the SOL and local school divisions were directed to incorporate the new SOLs into their curriculum programs.

THE IMPACT ON MY SCHOOL COMMUNITY

I have always been a "team player." Acknowledging that the SOLs were now a reality, I agreed to chair the Curriculum Revision Project in English K–12 for the Manassas City Schools. Our task was to align our current curriculum with the curriculum now established by the state Board of Education. When we finalized our document, I felt that we had been successful for a number of reasons: Teachers of students from kindergarten to 12th grade had an opportunity to discuss the diversity in our individual classrooms and with our individual students. We shared ideas and gained insights into the challenges of meeting the needs of each student at each level. We were able to acknowledge the impossibility of having each and every student at the same level in all skill areas at the same time because we understood developmental variables.

I failed, however, to recognize a problem that was inherent in the process of making our curriculum like that of the state's: By setting rigid terms for the curriculum, the state subtly disregarded the professional judgment of teachers. Although we discussed all of the most important issues as we wrote our document, the underlying assumptions driving the standards movement ignored those very issues. Hence, an apparent dismissal of the teachers' perspective had filtered down to my own school division as it strived to obey the state mandate.

This point truly hit home as we struggled with how to cover the considerable SOL-driven curriculum while retaining what we were currently teaching. For example, I have organized my English 11 curriculum to foster increasingly higher levels of critical thinking, particularly synthesis and evaluation. Both processes encourage divergent thinking and pose open-ended questions. Multiple-choice formats, however, rarely evoke divergent thinking because they always have a single right answer. In attempting to reconcile this curriculum content with that tested by the state, I shrugged my shoulders, saying to myself: "That's okay. I will continue to teach what I have always believed is important. I will continue to emphasize the skills and content that are essential for my students to master. This approach will surely satisfy the state." Somewhere in my heart—and in the hearts of other teachers with whom I talked—I knew I was better off following my own judgment because I believed the SOL initiative was doomed to failure. I did not anticipate the strong will of the Board of Education to dictate the content taught in each classroom. Nor was I prepared

for the subsequent pressure from central office personnel and school administrators to do whatever it takes to ensure that students' scores rise on the SOL
tests, despite whether the content addressed their needs and fostered their abilities.

Nevertheless, I continued to be a team player. I sincerely believed that as a
professional I had a "voice" that was respected by those who were not in the
classroom. When our school division submitted my name as a representative to
serve on a Virginia Content Review Committee of the testing questions for
English 11 Reading, I felt that it was an opportunity for me to exercise that
voice and to gain a new perspective on the future direction of the SOL testing
program. The state claimed that the committees were "comprised of classroom
teachers, curriculum specialists, and representatives of educational organizations," but our committee had only five members—four English teachers and
one English supervisor. These five people made decisions about the format of
the test questions, the standards that would not be tested, the importance of
some content over other content, and the baseline of what was to be mastered
by every 11th grader in the Commonwealth. Given the limited make-up of the
committee, I had to ask myself, "Why didn't the state mount a more extensive
review process that included input from many more Virginia teachers?"

At the first meetings in the fall of 1997, I was even more concerned when I
realized there were questions that would not be asked. The test developers were
measuring reading comprehension by testing children's memory and knowledge
of arbitrary details and literary devices. For instance, test questions included
factual, detailed questions on consumer product information such as warranties
and contracts. Thirty years of practice in the English classroom, as well as
numerous courses, readings, and staff development programs, have taught me,
however, that testing students' recall of discrete facts from material with little
or no relevance to them is a serious mistake. Such an approach simply cannot
determine whether students can make meaning from what they read or use that
meaning to inform their thinking and their lives.

Students, in fact, make meaning based on their individual backgrounds, prior
knowledge, and cultural understandings; in other words, each student reacts
differently to a reading piece. For example, when my students read John Stein-
beck's Depression-era novel, *Of Mice and Men*, they interview a family member
who had lived during that time period. Each student's personal account from
the interview sheds a different light on the novel, thus creating a variety of
opinions about the work's theme. Educators Mulcahy-Ernt and Ryshkewitch
(1994), who have written extensively about reading comprehension skill development for diverse students, support the use of teaching strategies to promote
"thinking critically, reflecting, connecting ideas with one's experience, elaborating concepts, using the text's ideas, and creating unique interpretations in
response to text" (p. 326). At the end of the first session of the Content Review
Committee, I expressed my concern to the test makers that the tests were only
assessing recall of factual knowledge. The representative from Harcourt Brace

simply responded that the directions regarding the testing format from the state Board of Education had tied their hands.

By the time we met again a month later, some of the field test information had been completed. We examined the results to see if the questions appeared to be fair in format and to look for unforeseen biases. I asked why none of the test questions addressed complicated thinking skills or individual reading comprehension but no one on the committee seemed interested in my concern. At the end of the question review session, the committee discussed releasing "lists of terms" to teachers as a resource for test preparation, but, to my knowledge, such a list has not been released. Although I understood that this list might encourage teachers to "teach to the test," teachers could also legitimately use it as a guide to ensure appropriate coverage of key concepts. At bottom, however, what irritated me most was the complete disregard for teachers' professional autonomy and judgment.

What was happening here? The state was forging ahead with a flawed instrument that would determine if a student graduated and if a school was accredited. Why wasn't someone in authority saying, "Wait a minute"? Why weren't they asking, "What do teachers think students can and should learn? After all, they're the ones working most closely with students."

I was even more disturbed when the state Board released a "blueprint" in which they listed certain of the SOLs excluded from the tests because they did not lend themselves to multiple-choice testing. These exclusions involve essential skills and abilities, ones my students will invariably use in their lives after leaving my classroom. For example, the following standards are excluded from the English 11 testing: the ability to work and learn with others, the ability to compare and contrast, synthesize, or see universal themes, and the ability to see information from different perspectives. Specifically, multicultural literature has been eliminated from the test despite increasing calls for America to be seen as a "salad bowl" rather than as a "melting pot."

I am struck more by what the writing portion of the English 11 tests fails to ask of students than what it does ask. For instance, it asks for neither persuasive nor evaluative writing. Students write neither business nor personal correspondence. Although required to name the parts of a research paper, they are not asked to demonstrate their abilities to collect, evaluate, and organize information—the essence of research. They are not asked about the importance of different cultures in the development of America nor to analyze the relationships among American literature, history, and culture. They are not asked to synthesize information in a logical sequence. These skills, to my mind, are much more important to lives lived outside of classrooms than differentiating between metaphors and similes, identifying the main characters in a short story, or knowing when to use who or whom. Moreover, the omitted skills are the ones most essential for the world of work and, more importantly, for participation in a democratic society.

One of my most successful learning experiences for students, one involving most of the excluded standards, was a persuasive letter-writing campaign to an appropriate government official concerning a topic about which the student was passionately concerned. Throughout subsequent units, the students referred to the letters they wrote and their evaluations of the replies they received. Moss (1994), in her article "Can There Be Validity Without Reliability," pointed out that "what isn't assessed tends to disappear from the curriculum" (p. 6). How, I wondered, might I prevent valuable life skills from vanishing from my own classroom?

When the results from the first testing in 1998 were released, 97% of the schools in Virginia had failed. Are that many young people in the state of Virginia failing? I think not! My students leave high school to become successful college students, working professionals in the community, caring parents, and involved citizens. I never perceived these students as "not making the grade," nor do I believe that they see themselves as failures either. The students did not fail the tests; the testing system failed them! Despite repeated attempts to explain that the tests ignore individual learning development, assess only mastery of concrete facts, and seem to be administered unfairly, these concerns seem to fall on deaf ears. When asked if the Board would consider relaxing its rules or changing the exams, state Board President Kirk T. Schroder responded, "Absolutely not, unequivocally no" (cited in Dewar & Peter, 1999, p. A6).

THE DILEMMA HITS MY CLASSROOM

Eventually, the impact of the SOL and its testing program filtered into my classroom—the last bastion for teacher autonomy. As a graduate student at GMU in 1999, I faced the dilemma created by the SOLs as I worked on a research project in my English 11 classroom. I spent the year utilizing strategies designed to develop individual student voice in speaking, writing, and reading comprehension, rather than focusing on lists of literary terms and specific facts and details. Unfortunately, personal voice or independent thinking is never mentioned as an objective in the SOL.

Despite that fact, I believe that my students and I learned immensely from the work that we did last year. At the conclusion of the school year, they assembled a portfolio of written work, chosen because it best reflected who they were and what they had learned. At the conclusion of the portfolio they composed an "exit paper" that focused on their perceptions of their personal and/or intellectual growth in English. I suggested that they center their paper on one or more overriding ideas that had emerged from the curriculum and had made a particular impact on them. In the portfolios, many students identified the cry for self-reliance and intellectual independence, central to the study of the American Transcendentalists, as the turning point in their development of their own voices. The most pervasive conclusion that my students seemed to reach was a belief in their own selves—a strong self-confidence in their own thinking.

The voices of the students express this growth best. Pam said that her "timid nature has developed into a more assertive personality." Marta said that I had provided the "space" to develop her thoughts. She recognized my belief that "projects and papers would improve [her] confidence" and asserted that they, in fact, "did." Tiffany said, "When I first joined this class, I felt out of place, and that I was not smart enough to become a 'part' of this class. . . . As I began to think, and to poetically express my feelings, I felt not only as a part of the class, but as a bold individual." Vivian, echoing Tiffany, also wrote of gaining confidence in her voice: "I am awakening my opinions and expressing them much more freely." An even stronger statement came from Patrick: "I have realized the immense power that I have, that every individual has. I am a person alive in my eyes." For Kate there had been a significant change: "I have learned to express myself, free of worrying about whether or not my opinion measures up to others' opinions." Brandi saw her growth metaphorically as she expressed such pleasure that "my heart has leaked into my hand."

The students had learned a great deal about themselves as well as information about American literature. I clearly believe that the development of personal voice was more valuable to students' learning than their mastery of arbitrary curriculum determined by an outside agency (the Board of Education). My dilemma crystallized. How can I arrive at a teaching philosophy that supports divergent student thought and also covers a state-mandated curriculum with a criterion-referenced, high-stakes test? What has happened to a respect for the practitioner's knowledge about what is best for his or her students? Why are the behaviors and values that professionals believe are most important and most successful for learning being ignored by the educational decision makers? Moss (1994) cited a study that "laments the fact that teachers' accounts of their own practices typically have no place in the discourse of schooling" (p. 9). She concluded that "similar concerns have been raised about the role of students in assessments that have consequences in their own lives" (p. 9). The reality is that the classroom teacher, in collaboration with the student and his or her parents, is the one best able to determine the needs of the individual student, utilize the most effective teaching strategies for the student and teacher, and accurately assess the learning progress of the student.

FURTHER CONCERNS

As the SOL movement escalates, so do my concerns, not only for my students but also for my entire school community. There is a narrow view of learning that is inherent to the SOL initiative. This model elevates four disciplines—math, English, science, and social studies—above other disciplines such as business, physical education, foreign language, the arts, and vocational training. But, as Levine (1996) suggested in *The Opening of the American Mind*, all knowledge relates to other knowledge; that is, it is interdisciplinary. Isolated units of knowledge become static and separate. What happens to a comprehensive high school program that does not integrate knowledge about adolescent development into the school's learning goals and curriculum? As school divisions allocate monies, responsibilities, and other resources, the SOL emphasis on four disciplines sends a message that has the potential to split a school's academic programs between the "haves" and the "have nots," between "those that matter" and "those on the margins."

Already, my own school division has budgeted a significant amount of money for a staff development program that focuses on the four content areas only. Other programs are losing financial support. The agenda items at faculty meetings and leadership team meetings are overwhelmingly crowded with information and discussion about the need to improve the scores in the four core areas. I see the restlessness in the faces of those not teaching the core subjects and dread the day that those feelings may turn to resentment or anger. It appears that the pressure to maintain a school's accreditation may eventually rest on the shoulders of the teachers of the core curriculum instead of being a goal of the entire school community. One example of this shift in educational perspective occurred when our school scrapped the plans to develop a senior interdisciplinary independent study program—especially supported by those in the arts and in vocational programs—in order to concentrate on raising the SOL scores.

The elementary schools are not immune from similar inequities or shifts in emphasis. For example, one school division in Virginia has overloaded the elementary classes that will not be tested on SOLs with more than 30 students and assigned no aides to those classes, whereas the third- and fifth-grade classes (the testing years) have 15 or fewer students with full-time aides.

I am also concerned about the students who are already marginalized—the limited English proficient students, the special education students, and the slower learners. We have been developing special programs and individual educational plans for these students for decades. Now, they are required to take a grade-level test or an end-of-course test regardless of these special adaptations. Although the Commonwealth is discussing exemption of their scores from the final school reporting, no long-range policy has been established. If the present system stays as it is, they will not receive a diploma unless they pass the standardized tests. Unfortunately, the state is setting these students up for failure by requiring that they take a test that they will find extremely difficult to pass. Additionally, they are required to be in school with little or no hope of their education being valued; there will be no verification of their real progress, however limited it may be. When test scores become the "be all and end all," then children who are unlikely to pass the tests are placed in danger of being ignored or dismissed. Ironically, on a larger scale, I fear that the SOL testing and accreditation program will eventually discredit the very educational system that it sought to strengthen. The state has relentlessly forged a path that is destined to frustrate students, teachers, administrators, and parents. What happens to the reputation and respect for a state that cannot accredit its schools? How will communities flourish if their schools are not accredited? How can parents trust the educational system that appears to be failing their children? Why would new businesses and industries want to locate in such a community? What happens to students who spend 12 or 13 years in school but are unable to pass six specific tests, whose contents have been arbitrarily determined to fit the mold of a mono-cultural educational viewpoint?

The ideology behind the state's program is accurately pegged in Levine's (1996) *The Opening of the American Mind*; he suggested that "teaching subjects in schools and colleges gives [the subjects] cultural legitimacy. And what we are witnessing in our society at present is a struggle over legitimacy" (p. 98). Those in decision-making positions in Virginia are afraid that their understandings of the world and what counts as knowledge are being challenged.

The admission that literature, history, and canons are more complex and more variable than [a universal literacy] entails a loss of control and acceptance of the truth that the academic world, like the larger universe, is more chaotic, less ordered, less predictable and more affected by such matters as geography, class, race, ethnicity, gender than many of us have been willing to accept. (Levine, 1996, p. 99)

We live in a multicultural society that must value diversity in learning styles, behaviors, and attitudes. Levine suggested that one cannot deny this complexity but must confront and comprehend it. Once rigid parameters are established on what someone must know, that content becomes arbitrary and prohibits free thought and creativity. Levine referenced the Carnegie Commission on Higher Education, whose members stressed the learning of process (curiosity, critical thinking, widening perspectives on self and culture) and of relevance (relating to students' lives and to the times in which it is taught). The Commission saw "preselected content" as being too extensive and lacking in depth.

I stand with Levine. The leaders of the Commonwealth of Virginia seem to deny the complexity of our multicultural society in favor of a traditional canon that has rendered members of our society invisible and silent (although there is some concession made to technological literacy). In doing so, they are handi-capping our students by de-emphasizing and negating the thinking processes essential for survival and success in the next century. Although as a teacher I can be "methodologically active" in my lessons, I am forced to make the cur-riculum "materially static" as suggested by Yancey (1998) in *Reflection in the Writing Classroom*. I recognize that SOL proponents may have good motives, such as ensuring appropriate sequencing of information, establishing a common culture, and ensuring the public schools' accountability. Addressing these issues, however, should not privilege memorization over critical and independent think-ing, or perpetuate a monocultural rather than multicultural view of society, or reward convergent over divergent thinking.

What To Do?

I believe that several steps can be taken to rectify many of the problems already created by the SOL and the testing/accreditation program. The Board of

Education needs not only to listen to the voices of teachers who are working with students every day, but also to respect their knowledge of how students develop and what students should learn. The autonomy of the teacher in the classroom is essential to effective teaching and learning. In addition, Board members need to listen to the experts in the field of education, including those who raise questions about the current testing format and the developmental learning needs of students. Universities should provide input about the relevance and importance of the standards as well as the accuracy of the assessments.

Furthermore, I believe there needs to be a shift in the paradigm that drives assessment. The current criterion-referenced test (whose content and format must be re-examined) should not be the only means of assessment. According to Moss (1994), "a growing number of educators are calling for alternative approaches to assessment that support collaborative inquiry and foreground the development of purpose and meaning over skills and content in the intellectual work of students and teachers" (p. 6). Portfolio assessment is central to fields such as art and writing and could apply to all content areas. In higher education, many support the concept of alternative assessments. For instance, graduate degrees and tenure awards frequently hinge on assessments made by panels and committees reviewing portfolios of academic work. In the public school realm, our neighboring state, Maryland, has an elementary testing program that evaluates the ability for groups of students to work together to solve problems. Students do not receive individual grades on content knowledge; the problem solving of groups of students in individual schools is evaluated and reported. There are numerous other examples of assessments better suited to foster significant student learning. The structure and underlying principles of Virginia's SOL program are not in the best interest of all students because they ignore fundamental facts about learning. First, individuals learn differently, and second, individuals bring unique experiences and interests to learning situations. One size *does not and cannot* fit all.

Henry David Thoreau, in his "Resistance to Civil Government," said that, "if one thousand, if one hundred, if ten men whom I could name,—if ten honest men only–ay, if one HONEST man" would stand up for his convictions, then the state will do what is right in answer to the people. Thoreau continued, "For it matters not how small the beginning may seem to be," it will bring change. My learning experiences in the IET program have enabled me to care for my students over the dictates of the state, to confront the deceit in a plan that inhibits student learning, to cry out for fairness and practical wisdom, and to evoke the courage to confront those who have lost sight of the true meaning of learning. I can only hope that others will join those of us who are making our voices heard so that together we can design an approach to ensuring both standards and accountability that truly supports the complexity of learning and the uniqueness of the individual teacher and student.

14

Leading a Transformative Innovation: The Acceptance of Despair

Hugh T. Sockett

As might be expected from the critique of teacher education adumbrated in chapter 1, this innovation represented a challenge to the culture of the college, later the Graduate School of Education (GSE), and the formal and informal roles of the faculty. The strategy for IET's growth as a structural ambition failed. However, we know that innovations are expensive and always extraordinarily fragile, although the job of the university is to nurture ideas. Where deliberate assaults on the innovation that do not address its ideas bring about the failure of innovation, there is at least a prima facie case for saying that the university's proper role has been corrupted and that such assaults are an assault on the academic freedom of the innovators.

These matters are dealt with in this chapter. The chapter's title deliberately reveals its primarily autobiographical character. I recall watching a TV interview with theologian Paul Tillich who described faith as the "acceptance of despair." I share with most people who attempt to innovate the need to articulate the core beliefs that drive the new practice to one's self and others. One must find a moral compass, and be a "true believer." Whatever the detail of the ideas, the moral focus has to be on the lives and welfare of those one serves, in this case, teachers and the children they teach. Innovators need to accept the vagaries of the human predicament, accepting that there is no special reason why your innovation should be any different from others that fail. Despair can arise from changes (like a recession) quite outside one's control, and from the machinations of others (which one expects). More despairing are the things within one's control that end up as errors and misjudgments, or signs of political myopia. Often, such errors are minor, but sometimes they are crass, and too often they are debilitating. One has to watch the tendency to believe one's motives are un-impeachable, even where the outcomes are disastrous.

Unlike regular managers, innovators cannot afford the luxury of error, perhaps because they don't have the institutional mechanisms for concealing it. One must also rely on one's intuition, one's ability for fast-paced decision making, and the constitutional ability to avoid fatigue occasioned by the nightly struggles for sleep as the problems cascade through one's mind. Intuition in innovation, I can now assert with hindsight, is as significant as rational analysis. My disappoint-ments in finding the right personnel to staff an innovation, for example, have come from succumbing to rational and political analysis of applicants that ran counter to my gut feeling. So the innovator has to accept across the board the despair (and the fate) of Sisyphus and the likelihood that, however near one thinks one is getting to the top of the slope, there's a 99% chance that the stone will roll back.

THE LOCAL CHALLENGE

At the end of the 1980s, a surfeit of books criticized the work of schools of education (e.g., Clifford & Guthrie, 1988; Goodlad, 1990). In particular, Good-lad's scholarly book *Teachers for Our Nation's Schools*, although written by a sympathetic observer, contained data that presented both universities and their schools of education as out of touch with the problems of schooling in the *fin de siècle* United States. The Holmes Group of Deans (Holmes, 1986, 1989) was launched in part to counter the critics, although the claims made for change by Shulman (1987) and others in this vanguard seemed to be at least overreaching and at worst, politically suicidal (Sockett, 1988b). The National Board for Pro-fessional Teaching Standards (1989) was founded in 1987 exemplifying the environment for teacher education reform.

I thus came to GMU in 1987 at a time of ferment and opportunity in the world of teacher education. For the 10 previous years, I had occupied two lead-ership posts that demanded reinventing institutions: first as director of the In-stitute for Continuing Education at the New University of Ulster in Londonderry, Northern Ireland, and second as dean of a (new) School of Education at the University of East Anglia in England (Sockett, 1988b, 1995). Both experiences gave me the opportunity to develop an intellectual and moral conception of leadership, but also gave me some experience of leading innovations.

Coming to the GMU College of Education and Human Services seemed a different kind of opportunity, free from the administrative chores of a deanship, for, under the transformative leadership of President Johnson (see chap. 1), the university was growing by leaps and bounds as a new American university. I was asked to establish a new center connecting school districts with the school of education in a research and development partnership, and later on a proposal to the president to found the Institute into which the center was eventually merged. Like many presidents interviewed by Goodlad (1990), President George

Johnson always seemed to me to be suspicious of the quality of the college work, in research and in practice, unsure of its ability to innovate, and he appeared unsympathetic to any claims that education was a discipline.

My appointment had a strong personal aspect that created tensions. It had come about as a result of the dean's head-hunting, and was made personally and institutionally complex by my immigrant status and the restricted positions I held that were necessary to meet visa regulations. Moreover, the dean had obtained resources for the position because, as he explained it to me, he had indicated to the president that I was a "systems-buster." A second source of tension was the financial basis for the center. This was never thoroughly settled: whether it was to be "self-financing," what the balance might be between hard and soft money, and how far it could partner with outside institutions or with other college activities (such as the outreach program staffed almost entirely by adjuncts) to make the best of resources.

Systems-busting, however, was the name of the game. The center's mission statement had been discussed and agreed among the college leadership, yet within 6 months, the chair of one of the college's departments said to me "your difficulty is that people won't work with you because you want them to change their roles." I thought this was only a symptom of deep-rooted conflicts—of epistemology, hierarchy, and ownership.

The Conflict of Epistemology

First there was the deep-rooted epistemological division between the traditional empiricist-positivist view of research and development to which the college leadership by and large subscribed and the various qualitative paradigms being developed, especially in curriculum evaluation and design (see chap. 1). I was on the wrong side, having written critically of such empiricist manifestations as rational planning in curriculum (Sockett, 1972), and I was on the way to clearing my head on what a moral epistemology of practice might look like (Sockett 1989, 1993). I was aligned with the few faculty, usually women, who came from other traditions, such as anthropology and child development, who supported my proposal to develop a reflective practice strand within the existing master's in education program, easily thrown out by the doyens of the dominant paradigm. A route for teachers who wanted to do classroom research and work with the center as part of that master's program was not opened.

The Conflict of Hierarchy

Second, the college's teacher education programs contained no hint of partnership with teachers, or school divisions. Attitudes to teachers were frankly, even strongly, hierarchical. "We produce the knowledge," another chair said to me once, "and the teachers carry it out." This attitude was in total contrast, it should be said, to the Writing Project, based in the university's English Department in the College of Arts and Sciences, where the partnership with such distinguished teacher-researchers as Marian Mohr and Marion McLean (1987) was wide-ranging and profound. Partnership was not a novelty at GMU, although it was in the college.

A major example of the hierarchical attitude was brought home to me by a comparison with my context in Great Britain. Many education faculty there travel from their campuses to urban and rural centers, usually in schools, often staying overnight, to provide accessible graduate study for teachers. This was seen as a matter of respect for teachers' work, a basis for the formation of partnerships, and, of course, no big deal. This practice was totally unknown in the college. To signal I was serious about partnership, I based myself off campus in a junior–senior high school, and visited schools and superintendents frequently.

The Conflict of Ownership

Third, the college felt it owned the center, even though it had financial support from outside, specifically in the part-time associate director (who was director of research and planning in Fairfax County) and in a 50% contribution to the center's administrative secretary. The myth of full ownership by the college led many members to feel that the college alone should determine the center's policy, irrespective of whether they as individuals were involved in the center's work. Finances apart, a partnership program has to have its agenda developed in a context of partnership, with the problems of accommodation to differing perspectives that would involve whoever was the formal owner. Universities are, in general, terrible partners because they always want to say what goes, and if they don't get their way, they take their ball away. The development details of the center's program are not germane to this chapter; suffice it to say, it was a difficult and painstaking business, involving numerous small initiatives to see which types of activity might fly.

THE FOUNDATION OF THE INSTITUTE

The center made some headway, however, and was welcomed by the local superintendents and the teachers' associations. In February 1990, at a lunch meeting for superintendents hosted by the president, the discussion focused on the difficulties facing school reform. I argued that there was no support for a university radical initiative to which his response was "if you come up with something radical, I'll fund it." This was the seed from which IET grew. But the president wanted something far more ambitious than the center, constrained as it was by its inability to break through the problem of faculty role and attitudes. The proposal for IET initially involved four sympathetic members of faculty, including the dean, although one former department chair, on seeing the initial draft, recanted, saying "I can't take part in this, I'm just not a radical person like you." Eventually 10 faculty (out of 30 or so) signed a proposal that IET become a recognized department of the college, a proposal made moot by the college leadership's decision to seek a department-less and renamed Graduate School of Education.

Shortly after the IET proposal was accepted by the president in 1990, the recession struck university budgets and the seven faculty positions for the IET under process of approval evaporated. "I'm sorry, but I hope you'll do what you can" was the signal of his and our disappointment. Moreover, the dean announced his return to the faculty after recuperation from a long period of illness. An interim dean was appointed for a year. A national search failed and the director of the Community College Program within the university, a person with no experience of teacher education, was appointed. The retiring dean had appointed an associate in his penultimate year of office, who was very strongly attracted by the potential of the center and contributed heavily to the ideas and development of IET as an institution. His forthrightness made him a strongly controversial figure in the now Graduate School for reasons mostly unconnected to IET, but he was told by a chair at the time that his association with IET was damaging his position in the college. These factors combined to create a long period of turbulence in the school's leadership, which was not a propitious time for an innovation to grow, especially one that had inherited hostility and whose ambitions were so wide-ranging.

Through that turbulent period, IET nevertheless took two major initiatives. First, it constructed a huge partnership of 57 organizations in a major bid for a $20 million grant from the New America Schools Development Corporation, and received ad hoc funding from the president to mount the bid. A win would have squelched the hostility, but we lost. Second, in cooperation with two school superintendents, IET put forward the proposal within the Graduate School for the school-based master's program with which this book has been primarily concerned. Permission was eventually granted by the relevant committee, after the proposal had been obliged to go through a set of hoops specially designed for it, with a limited number of thirty students. When 500 teachers expressed interest, the interim dean ignored the faculty, obtained two additional tenure-track positions and 143 students were enrolled. IET was therefore getting additional resources with a vengeance, exacerbating faculty complaints about resources, which had begun with the center.

The school's hostile response to these two developments became so virulent that the university decided to make IET organizationally autonomous, first within the Graduate School, but shortly thereafter, outside it. Although regarded as the manipulator of this, I, in fact, had no part in either of these decisions or the discussions that led to them. I later asked the provost why the university administration had decided to move IET. "Well, you're doing well and they hate you, Hugh, don't you know?" was his reply. Actually, I didn't. For part of my puzzlement and contributory to my despair was that there was never any serious *public* debate inside the Graduate School about anything that IET stood for, or indeed about the national need for teacher education reform. On two occasions at least, my presentations about IET to the faculty were politely received but largely ignored. No doubt IET was discussed, in meetings to which I was not invited, but serious attention to matters of epistemology, hierarchy, and ownership/partnership or matters of substance was never publicly undertaken by the whole faculty.

It was that lack of attention to the substance of IET's ambitions that made me realize that opposition is often not grounded in reason or in a commitment to improve education, but more often in self-serving politics. It is a peculiar weakness for intellectual institutions to be driven by personal animosities, especially as a dispute can then be labeled "personal" when, of course, it is nothing of the sort. It involves ideas and the power that comes from those ideas, which then become identified with one individual and his or her personal traits or attitudes. Although the provost had described the reasons for the move as personal, that could not have been the sole reason, for there are many kinds of loves and hatreds within the academy that don't require organizational solutions. But if it is the case that the development of IET ideas were being impeded by reactionary forces and personal hatreds, there is at least a case to be made and answered about academic freedom (see Part III).

Into the issues of epistemology, hierarchy, and ownership, therefore, came the turbulence of college leadership and the intensification of jealousies and hostilities driven by additional earmarked resources, layers of interpersonal distrust and dislike, and a steadfast refusal to open up the issues of intellectual substance to public debate and analysis. This was the local challenge that made me despair.

Why despair? First, I am saddened by intolerance of, or naked opposition to, intellectual developments and changes. It seems ubiquitous. In recent years a medical researcher who discovered that duodenal ulcers were caused by the heliobacter virus had difficulty getting papers published on the subject and was virtually ostracized in his own country. The Human Genome Project was fraught with personal hatreds and animosities founded in intellectual approaches to method. For instance, to quote one protagonist, "the publicly funded labs are angry and for reasons I can partly understand. We took it away from them. We took the big prize away from them, when they thought they would be the team that would do the whole human genome and go down in history. Pure and simple, they hate us" (Preston, 2000, p. 83).

Second, college faculty seemed at once jealous of the resources, respectful of the energy, unwilling to take part without special inducement, scornful of the ideas without engaging in discussion about them, and determined to oppose them. This combination left me baffled as to what to do.

Third, I despaired of making any impact on what seemed to me to be the disdain of many faculty for teachers. The old saw that "researchers work on teachers rather than with them" was reinforced as true for me by the opposition generated to my priority of working with them. It grieved me especially that, for the most part, the college leadership didn't seem to care much whether the program was good, good for teachers and good for children, so fixated were they by seeing me as the target.

Fourth, college faculty did not know how to discuss the shape and character of GMU either at university or college level. It was simply not a self-critical culture, which we struggled to build in IET. This source of despair may well be, I acknowledge, because I had spent most of my career fascinated by the character of the institutions in which I worked. Yet it seems immensely difficult for academics (1) to look at their organization as a practical theory about how best to organize themselves, (2) to get the detachment needed in contemplating that theory, and (3) to do this as a matter of course, not to protect themselves in such things as an accreditation review. Rather, such discussions were regularly infected by power bids and fratricidal hostility. Contrast that with the serious moral beauty of Deming's (Gabor, 1990) view of Total Quality Management: It is its democratic aspiration to have people define their own institution and contribute to its improvement. Its major rule is "drive out fear." Yet fear, as Cornford (1908) suggested, is the political motive of the academic, a fact made immensely paradoxical by the existence of tenure that only seems to heighten academic insecurity.

Yet finally, I despaired at the absence of an institutional ethos, a set of intellectual and moral standards befitting the community. I missed it, because I had been accustomed to it. Sometimes it had a mafia-like quality. Talking one winter evening with three very smart women members of the faculty, all of whom were generally supportive, but all of whom were up for promotion or tenure, I realized how insidious all this had become. They told me that they had been warned that support for IET would count against them. What was I to make of this as an example of the ethos of an intellectual community? Can one avoid despair at such a context?

GROWTH AND SURVIVAL

"If you pause you are sunk," President Johnson said in one of his twice-yearly reports to the faculty, which were a remarkable treat for those who had the pleasure of listening to them. George Johnson was an English scholar, but was also a brilliant self-deprecating raconteur, a man well on the way to proving that at GMU you could make a real silk purse out of a sow's ear. He always acknowledged the concern of many faculty for the speed of growth, at the funding of new rather than traditional academic units. As the country came out of the recession, he said bluntly: "We have come through a period of having to circle the wagons, but we are now on the road again, and those of you that get left behind will, I am afraid, just be left behind." More controversially, he believed in a chaos theory of organizations: that is, he liked people to run with the ball in space he had opened up. But you couldn't stop, he claimed, even though you might be pulled back, as in the recession of the early 1990s.

IET had a bad start as it was launched in the recession. Going ahead anyway, "If you pause . . ." was the IET strategy dominating its growth in the 1990s. It had several parts to it. First, we created business partners as a way of bridging the business–education gap, but also of using their influence. Second, we threw in our lot with the most radical of university opportunities, which other units might ignore. Of most importance was the university's interest in new forms of flexible and alternative staffing, a first mild experiment in expanding nontenured appointments. Given the student demand, we added faculty rapidly, and we also moved to a form of funding that connected closely our student enrollment figures with our revenue. We were also mobile, moving out to a new campus in temporary accommodation and providing student numbers crucial to state auditors. Third, we wrote a wide range of proposals, always in partnership, with a success rate of about 1 in 20, in areas germane to our interests.

The target was to get IET established as a university institute, which would give us the equivalent status of a school or college, realizing our institutional ambition. Such institutes were developed by Johnson as organizational homes to build initiatives that proved difficult to accommodate within existing schools or colleges, a common practice across business and industry. The IET strategy was worked through with the president and the provost, with strong support from the business people with whom we worked. The key was, as Johnson put it, "faculty heft." For faculty appointments we were specifically interested in people who would be *persona grata* in other academic units. The idea was to develop long-term academic links across the university, so that IET would reach across the institution, not be constrained within its own walls like the (now) Graduate School of Education.

Yet the problems associated with fast growth beset us. Bringing in new faculty on an annual basis, especially to an organization with a strong ethos, simply does not allow for an effective period of reflective socialization. Some appointees did not fit with us and moved on. New faculty were also encouraged to use the space created to develop their ideas and interpretations which, because of time and other pressures, proved difficult. Instead of being able to build a close community, we suffered some fragmentation (see chap. 12), especially as our fast growth strategy demanded working on two campuses. Furthermore, new faculty getting their feet wet could not be expected to meet the demands of external work, linking with business as we had originally hoped. Yet moving more slowly would allow the target of proper independent status to recede far too far into the distance.

The effect of fast growth on my leadership was dramatic. Seeking to preserve the integrity of the developing idea, I tried to walk on water (see Goodlad, 1990, p. 142). I kept up strong business relationships. I taught full time and was a full-time administrator. To protect inexperienced faculty, I was single-handedly responsible for student recruitment. And I could not pause, developing ideas for links with the university's Center for Field Studies with Bahamian teachers, providing support and ideas for the Urban Alternative, attending superintendents' conferences, visiting school teams, trying to write books and papers, and so on. I spent much of the time, too, ensuring that my links to the various parts of the university administration were strong. Yet, somehow, it all worked. That is, we did receive the president and provost's assent to becoming a university institute.

We had many disappointments in the process of growth, of course, but despair was also around the corner. Two days before the provost was to present the recommendation to the university Board of Visitors that IET become a university institute, he pulled the matter off the agenda. The "organizational change" had not been open to consultation with Senate as the newly amended Faculty Handbook demanded. So procedures had to be invented. It was decided to hold a Town Meeting, chaired jointly by the provost and the chair of Senate (a bizarre proceeding if ever there was one), before the matter went to Senate. Just as I had been deeply shocked by the conversation with my three women colleagues some years earlier, I was astonished at that meeting by the malice and the wretchedness of the comments on the proposal by members of the Graduate School of Education at this meeting. I can say no more about their comments than that they were predominantly a catalogue of downright lies, personal attacks, and manifest irrelevancies. I was amazed by the intensity of what was now simply a vendetta.

And Johnson announced his retirement 2 weeks later, just before the Senate held a special meeting to discuss IET as an institute. This retirement unblocked two decades of resentment. It let loose all those who, although they had personally profited from his build-up of the university, wanted to settle some old scores and bring to the university a somnolent mediocrity. Moreover, the composition of the Board of Visitors was changing under a Republican governor, bringing to its counsels a different temper and an interventionist style. The president could have ignored the Senate's decision (by a very small majority) not to make IET a university institute. But, as he lamented to me at an early morning meeting, times had changed and the turbulence surrounding his retirement was such that he could not bring the proposal to give IET full powers as an institute to the Board.

IET was thus forced to pause. One immediate question for me was whether my leadership had brought it to this terminus. I had with some success negotiated the politics of the environment. I had never thought of myself as a person who believed that sweet reason alone could change people's minds. Rather, if you had passion and commitment, there would be those who would want to join you and those who would watch you with amusement. Few would throw landmines at you. The despair mounted in this way. Rather than ignoring the presence of IET, which was now an imagined threat following the defeat of the Institute proposal, GSE's leadership became increasingly angered by our success and its high-risk fast growth strategy. That venom was apparent in many documents, public and private. When, in the new president's first year, unit self-studies became the order of the day, the cross-university group assessing IET systematically misrepresented our work in criticisms apparently culled from Graduate School advice. Indeed, as I wrote to a new provost, that assessment was an intellectual disgrace as a public document in a university.

I personally was the consistent, if not the fully acknowledged, target. The ambitious style of my leadership clearly contained the seeds of failure. Not because I stamped on toes, dearly as I would love to have done, but because I became a focus for attack and the quality of the work and the ideas were never cogently examined or even discussed. Fast growth demanded more prominent leadership and activity, which drove up the level of personal animosity. My strong leadership, or my execution of it, seemed to me becoming a continuing source of IET's failure to get established. Either people did not care about intellectual integrity, or they did not understand the ideas behind IET, so they attacked me.

So there is also despair, when one's own personality is under attack, in not really understanding what it is about you that makes purportedly intelligent people hate you. Some people have suggested that by starting an institution based on criticism of current practice, by suggesting changes in roles, I frightened them. Maybe, but what has happened to the institutional culture if people in a university of all places get so vindictive about new ideas? And why do university administrators reinforce this nonsense by regarding all disputes as interpersonal, to be swept away by a new broom of reorganization?

For the IET innovation described an organization, not just a program (see chap. 1). It was thus a mix of ideas—about the university's relation to public education, about professional education, about the interplay of university and community, about teacher education practices, about alternative epistemological bases and institutional shape, and in the end about the moral responsibility of teacher education to those they teach. When IET was originally shifted out of the Graduate School, the move was to protect the ideas and thereby the academic freedom of those involved, at that stage primarily myself, but also the fledgling possibilities of a new institution. The university could nurture what the Graduate School of Education, for whatever reason, could not. Once the attempt to become a university institute failed and a new president was appointed, IET's future would depend on his leadership. Suffice it to say that IET first went through a protracted period of discussion with the university in which it was given autonomous affiliated status within the Graduate School. After my resignation as director on grounds of illness, the agreement was unilaterally torn up and none of its hard-debated understandings respected. Although not quite asset-stripping the institute, the school has supported only its role as an innovative teacher education program, failing to support, for example, the Urban Alternative program. As I contemplate the history and work of IET, I have asked myself whether it would be fair to claim that my academic freedom was seriously denied and whether this is not the root of my despair since it is the lynchpin of intellectual life.

ACADEMIC FREEDOM AND THE PROFESSIONAL EDUCATION INNOVATOR

The rationale for academic freedom is the application of the principle of free speech to an organization whose purpose is ideas, but whose management and locus of financial control may be political (as in a state university) or ideological (as in a religious foundation). Tenured or untenured, you can't be fired for speaking your mind and disagreeing with those who give you your paycheck. And this applies whatever the personal temperament, characteristics, propensities, physiognomy, gender, race, and class of the speaker. It can be denied, for example, where a young scholar is told by a dean that to pursue a particular line of inquiry would be unacceptable, or it can be undermined, by attacking an individual's integrity.

Academic Freedom and Institutional Regulations

Academic freedom can be conceived as a right in two ways. First, it has been conceived as a *special right*, that is, one pertaining simply to universities as institutions and not the privilege of, say, an independent scholar, poet, or artist (like Robert Mapplethorpe). I have discussed elsewhere the weaknesses of this special right theory (Sockett, 1977), as I believe we should regard academic freedom as a *general* right. The difference can be summarized as follows: Academic freedom within the special right theory looks primarily to the special freedoms academics have in their roles and in the institution of which they are a part. The general right theory regards academic freedom as general intellectual freedom. This is a right in a democratic society (and thereby applicable to Mapplethorpe) and such limitations as there may be on it can be justified only insofar as they make the pursuit of knowledge procedurally and organizationally possible. Academic freedom is therefore the civil liberty of the democrat, tempered by institutional regulations.

Yet, like all profound principles, we must want the sustenance of the principle more than we want our own profit from it. Academics must protect it for themselves and each other, on the old principle that I may hate what you say, but I will defend to the death your right to say it. That is a relatively easy matter when we are dealing with theory. We can all admire the ground-breaking controversial work of a historian, a political scientist, a literary critic, Marxist or liberal, and, of course, the natural or physical scientist where their work is fundamentally theoretical. Moreover, the university as an organization need provide only an office, a salary and a requirement to teach. The matter is different, as we will see, when one comes to intellectual activities that are practical, like professional education, or in this case, teacher education or the foundation of a new institution. Supporting a person's academic freedom here does demand more than an office and a salary if the ideas are to be tested.

If the general right theory is appropriate, namely that academic freedom is the civil liberty of the democrat tempered by institutional regulations, then we need to understand what institutional regulations are. They will cover (a) such matters as the individual's contract with the institution for teaching, research, and service and (b) the regulations of governance that determine the activities of the larger and smaller corporate bodies thay make up the body politic of the institution. Under the regulations of governance will be rules for the distribution of resources and there will be designated people in roles (like deans and department chairs) empowered to decide and/or execute allocation decisions.

University management systems combine a committee system with personal discretion for office-holders. As a device for action, committees are frequently clumsy and slow, especially attractive to people with nothing else to do or the bureaucratic mindset of the gatekeeper or guardian. What do we have to do, we have too often to ask, to "get it through" this or that committee? Committees can rapidly become tools for control and stifling of innovation. Nor is it an integral part of democratic folklore that there must be committees, especially of this sort. The problem is to find functioning systems consonant with the highest common denominator, not the lowest common factor, of democratic ideals. For instance, a wisely led committee can use regulations as enabling devices, not as obstacles, using the tools the regulations provide to support rather than suppress innovation. For, of course, laws don't dictate their own application. Each and every case demands interpretation. Gatekeepers and guardians (the kiss of death to an intellectual community) can be transformed into creative enablers.

The stance then becomes "How can we help X to do Y?" not "Do X's proposals for Y meet our interpretation of the rules?" which defines regulations as opportunities not obstacles. Within that frame, the challenge is to balance the individual's rights with the institutional regulations. Overemphasis on the latter, in my view, puts bureaucracy above ideas. As a center of ideas, the university's task must be to put all regulations in the service of ideas and provide space for innovations to flourish. Where committees act like gatekeepers and guardians, they manifest a fear of change, a fear of ideas, and a conservative political motivation that becomes institutional timidity. The regulations matter, of course, for an intellectual community has to find an appropriate *modus operandi*. But when they become overregulated by gatekeepers and guardians, they reduce mutual trust to a matter of a successful process. The weight has to be put on the side of the ideas, not the mechanism of permissions. That applies to individuals exercising judgment and university institutions coming to corporate decisions.

Academic Freedom and the Practical Innovator

The academic freedom of the professional educator or practical innovator in a university is different from the theoretical because of the demands he or she makes on resources beyond the office and the salary. If a professional educator has (moral and epistemological) ideas for a new degree design within a new institution, there are obviously resource implications. These are practical not theoretical ideas. Presumably nobody in a university would say that a professional educator should not have a right in principle to explicate or to experiment with these practical ideas or to work them out. Maybe in principle, but what would defeat the application of this principle?

First, it could rightly be argued that the principle cannot be upheld where a program idea is not congruent with the institution's existing ideological frame. If a faculty member at a religious institution responsible for the training of ministers loses his or her faith, and wants to run a program proving God does not exist, the institution would, with justification, deny him or her the right. That action clearly does not defeat the individual's right in principle, it merely describes the authority of the institution and its right, where justified, to override the claims of the individual that run counter to its ideology.

Second, it could rightly be argued that the principle gives the professional education innovator a blank check. That would, of course, make nonsense of any institution's operations and regulations, and, pragmatically, there won't be enough to go round anyway. Yet the blank check issue, closely examined, extends the principle. For, on the basis that the individual who wills the ends wills the means, if I have a formal right to the freedom to express and develop practical ideas in principle, that must extend to a formal right to the resources in principle, too. Without it, for the professional education innovator, the formal right of academic freedom is just an empty gesture. Manifestly, in the day-to-day practical judgments of priority that have to be made in the management of resources under institutional regulations, the individual may not yet, perhaps never, get funding for his or her ideas. The principle, seen now as a right to express ideas for practice and to have the resources to carry them out, is not defeated: Rather, it simply comes into conflict with other priorities (themselves originating in other principles). At this stage, it is important for these priorities to be determined on rational nonarbitrary grounds.

In summary, there seems to be a general right of academic freedom for the professional educator to do such things as construct and implement degree or institutional designs, which carries with it the right to resources. There are three provisos:

1. Some institutions are established for a clear specific ideological purpose.
2. Resources are managed through the establishment of priorities, the denial of which does not undermine my formal right to them.
3. Such priorities are determined on rational nonarbitrary grounds.

How Can Academic Freedom be Denied or Undermined?

My claim is that professional education innovators have the right to academic freedom, which carries with it the right to resources. I have indicated that everyone in a university has a moral interest (and a prudential self-interest) in sustaining academic freedom. Institutions have a corresponding duty in principle to provide resources. Academic freedom simply can be denied, as in the case just cited, but that does not concern us here. Yet it can also be undermined, and I turn finally to reflect on whether and how, seeing myself as an example of an innovator in professional education, my academic freedom was undermined. To do this, we can examine what happened in the light of the three provisos.

Proviso 1 acknowledges that some institutions are established for a clear specific ideological purpose, which gives them a prima facie right to deny academic freedom to an individual. A public university is not ideologically free, of course, although the rhetoric (and the rhetoric of academic freedom) suggests that it is. Indeed, as indicated in chapter 1, the dominant epistemological paradigm amounts to an ideology open to challenge. Characteristics of this ideology are enshrined in institutional practices (e.g., student evaluations of teaching, bureaucratic management), but also in the institutional ethos. The job of the academic unit is, however, at least to hold the ring and to welcome dissenting voices if intellectual integrity and academic freedom are to be sustained. Although the Graduate School of Education was supposedly ideologically free, and expected to support new ideas, I was constantly under serious pressure to conform because I didn't subscribe to the dominant paradigm.

Proviso 2 states that resources are managed through the establishment of priorities, the denial of which does not undermine an individual's formal right to them. An institution will have to weigh the respective merits of different priorities, and in political reality debates over resources cannot be free of individual judgments and preferences. In my own case, and in the case of IET, resources were provided more by university intervention and support than distribution within the Graduate School. After the initial failure to get the full complement of resources from the university, IET later became self-supporting and took its own risks in a form of financing and staffing. But could an innovator claim not merely resources but some special status as part of his or her right? Specifically, is it justifiable to claim that my academic freedom was undermined by IET not becoming a university institute? No, of course not. For here the levels of complexity about priorities are much deeper, covering university as well as unit politics.

Proviso 3 states that such priorities are determined on rational nonarbitrary grounds. In a university, that must include formal and informal inclusive dialogue. This is where personalities, not just judgments and preferences about unit needs, are most insidious because animosities (or the preferences expressed in patronage) have little or nothing to do with the quality of the ideas. This is not to assert that the messenger and the message are somehow disembodied. Passion for ideas is tied up with their content. Yet academics (of all people) must focus on questions of the quality of ideas. While expecting personal passions and idiosyncrasies to influence debate and discussion without prejudice to specific proposals, they must attend to their professional obligations to put them aside.

That many people find this difficult is no response. They (and we) all need to learn. If university faculty find it impossible and define all disputes as personal, they are simply in the wrong business.

To clarify my particular position, we need to revisit the history briefly. The administrative decision to shift IET out of the Graduate School was a direct product of the school leadership's failure to support IET as a continuing presence in the school. The innovation suffered direct tissue rejection, so the school was no longer formally concerned. The university administration could not guarantee that the degree and the ideas it was generating within the school would be protected and nurtured. Yet after the university made this judgment on priorities, the Graduate School responded with the kind of personal venom on public display at the Town Meeting, and many other cases were brought to my attention of Graduate School faculty disparaging and undermining the program outside the university. So the university administration was justified in its implicit claim that the Graduate School would not or could not protect the academic freedom of some of its faculty and thereby would be unlikely to provide it with the resources needed.

The Graduate School of Education, however, had the right to refuse the program a priority status, assuming they had engaged in dialogue leading to decisions made on rational nonarbitrary grounds. It had absolutely no right, once the university had made the shift, to attack IET in the squalid way its leaders did and thereby undermine my academic freedom (and that of others). Their duty was to support the university's decision. I suggest that my academic freedom to be a professional innovator was seriously undermined by those in the formal and cultural leadership of the Graduate School. They failed to protect the original innovation. They failed to recognize they had a duty to do so. They scrambled rather than disentangled personal and intellectual issues, so that once IET was separated, they tried regularly to undermine it. They made it politically impossible to build partnerships with sympathetic faculty in the school. When the issue of its institutional future was raised in the university, they systematically bled their case into a personal vendetta. Either out of intention or incompetence, they failed to understand IET as an idea, and on frequent public occasions demonstrated that ignorance. Above all, they never promoted discussion of the complex of ideas IET raised, which is at the core of a university's purpose.

Academic Freedom and Social Responsibility

As a strictly personal matter, of course, my claim is in the "hill of beans" category. It matters not one whit. Yet as an example of what happens to innovations, it is important and a salutary warning. Take heed, young man or woman innovator! Be warned of the despair that awaits you!

First, the intellectual responsibility of the academic is to critique his or her institution within the principles of intellectual and moral integrity. If my account of the history of this innovation is broadly correct, it demonstrates just how badly needed an established critical culture is and, of course, how difficult it is to achieve.

Second, the purpose of publicly funded university institutions is to contribute to the public good, not to provide an arena for intellectuals to have fun at the expense of others. Academic freedom carries with it social responsibility too. Universities have huge potential for impact on social life, especially on schools and teacher education, whatever their actual achievements. From the outset, the IET program was recognized as valuable by the teachers who came to study with us, by the principals who saw the impact they had on their schools, even by children who saw their teacher re-energized and re-vitalized by the moral and intellectual experience they had in the program. Superintendents agreed. Visitors came to the program from home and abroad and the program became a prototype for others. Most teachers claimed and many documented the impact the program had on children's performances (see chap. 7 and 8).

Yet the program also sprang from the concept of IET as an organization, with outreach planned to families and communities, with internal relationships re-formed and recreated, and continued with alumni, with all the characteristics of an alternative to the dominant paradigm. IET faculty, myself included, worked extraordinarily hard to build this vision and were rewarded by the enthusiasms of our professional colleagues from the classrooms. At least 30 teachers had their work with us published.

The most remarkable and despairing feature of the innovation, therefore, is not that an individual's academic freedom was undermined, although it was, and not that there was no self-critical culture established where there should have been. Rather, a highly successful innovative program of quality with great influence on the lives of teachers and children was constantly under attack by a Graduate School of Education leadership. What can we make of this? Especially in teacher education, I think, institutions need to open up ways for individuals to use their academic freedom to realize their social responsibilities to public education. No form of organization, of course, guarantees productive ideas or ideas which are beyond criticism. But if teacher education institutions cannot face up to the prolixity of ideas and the value of bold initiatives, they are opting for increasing irrelevance to the educational world. If the institutions cannot raise their sights above personal in-fighting to an institutional commitment to improving public education, they will continue to deserve the excoriations and criticism presently meted out to them.

So we need many alternative ways of doing things if we want to find out what an institution is capable of. The story in this book is merely one of those alternatives. Sadly, Johnson's vision (like many an innovation) is being dismantled with the speed of a marquee disappearing after a society wedding. In its place is being erected a smokestack view of the organization with its traditional lines of control and its extraordinary ability to scotch the emergence of ideas about educational institutions which are so desperately needed in this society.

But I write as though IET has had no life after the failure to gain institute status. Its ambitions have been drastically curtailed, although that is another story and I have only been marginally involved in it. The final part of the lesson is now clear, however. The heart of the problem is that the dominant empiricist paradigm finds its organizational form, even in teacher education, in a bureaucracy neutral and unself-critical about its moral purpose. It has also socialized people into rigid patterns of control and a set of static and unimaginative moral and political habits. Increasing numbers of teacher educators reject this paradigm, and the institutions it has spawned. We embrace the immense challenge of a moral epistemology and institutions to match it. We realize you can't reform teacher education. You can only transform it.

Appendix

STAGES OF WRITING DEVELOPMENT (PRINCE WILLIAM COUNTY PUBLIC SCHOOLS)

Pre-Emergent (Scribble)

- Uses paper and pencil
- Movements of writing utensils are uncontrolled and random
- Ability to read or explain writing is not yet observed
- Letter symbols are beginning to become apparent

Emergent (Functional Scribble)

- Ideas may not be readily apparent to an observer
- Left to right progression may not be consistent
- May be able to read or explain own writing to an audience
- Appears to use letter forms and drawings to communicate meaning

Dependent (Combination)

- Strings letters and begins to form words
- May forget what is written after a period of time
- Uses simple and known vocabulary

- May rely on classroom print
- Inventive spelling has beginning or ending sounds

Developing (Restricted)

- Begins to take more risks by writing simple sentences
- Can read own writing back to an audience
- Space between words to produce a reliable manuscript
- Rereads to check meaning
- Begins to incorporate vowels in inventive spelling

Independent (Expanded)

- Begins to match oral language to writing
- Understands, "If I can think it, I can say it; if I can say it, I can write it; if I can write it, I can read it."
- Utilizes a sort of organizational plan to write
- Begins to take risks when writing
- Begins to make corrections while writing
- Writes for a variety of purposes (including to express personal experiences, to learn, to respond)
- Writes in a variety of forms (including journals and logs)
- Develops a sense of authorship and voice
- Develops further knowledge of spelling conventions
- Varies sentence structure (may include fragments and spelling errors)

DESCRIPTION OF RICHARD GENTRY'S SPELLING STAGES

Prephonemic spelling—Children scribble, form letters, and string letters together but without awareness that letters represent phonemes or speech sounds. Typically seen in preschoolers and beginning kindergarteners.

Early phonemic spelling—There is limited attempt to represent phonemes with letters, for example, using one or two letters for a word ("m" for "my" and "nt" for "night"). Early phonemic spelling is typical of many kindergarten and beginning first grade children.

Phonetic (or letter-name) spelling—The child uses letters for phonemes—for example, "lik" for "like" and "brthr" for "brother." The child represents most phonemes, understands the concept of a word but is not quite reading yet.

Transitional spelling—In this stage, children are internalizing much information about spelling patterns, and the words they write look like English words. For example, the child may write "skool" for "school" and "happe" for "happy." Rules are employed, but not always correctly. This stage usually includes first through third graders.

Standard spelling—At this stage, children spell most words correctly. "We have found this stage occurs by the middle to the end of third grade or in fourth grade." (Routman, 1991, p. 239)

References

Appiah, K.A., & Gutmann, A. (1996). *Color conscious: The political morality of race.* Princeton, NJ: Princeton University Press.

Apple, M.W., & Beane, J.A. (1995). *Democratic schools.* Alexandria, VA: Association for Supervision and Curriculum Development.

Arendt, H. (1958). *The human condition.* Chicago: University of Chicago Press.

Ashton-Warner, S. (1963). *Teacher.* New York: Simon & Schuster.

Atwell-Vasey, W., Gerow, S., Sevcik, A., Sockett, H., & Wood, D. (1995). *Beliefs and principles in IET practice.* Fairfax, VA: George Mason University, Institute for Educational Transformation (IET).

Avery, C. (1993). *And with a light touch.* Portsmouth, NH: Heinemann.

Barber, B.R. (1997). Public schooling: Education for democracy. In J.I. Goodlad & T.J. McMannon (Eds.), *The public purpose of education and schooling* (pp. 21–32). San Francisco: Jossey-Bass.

Barnard, D. (1995). Writing in Art. In the Institute for Educational Transformation (Eds.), *Research in practice—Cohort III* (unpublished anthology). Fairfax, VA: George Mason University.

Bauman, R. (1982). Ethnography of children's folklore. In P. Gilmore and A. A. Glatthorn (Eds.), *Children in and out of school: ethnography and education.* (Washington, DC: Center for Applied Linguistics), 172–186.

Belenky, M.F., Clinchy, B.M., Goldberger, N.R., & Tarule, J.M. (1986). *Women's ways of knowing.* New York: Basic Books.

Blum, L. (1998, April). *The significance of race and philosophy.* Paper presented at the Philosophy and Education Colloquium, Teachers College, Columbia University, New York.

Boal, A. (1995). *The rainbow of desire: The Boal method of theatre and therapy.* New York: Routledge.

Bohm, D. (1996). *On dialogue*. New York: Routledge.

Bok, S. (1978). *Lying: Moral choice in public and private life*. New York: Pantheon Books.

Bok, S. (1983). *Secrets: On the ethics of concealment and revelation*. New York: Pantheon Books.

Booth, W.C., Colomb, G.G., & Williams, J.M. (1995). *The craft of research*. Chicago: University of Chicago Press.

Bourne, R. (1916). Trans-national America. In W. Sollers (Ed.), *Theories of ethnicity: A classical reader* (pp. 93–108). New York: New York University Press.

Braxton, J., & Bayer, A. (1999). *Faculty misconduct in collegiate teaching*. Baltimore, MD: Johns Hopkins University Press.

Browning, F. (1996). *A queer geography: Journeys toward a sexual self*. New York: Noonday Press.

Bruner, J. (1996). *The culture of education*. Cambridge, MA: Harvard University Press.

Calkins, L., Montgomery, K., Santman, D., & Falk, B. (1998). *A teachers' guide to standardized reading tests: Knowledge is power*. Portsmouth, NH: Heinemann.

Campbell, M. (1993). *Powerful learning experiences. Expeditionary learning*. Outward Bound Online Archive, URL: http://www.gmu.edu/~amoore2iet/campbell.html.

Clifford, G., & Guthrie, J.W. (1988). *Ed school: A brief for professional education*. Berkeley: University of California Press.

Cochran-Smith, M., & Lytle, S.L. (1992). *Inside–outside: Teacher research and knowledge*. New York: Teachers College Press.

Cochran-Smith, M., & Lytle, S.L. (1999). The teacher research movement: A decade later. *Educational Researcher, 28*(7), 15–25.

Cohn, M.M., & Kottkamp, R.B. (1993). *Teachers: The missing voice in education*. Albany: State University of New York Press.

Cornford, F.M. (1908). *Microcosmographia academica*. Cambridge: Cambridge University Press.

Courter-Folly, D. (1995). Active learning. In the Institute for Educational Tranformation (Eds.), *Research in practice—Cohort III* (unpublished anthology). Fairfax, VA: George Mason University.

Cowley, J. (1983). *Dan, the flying man*. Hong Kong: Shortland Publications.

Dalton, H. (1995). *Racial healing: Confronting the fear between Blacks and Whites*. New York: Anchor Books Doubleday.

Dalton, J., & Watson, M. (1997). *Among friends: Classrooms where caring and learning prevails*. Oakland, CA: Developmental Studies Center.

Darder, A. (1991). *Culture and power in the classroom: A critical foundation for bicultural education*. New York: Bergin & Garvey.

Darling-Hammond, L. (1994). Developing professional development schools: Early lessons, challenge, and promise. In L. Darling-Hammond (Ed.), *Professional development schools* (pp. 1–27). New York: Teachers College Press.

Darling-Hammond, L. (1997a). Reforming the school reform agenda: Developing capacity for school transformation. In E. Clinchy (Ed.), *Transforming public education* (pp. 38–55). New York: Teachers College Press.

Darling-Hammond, L. (1997b). *The right to learn: A blueprint for creating schools that work*. San Francisco, CA: Jossey-Bass.

Delpit, L. (1995). *Other people's children: Cultural conflict in the classroom*. New York: The New Press.

Deming, W.E. (1995). *The new economics: For industry, government, education.* Boston: MIT Press.

DeMulder, E.K., & Eby, K.K. (1999). Bridging troubled waters: Learning communities for the 21st century. *American Behavioral Scientist, 42*(5), 892–901.

Dewar, H., & Peter, B. (1999, January). 97% fail first round of key tests in Virginia. *The Washington Post*, pp. A1, A6.

Dewey, J. (1919). *The child and the curriculum.* Chicago, IL: The University of Chicago Press.

Dewey, J. (1934). *Art as experience.* New York: Perigee.

Dewey, J. (1938). *Experience and education.* New York: Macmillan.

Dewey, J. (1954). *The public and its problems.* Athens: Ohio University Press.

Dewey, J. (1985). *Democracy and education.* Carbondale: Southern Illinois Press. (Original work published 1916)

Dewey, J. (1990). *The school and society. The child and the curriculum.* Chicago, IL: University of Chicago Press. (Original work published 1902)

Dickens, C. (1854). *Hard Times.* New York: Penguin Books.

Diegmueller, K. (1995) Expletives deleted. *Education Week, 14*(39), p. 36.

DuBois, W.E.B. (1903). *The souls of Black folk.* New York: Signet Classics.

Eisner, E. (1985). *Learning and teaching the ways of knowing.* Chicago, IL: University of Chicago Press.

Elbaz, F. (1983). *Teacher thinking: A study of practical knowledge.* New York: Nichols.

Elliott, J. (1991). *Action research for educational change.* Buckingham: Open University Press.

Farkas, S., Johnson, J., & Foleno, T. (2000). *A sense of calling: Who teaches and why.* New York: Public Agenda Foundation.

Fenstermacher, G.D., & Goodlad, J.I. (1997). *On knowledge and its relation to the human conversation. Work in Progress Series* (No. 6). Seattle, WA: Institute for Educational Inquiry.

Finn, C.E. (1991). *We must take charge: Our schools and our future.* Glencoe, IL: The Free Press.

Fisher, B. (1991). *Joyful learning.* Portsmouth, NH: Heinemann.

Fitzgerald, F.S. (1925). *The great Gatsby.* New York: Charles Scribners Sons.

Freire, P. (1970). *Pedagogy of the oppressed.* New York: Continuum.

Gabor, A. (1990). *The man who discovered quality: How W. Edwards Deming brought the quality revolution to America—The Stories of Ford, Xerox & GM.* New York: Crown.

Gallas, K. (1991). Arts of epistemology: Enabling children to know what they know. *Harvard Educational Review, 61*(1), 19–31.

Garcia, E.E. (1997). The education of Hispanics in early childhood: Of roots and wings. *Young Children, 52*(3), 5–14.

Geertz, C. (1973). Thick description: toward an interpretive theory of culture. In C. Geertz, *The Interpretation of Cultures: Selected Essays.* (New York: Basic Books), 3–30.

Genesee, F. (1994). *Educating second language children: The whole child, the whole curriculum, the whole community.* Cambridge: Cambridge University Press.

Gerow, S. (1996). *Teacher researchers in school-based collaborative teams: One approach to school reform.* Unpublished doctoral dissertation, George Mason University, Fairfax, VA.

Gilbert, L. (1992). *Teachers' experiences of peer coaching in one ethnically diverse urban public high school.* Unpublished doctoral dissertation, Syracuse University, Syracuse, NY.

Gilligan, C. (1982). *In a different voice.* Cambridge, MA: Harvard University Press.

Giroux, H. (1988). *Teachers as intellectuals: Toward a critical pedagogy of learning.* Westport, CT: Bergin & Garvey.

Giroux, H. (1992). *Border crossings: Cultural workers and the politics of education.* New York: Routledge.

Gitlin, A., Bringhurst, K., Burns, M., Cooley, V., Myers, B., Price, K., Russell, R. and Tiess, P. (1992). *Teachers' Voices for School Change: An Introduction to Educative Research.* New York, NY: Teachers College Press.

Givens-Generett, G. & Hicks, M. (2001, February). *Is there life after transformation? The struggle to remain hopeful in oppressive contexts.* Paper presented at the Dogwood Conference on Educational Studies at Emory University, Atlanta, GA.

Goldberg, D.T. (1995). *Multiculturalism: A critical reader.* Cambridge, MA: Blackwell.

Goldenberg, I. (1978). *Oppression and social intervention.* Chicago, IL: Nelson-Hall.

Gonzalez, J., & Darling-Hammond, L. (1997). *New concepts for new challenges: Professional development for teachers of immigrant youth.* Washington, DC: Center for Applied Linguistics.

Goodlad, J.I. (1984). *A place called school: Prospects for the future.* New York: McGraw-Hill.

Goodlad, J.I. (1990). *Teachers for our nation's schools.* San Francisco, CA: Jossey-Bass.

Goodlad, J.I. (1994). *Educational renewal.* San Francisco, CA: Jossey-Bass.

Goodlad, J.I., & Keating, P. (Eds.). (1991). *Access to knowledge: An agenda for our nation's schools.* New York: College Entrance Examination Board.

Goodlad, J.I., Soder, R., & Sirotnik, K.A. (Eds.). (1990). *The moral dimensions of teaching.* San Francisco, CA: Jossey-Bass.

Gouinlock, J. (1994). *The moral writings of John Dewey.* Amherst, NY: Prometheus Books.

Gould, S.J. (1996). *The mismeasure of man.* New York: Norton.

Graph, G. and Phalen, J. (1995) *The adventures of Huckleberry Finn: A case study in critical controversy.* New York, NY: St. Martins.

Greene, M. (1988). *The dialectic of freedom.* New York: Teachers College Press.

Greene, M. (1995). *Releasing the imagination: Essays on education, the arts, and social change.* San Francisco, CA: Jossey-Bass.

Grumet, M.R. (1988). *Bitter milk: Women and teaching.* Amherst: University of Massachusetts Press.

Gutmann, A. (1999). *Democratic education.* Princeton, NJ: Princeton University Press.

Habermas, J. (1991). *Moral consciousness and communicative action.* Cambridge: MIT Press.

Hagerty, P. (1992). *Readers' workshop—Real reading.* New York: Scholastic.

Hamlyn, D. W. (1978) *Experience and the growth of understanding.* London and Boston: Routledge & Kegan Paul.

Hansen, D. (1998). The moral is in the practice. *Teaching and Teacher Education, 14*(6), 643–655.

Harding, S. (1991). *Whose science? Whose knowledge? Thinking from women's lives.* Ithaca, NY: Cornell University Press.

Hare, A., Blumberg, H. and Goffman, E. (1988). *Dramaturgical analysis of social interaction.* New York: Praeger.

Heron, J. (1992). *Feeling and personhood (Psychology in another key).* Newbury, CA: Sage.

Hersch, P. (1998). *A tribe apart: A journey to the heartland of American adolescence.* New York: Fawcett.

Hicks, M., Foster, M., Williams, C., & Wood, D.R. (2000, February). *Awakening moral sensibilities through aesthetic experiences: Integrating the arts in teacher education.* Paper presented at the meeting of the American Association of Colleges for Teacher Education, Chicago, IL.

Hicks, M., Sockett, H. (2000). *Transformation as an educational aim in teacher education.* Unpublished paper.

Hicks, M., & Wood, D.R. (2000, April). *Opening aesthetic gateways to moral practices in teacher education programs.* Paper presented at the annual meeting of the American Educational Research Association, New Orleans, LA.

Hill-Collins, P. (1986). Learning from the outsider within: The sociological significance of Black feminist thought. In M. Fonow & J. Cook (Eds.), *Beyond methodology: Feminist scholarship as lived research* (pp. 35–59). Bloomington: Indiana University Press.

Hirsch, E.D. (1996). *The schools we need and why we don't have them.* New York: Doubleday.

Hochschild, A.R. (1983). *The managed heart.* Berkeley, CA: University of California Press.

Hollingsworth, S. (1992) Learning to teach through collaborative conversation: a feminist approach. *American Educational Research Journal, 29*(2), 373–404.

Hollingsworth, S. and Sockett, H. T. (eds) (1994). *Teacher research and educational reform, 93rd Yearbook, Part 1, of the National Society for the Study of Education.* Chicago, IL: NSSE.

Holmes Group. (1986). *Tomorrow's teachers.* East Lansing, MI: Author.

Holmes Group. (1989). *Tomorrow's schools.* East Lansing, MI: Author.

Institute for Educational Transformation, (IET) (1995) *Beliefs and Principles in IET practice.* Fairfax, VA: George Mason University.

Jackall, R. (1988). *Moral mazes: The world of corporate managers.* Oxford: Oxford University Press.

Jackson, P.W. (1968). *Life in classrooms.* New York: Holt, Rinehart & Winston.

Jacobs, M. (1997). Teachers and the public. Unpublished lecture. Initiatives in Educational Transformation, Fairfax, VA.

Jacobson, S.L., Emihovich, C., Helfrich, J., Petrie, H.G., & Stevenson, R.B. (1998). *Transforming schools and schools of education.* Thousand Oaks, CA: Corwin.

Jarvis, P. (1992). *Paradoxes of learning: On becoming an individual in society.* San Francisco, CA: Jossey-Bass.

Johnson, D., & Johnson, R. (1989). *Cooperation and competition: Theory and research.* Edina, MN: Interaction Book.

Johnson, D., & Johnson, R. (1990). *Circles of learning: Cooperation in the classroom.* Edina, MN: Interaction Book.

Jones, E.P. (1994). The first day. In T. Wolfe (Ed.), *Vintage book of contemporary American short stories* (pp. 286–290). New York: Vintage Contemporaries.

Jordan, K.L. (1993). *A naturalistic study of educational team efficacy*. Unpublished doctoral dissertation, Brigham Young University, Provo, UT.

Kallen, H. (1915). Democracy versus the melting-pot: A study of American nationality. In W. Sollers (Ed.), *Theories of ethnicity: A classical reader* (pp. 67–92). New York: New York University Press.

Kazantzakis, N. (1960). *The saviors of God: Spiritual exercises*. New York: Simon & Schuster.

Kegan, R. (1982). *The evolving self: Problem and process in human development*. Cambridge, MA: Harvard University Press.

Kincheloe, J. L. and Mclaren, P. L. (1994). Rethinking critical theory and qualitative research. In N. Denzin and Y. Lincoln (eds), *Handbook of Qualitative Research* (Thousand Oaks, CA: Sage), 138–157.

Kinlaw, D. (1992). *Continuous improvement and measurement for total quality: A team-based approach*. San Diego, CA: Pfeiffer.

Kohlberg, L. (1970). *Education for justice: A modern statement of the Platonic view*. Cambridge, MA: Harvard University Press.

Kohn, A. (1998). *What to look for in a classroom*. San Francisco, CA: Jossey-Bass.

Lagemann, E.C. (2000). *An elusive science: The troubling history of education research*. Chicago, IL: University of Chicago Press.

Leiberman, A. (1986). Collaborative research: Working with, not working on. *Education Leadership, 43*(5), 28–32.

LePage, P., Boudreau, S., Maier, S., Robinson, J., & Cox, H. (2001). Exploring the complexities of K–12 faculty and college faculty relationships in a nontraditional professional development program. *Teaching and Teacher Education, 17*(2), 195–211.

LePage, P., Decker, K., & Maier, S. (2001, March). *Developing and nurturing teacher leadership: Opening up dialog about sensitive moral issues and governance*. Paper presented at the meeting of the American Association of Colleges for Teacher Education. Dallas, TX.

LePage, P., & Kirk, D. (1999). *Initiatives in Educational Transformation alumni survey*. Fairfax, VA: Initiatives in Educational Transformation, George Mason University.

LePage, P., & Sockett, H. (in press). *Educational controversies: Towards a discourse of reconciliation*. London: Routledge.

Levine, L. (1996). *The opening of the American mind*. Boston, MA: Beacon Press.

Lieberman, A. (1990). *Schools as collaborative cultures: Creating the future now*. New York: The Falmer Press.

Lieberman, A., & Miller, L. (1992). *Teachers, their world and their work: Implications for school improvement*. New York: Teachers College Press. (Original work published 1984)

Lortie, D. (1975). *Schoolteacher: A sociological study*. Chicago, IL: University of Chicago Press.

Macgillivary, L. (1997). Do what I say, not what I do: An instructor rethinks her own teaching and research. *Curriculum Inquiry, 27*(4), 469–488.

MacIntyre, A. (1984). *After virtue*. Notre Dame, IN: University of Notre Dame Press.

Maeroff, G.I. (1993). *Team building for school change: Equipping teachers for new roles*. New York: Teachers College Press.

Martin, J.R. (1992). *The schoolhome: Rethinking schools for changing families*. Cambridge, MA: Harvard University Press.

McCollum, P. (1996, November/December). Obstacles to immigrant parent participation in schools. *Intercultural Development Research Association Newsletter*.

McIntosh, P. (1988). *White privilege and male privilege: A personal account of coming to see correspondences through work in women's studies* (Paper No. 189). Wellesley, MA: Wellesley Center for Research on Women.

McKeon, R. (1944). Discussion and resolution in political conflicts. *Ethics, LIV*, 235–262.

McLaren, P. (1993). *Schooling as a ritual performance: Towards a political economy of educational symbols and gestures*, 2nd ed. New York: Routledge.

McLaren, P. (1994). *Life in schools: An introduction to critical pedagogy in the foundations of education*. New York: Longman.

McTaggart, R. (1994). Participatory action research: issues in theory and practice. *Education Action Research, 2*(3), 313–347.

Meier, D. (1995). *The power of their ideas: Lessons for America from a small school in Harlem*. Boston, MA: The Beacon Press.

Miller, J.B. (1991). The development of women's sense of self. In J. Jordan, A. Kaplan, J. Miller, I. Stiver, & J. Surrey (Eds.), *Women's growth in connection: Writings from the Stone Center* (pp. 11–26). New York: Guilford Press.

Minnich, E. (1990). *Transforming knowledge*. Philadelphia: Temple University Press.

Mohr, M.M., & MacLean, M.S. (1987). *Working together: A guide for teacher researchers*. Urbana, IL: National Council for Teachers of English.

Moje, E.B., Southerland, S., & Wade, E. (1999). Researching case pedagogies to inform our teaching. In M.A. Lundeberg, B.B. Levin, & H.L. Harrington (Eds.), *Who learns what from cases and how? The research base for teaching and learning with cases* (pp. 73–94). Mahwah, NJ: Lawrence Erlbaum Associates.

Moody-Adams, M. (1997). Race, class, and the social construction of self-respect. In J. Pittman (Ed.), *African-American perspectives and philosophical traditions* (pp. 251–266). New York: Routledge.

Morrison, T. (1973). *Sula*. New York: Penguin Books.

Moss, P. (1994). Can there be validity without reliability? *Educational Research, 23*(2), 5–12.

Mulcahy-Ernt, P., & Ryshkewitch, S. (1994). Expressive journal writing for comprehending literature: A strategy for evoking cognitive complexity. *Reading and Writing Quarterly: Overcoming Learning Disabilities, 10*, 324–342.

Nagel, E. (Ed.). (1950). *Mill's philosophy of scientific method*. New York: Hafner.

National Board for Professional Teaching Standards. (1989). *Towards high and rigorous standards for the teaching profession*. Detroit, MI: Author.

National Council for Teacher Accreditation. (2000). Available online: http://www.ncate.org/2000/2000stds.pdf.

Noddings, N. (1984). *Caring: A feminine approach to ethics and moral education*. Berkeley: University of California Press.

Noddings, N. (1992). *The challenge to care in schools: An alternative approach to education*. New York: Teachers College Press.

Noddings, N. (1997). A morally defensible mission for the schools in the 21st century. In E. Clinchy (Ed.), *Transforming public education* (pp. 27–37). New York: Teachers College Press.

Noddings, N. (1988). An ethic of caring and its implications for instructional arrangements. *American Journal of Education, 96*(2), 215–230.

Oakes, J., & Lipton, M. (1999). *Teaching to change the world.* New York: McGraw-Hill.

Oakeshott, M. (1967). Rationalism in politics and other essays. In R.S. Peters (Ed.), *Psychology and ethical development* (pp. 433–457). London: Allen & Unwin.

Ogbu, J.U. (1990). Overcoming racial barriers to equal access. In J.I. Goodlad & P. Keating (Eds.), *Access to knowledge: An agenda for our nations' schools* (pp. 59–89). New York: College Entrance Examination Board.

Olsen, T. (1961). I stand here ironing. In *Tell me a riddle* (pp. 9–21). New York: Dell Publishing Company, A Laurel Edition.

Paley, V.G. (1979). *White teacher.* Cambridge, MA: Harvard University Press.

Paulsen, G. (1991). *Woodsong.* New York: Penguin Books.

Perry, W.G. (1970). *Intellectual and ethical development in the college years.* New York: Harcourt Brace Jovanovich College Publishers.

Peters, R.S. (1966). *Ethics and education.* London: Allen & Unwin.

Piaget, J. (1973). *To understand is to invent.* New York: Grossman.

Polanyi, M. (1958). *Personal knowledge.* Chicago, IL: University of Chicago Press.

Prawat, R.S. (1992). Teachers' beliefs about teaching and learning: A constructivist perspective. *American Journal of Education, 100*(3), 354–395.

Prawat, R.S. (1993). The value of ideas: problems versus possibilities in learning. *Educational Researcher, 22* (6), 5–16.

Preston, R. (2000, June 12). The genome warrior. *The New Yorker,* pp. 66–78.

Prince William County Public Schools. (1995). *Potomac view K–5 cumulative portfolio—writing across the curriculum.* Prince William County, VA.

Putnam, R. (2000). *Bowling alone: The collapse and revival of American community.* New York: Simon & Schuster.

Reason, P. (1994). Three approaches to participatory inquiry. In N.K. Denzin & Y.S. Lincoln (Eds.), *Handbook of qualitative research* (pp. 324–339). Thousand Oaks, CA: Sage.

Reason, P., & Hawkins, P. (1988). Storytelling as inquiry. In P. Reason (1988). *Human inquiry in action—Developments in new paradigm research.* London: Sage.

Reich, P.A. (1986). *Language development.* Englewood Cliffs. NJ: Prentice-Hall.

Renyi, J. (1993). *Going public: Schooling for a diverse democracy.* New York: The New Press.

Rigsby, L., & DeMulder, E. (1998, April). *Teachers' voices interpreting change.* Paper presented at the annual meeting of the American Educational Research Association, San Diego, CA.

Robinson, P., & LePage, P. (submitted). Implementing nontraditional ideas in a traditional "space" rethinking computer conferencing in teacher education. *Teacher Education Quarterly.*

Rodriguez, R. (1982). *Hunger of memory: The education of Richard Rodriguez.* New York: Bantam Books.

Rose, M. (1995). *Possible lives: The promise of public education in America.* New York: Houghton Mifflin.

Routman, R. (1991). *Invitations: Changing as teachers and learners K–12.* Portsmouth, NH: Heinemann.

Rowland, E.F. (1993). *Teacher study groups: A case study.* Unpublished doctoral dissertation, University of North Texas, Denton.

Sarason, S.B. (1982). *The culture of the school and the problem of change.* Boston, MA: Allyn & Bacon.

Sarason, S.B. (1991). *The predictable failure of educational reform.* San Francisco, CA: Jossey-Bass.

Sarason, S.B. (1996). *Revisiting the culture of the school and the problem of change.* New York: Teachers College Press.

Scheffler, I. (1985). *Of human potential: An essay in the philosophy of education.* Boston, MA: Routledge & Kegan Paul.

Schon, D.A. (1983). *The reflective practitioner: How professionals think in action.* New York: Basic Books.

Schon, D.A., & Rein, M. (1994). *Frame reflection: Toward the resolution of intractable policy controversies.* New York: Basic Books.

Schwartz, S., & Pollishuke, M. (1991). *Creating the child-centered classroom.* New York: Richard C. Owen.

Searle, J.R. (1994). *The rediscovery of the mind.* Cambridge, MA: MIT Press.

Seuss, Dr. (1937). *And to think that I saw it on Mulberry Street.* New York: Vanguard Press.

Sevcik, A. (1984). Thinking about names. *ETC. A Review of General Semantics, 41*(4), 387–388.

Sevcik, A., Robbins, B., & Leonard, A. (1997). The deep structure of obscene language. *Journal of Curriculum Studies, 29*(4), 455–470.

Shulman, L.S. (1987). Knowledge and teaching: Foundations of the new reform. *Harvard Educational Review, 57*(1), 1–22.

Sizer, N.F. (1970). *Five lectures by James M. Gustafson, Richard S. Peters, Lawrence Kohlberg, Bruno Bettelheim and Kenneth Keniston on moral education.* Cambridge, MA: Harvard University Press.

Skinner, B.F. (1975). *Beyond freedom and dignity.* New York: Knopf.

Slater, J.J. (1996). *Anatomy of a collaboration. Study of a college of educationa/public school partnership.* New York: Garland.

Slavin, R. (1990). *Cooperative learning: Theory research, and practice.* Englewood Cliffs, NJ: Prentice-Hall.

Slavin, R. (1991). Synthesis of research on cooperative learning. *Educational Leadership, 47*(1), 71–82.

Smith, F. (1995). Overselling Literacy. In F. Smith, *Between hope and havoc: Essays into human learning and education.* Portsmouth, NH: Heinemann.

Sockett, H. (1972). Curriculum planning: Taking a means to an end. In R.S. Peters (Ed.), *The philosophy of education* (pp. 150–163). Oxford: Oxford University Press.

Sockett, H. (1977, January). *Academic freedom and social responsibility.* An inaugural lecture. The New University of Ulster, Ireland.

Sockett, H. (1988a). Education and will: Aspects of personal capability. *American Journal of Education, 98*(2), 195–215.

Sockett, H. (1988b). Has Shulman got the strategy right? *Harvard Educational Review, 57*(2), 208–215.

Sockett, H. (1988c). What is a school of education? In P. Gordon (Ed.), *The study of education. Vol. III: The changing scene*. London: The Woburn Press.

Sockett, H. (1989). A moral epistemology of practice? *Cambridge Journal of Education, 19*(1), 33–41.

Sockett, H. (1993). *The moral base for teacher professionalism*. New York: Teachers College Press.

Sockett, H. (1994, October 19). "School-Based" master's degrees. *Education Week*, p. 35.

Sockett, H. (1995). Storming the tower of Babel: A British experience in ed school reform. In L.S. Bowen (Ed.), *The wizards of odds: Leadership journeys of education deans* (pp. 37–49). Washington, DC: American Association of Colleges for Teacher Education.

Sockett, H. (1996, October). *Lies, secrets, partnerships and institutions*. Paper presented to the Curriculum and Pedagogy Institute of the University of Alberta, Alberta, Canada.

Sockett, H., & LePage, P. (2001, April). *The missing language of the classroom*. Paper presented at the annual meeting of the American Educational Research Association, Seattle, WA.

Sollors, W. (Ed.). (1996). *Theories of ethnicity: A classical reader*. New York: New York University Press.

Solomon, R.P. (1992). *Black resistance in high school: Forgoing a separatist culture*. Albany: State University of New York Press.

Solomon, W. (1995). *Black resistance in high school*. Albany: SUNY Press.

Spring, J. (1999). *Wheels in the head: Educational philosophies of authority, freedom, and culture from Socrates to human rights*. New York: McGraw-Hill College.

Stout, J. (1988). *Ethics after Babel: The languages of morals and their discontents*. Boston, MA: Beacon Press.

Suskind, R. (1999). *A hope in the unseen: An American odyssey from the inner city to the Ivy League*. New York: Broadway Books.

Taylor, C. (1991). *The ethics of authenticity*. Cambridge, MA: Harvard University Press.

Taylor, C. (1994). *Multiculturalism: Examining the politics of recognition*. Princeton, NJ: Princeton University Press.

Taylor, D. (1993). *From the child's point of view*. Portsmouth, NH: Heinemann.

Tom, A. (1984). *Teaching as a moral craft*. New York: Longman.

Vygotsky, L.S. (1978). *Mind in society: The development of higher psychological processes*. Cambridge, MA: Harvard University Press.

Walker, A. (1982). *The color purple*. New York: Pocket Books.

Waller, W. (1967). *The sociology of teaching*. New York: Wiley. (Original work published 1932)

Watson, W. (1993). *The architectonics of meaning*. Chicago, IL: University of Chicago Press.

Wiggins, G.P. (1993). *Assessing student performance: Exploring the purpose and limits of testing*. San Francisco, CA: Jossey-Bass.

Wilentz, E.S. (1993). *The noneducation of America's children*. Washington, DC: U.S. Department of Education.

Wood, D. (1996). An inquiry into North American dreams. *JCT: An Interdisciplinary Journal of Curriculum Studies, 12*(2), 39–43.

Wood, D.R. (2001, March). *Teacher research—liberation or license? Confessions for a teacher educator.* Paper presented at the meeting of the American Association of Colleges for Teacher Education. Dallas, TX.

Wood, D.R., & Lieberman, A. (2000). Teachers as authors: The National Writing Project's approach to professional development. *International Journal of Leadership in Education, 3(3),* 255–273.

Wooten, C.C. (1993). *The team: An ethnographic account of teachers in an urban high school program for at-risk students.* Unpublished doctoral dissertation, University of Pittsburgh, Pittsburgh, PA.

Yancey, K.B. (1998). *Reflection in the writing classroom.* Logan: Utah State University.

Young, I.M. (1990). *Justice and the politics of difference.* Princeton, NJ: Princeton University Press.

Index

About the Editors and Contributors

DEBORAH BARNARD has been teaching fine arts at the middle school level for 18 years in Prince William County, Virginia. She earned a BA in art education from James Madison University and an M.Ed in curriculum and instruction at George Mason University (GMU) in 1994. With Deborah Courter-Folly, she has presented research at Virginia Middle School conferences and at the fourth annual International Conference on Teacher Research at National-Louis University in 1997.

DEBORAH COURTER-FOLLY has been teaching middle school in central and northern Virginia for 17 years. She has taught sixth-grade language arts, science, and math. She earned her BA in education and psychology at SUNY Stonybrook and an M.Ed in curriculum and instruction at GMU in 1994. With Deborah Barnard, she has presented research at Virginia Middle School conferences and at the fourth annual International Conference on Teacher Research at National-Louis University in 1997.

ANN CRICCHI is an adjunct instructor in the Initiatives in Educational Transformation (IET) program. Cricchi received a BA summa cum laude degree from Marygrove College, Detroit, Michigan, and was a Fulbright Scholar at the University of Southampton, England. She received a master of science in education degree from Old Dominion University, Norfolk, Virginia. Her teaching career included positions as an English teacher, a secondary reading specialist, and assignments in the central offices of Charleston County, and Fairfax County, VA. After retirement from Fairfax County Public Schools in 1995, she joined the IET adjunct faculty staff and worked for 4 years in the school-based master's program.

ELIZABETH K. DEMULDER is an associate professor with IET in the Graduate School of Education at GMU. She earned a PhD in developmental psychology from St. John's College, Cambridge University. Dr. DeMulder was a Staff Fellow in the Laboratory of Developmental Psychology at the National Institute of Mental Health and came to GMU in 1994 under the auspices of the National Science Foundation's Visiting Professorships for Women Program. Dr. DeMulder's research concerns the study of interpersonal relationships and early risk and protective conditions in children's development and education. Her primary research focus is on attachment processes in children's early social and emotional development. She is involved in community-based intervention research through IET's Urban Alternative initiative. Her publications include articles in *Developmental Psychology, Development and Psychopathology, The Journal of Abnormal Child Psychology, The Journal of Personality Disorders,* and *American Behavioral Scientist.*

SHARON J. GEROW is an adjunct professor at GMU and the English Department chairperson at a large public high school in Virginia. She received her bachelor's degree from Ohio State University and her master's and PhD from GMU. She has more than 25 years of teaching experience in secondary schools and 7 years in graduate school. She has published several articles on collaboration and reflective practice research. In 1991, she received the Virginia Governor's Outstanding Educator's Award for excellence in teaching. For her 1997 dissertation, entitled "Teacher Researchers in School-Based Collaborative Teams: One Approach to School Reform," she studied 31 school-based collaborative teacher researcher teams during their first year in IET's master's program as they conducted their individual teacher researcher studies into classroom practice.

RITA E. GOSS is currently a first-grade teacher in Prince William County, Virginia. After earning a BS in early childhood education from GMU, she has spent the past 9 years as an educator. In 1997, she completed her master's degree in curriculum and instruction from GMU through the IET. She presented her master's thesis at the University of Pennsylvania Ethnography in Education Conference. She is presently working toward a doctorate in educational leadership.

DAVID T. HANSEN is professor of Education and Philosophy at Teachers College, Columbia University. He is co-author with Philip W. Jackson and Robert Boostrom of *The Moral Life of Schools* and author of *The Call to Teach* and *Exploring the Moral Heart of Teaching.*

MARK A. HICKS is assistant professor of educational transformation at GMU in Arlington, Virginia. As a philosopher-activist, he is keenly interested in the process of social and intellectual transformation in democratic environments, and focuses his research and teaching along those lines. Of particular concern are issues at the intersection of individual and group identity, notably exceptionalities such as race, class, gender, sexual orientation, and spirituality. He completed his doctorate degree in philosophy and education at Columbia University's Teachers College while he was a research fellow for the Andrew Mellon Foundation.

MARGARET KAMINSKY has been a high school English teacher at Osbourn High School in Manassas, Virginia, since 1969. She has been English Department supervisor for more than 20 years as well as having chaired two division-wide curriculum writing projects and three K–12 textbook adoption committees. She has also served as summer school principal and as coordinator of the secondary gifted program. Within the past several years, she has conducted numerous workshops for teachers in Virginia and three other states on teaching strategies and curriculum planning for extended block scheduling. She was a member of the Executive Board of Virginia Teachers of English and is a past president of the Northern Virginia region of that organization. In 1986, she received the Agnes Meyer Outstanding Teacher Award, an annual award sponsored by *The Washington Post*. In 1988, Ms. Kaminsky was named Outstanding Teacher of the Gifted by the Northern Virginia Council on Gifted Education. She received her master's degree in 1999 from GMU under the IET program. Currently, she works as a member of the teaching team of professors in that GMU master's program as well as continuing to teach in a public high school.

PAMELA C. LEPAGE is an assistant professor with IET at GMU. After teaching in special education for 11 years, she earned a PhD in education from the University of California, Berkeley, and San Francisco State University. Before coming to GMU, she taught at a number of universities including San Diego State University, San Francisco State University, and George Washington University. She has written numerous articles and recently won an award for her book published in 1997 entitled, *From Disadvantaged Girls to Successful Women: Education and Women's Resiliency*. In addition, she just recently completed a book with Hugh T. Sockett entitled, *Educational Controversies: Towards a Discourse of Reconciliation*.

LEO RIGSBY is associate professor and director of Initiatives in Educational Transformation (successor organization to the IET). He came to IET after a 30-year career in teaching and research in sociology to intensify his work with teachers. He is editor of *School-Community Connections: Exploring Issues for Research and Practice*. Other recent publications have been focused on adolescent development and on resilience. His current research centers on two areas. The first is a series of papers on the professional development of teachers within the IET master's program. These papers are action research on the program and its pedagogy. The other research focuses on the transition from preschool to kindergarten of children from a preschool for non-English-speaking families. This research has a community/family outreach component. In collaboration with Elizabeth K. DeMulder, Rigsby is working on a book reporting this research.

DONNA V. SCHMIDT is a first-grade teacher and primary team leader at Samuel W. Tucker Elementary School in Alexandria, Virginia. She earned her bachelor's degree in early childhood education at Wheelock College in 1971 and her master's degree at the IET, GMU, in 1998. She has taught pre-kindergarten, kindergarten, first, second, and fifth grades, and talented and gifted classes.

ANN SEVCIK is retired. She earned her bachelor's degree in philosophy and intellectual history at the University of Michigan (Ann Arbor) in 1960. For 14 years, she taught social studies in Fairfax County (VA) Public Schools, continued to participate in GMU programs for teachers, such as the Northern Virginia Writing Project, and published classroom research, primarily on issues in the moral domain of teaching and learning. She joined GMU's Center for Applied Research and Development in1987. Drawing on work in CARD's Ethos Partnership, a collaborative, team-based research project involving eight Fairfax County schools, she earned a master's degree in qualitative analysis in 1990 from Norwich University (Montpelier, VT). She participated in planning IET's School-Based Master's Program and was a member of the program's first teaching team. She continued to teach and write in the program until she retired in 1999 and currently participates in the academic life of Chatham College (Pittsburgh, PA).

RENEE SHARP is the Network Resource Teacher at Cora Kelly Magnet School in Alexandria, Virginia. She earned a bachelor's degree in elementary education at Hampton University in 1973 and her master's degree at the IET, GMU, in 1998. For 14 years before becoming the network resource teacher, Renee taught third and fourth grades. While teaching in the classroom, she realized that technology provided opportunities for success for students struggling in traditional classrooms. When the opportunity arose, she set up and developed a technology integration curriculum for the school's computer lab. While in the computer lab, she taught students in Grades 2 through 6. As network resource teacher, she assists teachers in developing creative ways to use technology in the classroom.

HUGH T. SOCKETT is professor of education at GMU working in the Department of Public and International Affairs of the College of Arts and Sciences. He earned his bachelor's degree at Oxford, has master's degrees from London, Oxford, and Cambridge, and completed his PhD in 1974 at the University of London. Before coming to GMU in 1987, he was dean of education at the University of East Anglia (UK). He was director of the Institute of Continuing Education at the New University of Ulster based in Londonderry from 1975 to 1980. At GMU, he was founding director of the Center for Applied Research and Development (CARD) which was merged into the Institute for Educational Transformation (IET), which he also directed from 1991 to 1998. He resigned as director in February 1998 and joined the Department of Public and International Affairs in July 1999. He has published numerous articles and four books, including *The Moral Base for Teacher Professionalism* (1993). With Pamela C. LePage-Lees, he has recently completed a book entitled *Educational Controversies: Towards a Discourse of Reconciliation.*

KRISTIN S. STAPOR has spent the past 12 years teaching kindergarten in Prince William County, Virginia. She earned a BS in family and child development with an Early Childhood Education option from Virginia Technological Institute in 1988. In 1997, she completed her master's degree in curriculum and instruction from GMU through the IET. She presented her master's thesis at the 19th annual Ethnography in Education Research Forum at the University of Pennsylvania. She is continuing to utilize her skills as a teacher researcher and early childhood specialist by conducting in-service programs and expanding current teaching models in her school district.

TRACY STEPHENS is a primary teacher at George Mason Elementary School in Alexandria, Virginia. She earned a bachelor's degree in history, geography, and political science, and secondary education at Georgian Court College in 1992 and a master's degree at the IET, GMU, in 1998. She is pursuing a doctoral degree in educational administration and policy studies at George Washington University. She has taught primary, intermediate, multiage, and special education programs in the public schools for 8 years and is committed to helping teachers create effective instructional programs for all children through their collaborative efforts.

DIANE R. WOOD is an assistant professor with IET at GMU. After a 20-year career as a high school English teacher and administrator, she earned a 1996 doctorate at Teachers College, Columbia University where she worked as a researcher at the National Center for Restructuring Education, Schools, and Teaching. Her research interests include narrative inquiry, feminist theory, arts-integrated curriculum, and democratic schooling practices. Her articles have appeared in *Harvard Educational Review, JCT*, and *Anthropology and Education*. Recently, she completed a 2-year study with Ann Lieberman on the professional development approach of the National Writing Project. Currently, Wood is working on a book that focuses on narrative as a discourse for online teacher collaboration.